W9-CHI-262

JUAN DE FUCA'S STRAIT

FEB 1 4 2014

910.916432 Gou

Gough, B.
Juan de Fuca's Strait.

PRICE: $32.42 (3559/he   )

Also by Barry Gough

The Royal Navy and the Northwest Coast of North America, 1810—1914
To the Pacific and Arctic with Beechey
Distant Dominion
The Northwest Coast: British Navigation, Trade and Discoveries to 1812
Gunboat Frontier: British Maritime Authority and Northwest Coast Indians
First Across the Continent: Sir Alexander Mackenzie
HMCS Haida: *Battle Ensign Flying*
Fighting Sail on Lake Huron and Georgian Bay: The War of 1812
and its Aftermath
Through Water, Ice and Fire: Schooner Nancy *of the War of 1812*
Fortune's a River: The Collision of Empires in Northwest America
Historical Dreadnoughts: Arthur Marder, Stephen Roskill
and Battles for Naval History

JUAN DE FUCA'S STRAIT

Voyages in the Waterway of Forgotten Dreams

Barry Gough

HARBOUR PUBLISHING

Copyright © 2012 Barry Gough
First paperback printing, 2013
1 2 3 4 5 — 17 16 15 14 13

All rights reserved. No part of this publication may be reproduced, stored in a retrieval system or transmitted, in any form or by any means, without prior permission of the publisher or, in the case of photocopying or other reprographic copying, a licence from Access Copyright, www.accesscopyright.ca, 1-800-893-5777, info@accesscopyright.ca.

Harbour Publishing Co. Ltd.
P.O. Box 219, Madeira Park, BC, V0N 2H0
www.harbourpublishing.com

Front cover collage, detail from watercolour "June 9, 1792 — HMS *Discovery* & *Chatham* in Rosario Strait" by Steve Mayo (2012), courtesy the artist. Crackle texture courtesy Joseph Francis. Back cover and inside cover detail from "Num. 2 CARTA ESFÉRICA de los Reconocimientos hechos en la Costa N.O. DE AMÉRICA en 1791 y 92 por las Goletas Sutil y Mexicana y otros Buques de S.M." (Espinosa y Tello, 1802), courtesy David Rumsey Map Collection.

Edited by Audrey McClellan
Index by Stephen Ullstrom
Maps pp. 10–11 by Roger Handling
Dust jacket design by Anna Comfort O'Keeffe
Text design by Mary White
Printed and bound in Canada

Harbour Publishing acknowledges financial support from the Government of Canada through the Canada Book Fund and the Canada Council for the Arts, and from the Province of British Columbia through the BC Arts Council and the Book Publishing Tax Credit.

Library and Archives Canada Cataloguing in Publication

Gough, Barry M., 1938–, author
    Juan de Fuca's Strait : voyages in the waterway of forgotten dreams / Barry Gough.

Includes bibliographical references and index.
ISBN 978-1-55017-573-8 (bound).—ISBN 978-1-55017-617-9 (pbk.)

    1. Juan de Fuca, Strait of (B.C. and Wash.)—Discovery and exploration.
2. Navigation—History. 3. Explorers—Spain—History. 4. Explorers—Great Britain—History. 5. Spain—History, Naval. 6. Great Britain—History, Naval.
I. Title.

FC3821.2.G69 2012   910.9164'32   C2012-904296-X

To Robin Inglis
and the memory of Freeman M. Tovell

The earth is placed in the central region of the cosmos, standing fast in the centre, equidistant from all other parts of the sky . . . It is divided into three parts, one of which is called Asia, the second Europe, the third Africa . . . Apart from these three parts of the world there exists a fourth part, beyond the ocean, which is unknown to us.

—Isidore of Seville, *Etymologies* (circa AD 600)

Still Fame will grow, if once abroad it flie,
Whether it be a troth, or a lie

—Michael Drayton (1563–1631)

History is what happened and what continues to happen on and on through time. But it is also layered in strata that lie beneath the ground we walk upon, and the deeper the roots of our being reach down into those unfathomable layers of history—which lie beyond and below the fleshly confines of our ego and yet determine and nourish it . . .—the more weighed down with meaning is our life and all the more dignity attaches to the soul of our flesh.

—Thomas Mann, *Joseph and His Brothers*

Watercolour by Gordon Miller: Santa Saturnina *and longboat off Saturna Island.*
COURTESY OF GORDON MILLER

Contents

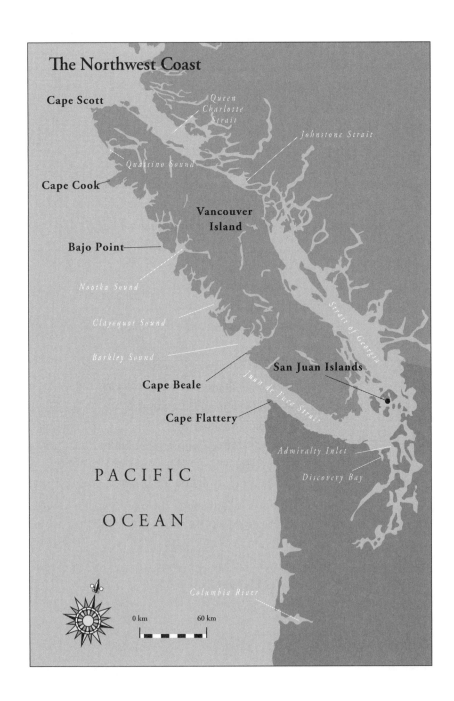

The Northwest Coast

Cape Scott

Queen
Charlotte
Strait

Johnstone Strait

Quatsino Sound

Cape Cook

Vancouver
Island

Bajo Point

Nootka Sound

Clayoquot Sound

Barkley Sound

Cape Beale

San Juan Islands

Juan de Fuca Strait

Cape Flattery

Strait of Georgia

Admiralty Inlet

Discovery Bay

PACIFIC

OCEAN

Columbia River

0 km   60 km

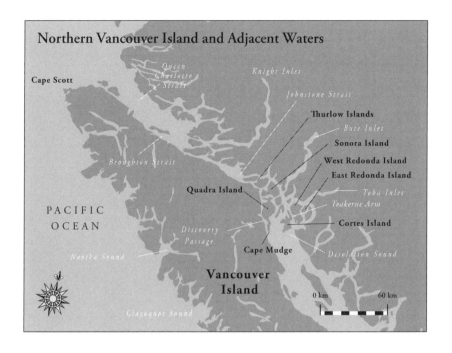

Northern Vancouver Island and Adjacent Waters

Cape Scott

Queen Charlotte Strait

Knight Inlet

Johnstone Strait

Thurlow Islands

Bute Inlet

Sonora Island

West Redonda Island

East Redonda Island

Broughton Strait

Quadra Island

Toba Inlet

Teakerne Arm

PACIFIC OCEAN

Discovery Passage

Cortes Island

Nootka Sound

Cape Mudge

Desolation Sound

Vancouver Island

0 km   60 km

Clayoquot Sound

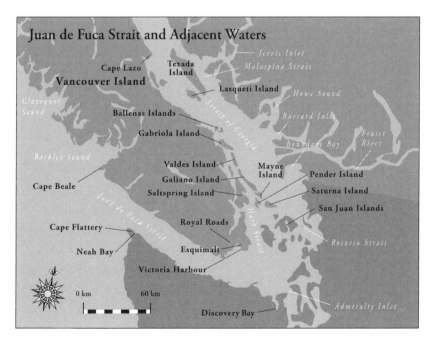

Juan de Fuca Strait and Adjacent Waters

Jervis Inlet

Cape Lazo

Texada Island

Malaspina Strait

Vancouver Island

Lasqueti Island

Howe Sound

Clayoquot Sound

Ballenas Islands

Strait of Georgia

Burrard Inlet

Gabriola Island

Fraser River

Boundary Bay

Barkley Sound

Valdes Island

Mayne Island

Pender Island

Cape Beale

Galiano Island

Saltspring Island

Saturna Island

San Juan Islands

Juan de Fuca Strait

Haro Strait

Cape Flattery

Royal Roads

Rosario Strait

Neah Bay

Esquimalt

Victoria Harbour

0 km   60 km

Discovery Bay

Admiralty Inlet

FOREWORD

*S*ome forty years ago, the western entrance of Juan de Fuca Strait became, for me, a place of intense focus. The occasion was purely personal but was imbued with apprehension, as my older brother Paul, on a solo non-stop passage from Panama to Victoria in a gaff-rigged ketch, was long overdue. Almost four months had elapsed since his departure from Balboa and, more to appease my mother than in any hope of a happy resolution, I asked the Canadian Coast Guard to notify shipping in the area. Before long, reports started to come in of a small, barnacle-encrusted, seaweed-festooned sailing vessel that had been flushing in and out of the strait for some days.

Engineless, and with only a shortwave receiver for weather reports and time signals, Paul had to endure the frustration of making advances with the favouring westerlies and nearly as impressive retreats when millions of gallons of water emptied out into the Pacific on the ebb, unable to communicate with fellow mariners or family ashore or to stem the tide when the wind failed. Nevertheless, he inched his way eastward until a compassionate pilot boat threw him a tow line and hauled him into Victoria.

Now the accepted practice of sailing vessels outward bound from Panama for Juan de Fuca is to work offshore in the direction of Hawaii and then proceed in a clockwise direction around the top of the North Pacific High. In Paul's case, he had been tempted to cut the corner and found himself becalmed for days on end. Taking advantage of his immobility, te-redo worms had managed to penetrate his planking and threatened to sink him well offshore until Paul took his ration of emergency candles, put his ship on the other tack, and poured hot wax into the wormholes, enabling him to complete his epic voyage.

Until fairly recently, then, it was possible to experience first-hand the vicissitudes that were the common lot of the first explorers under sail, except of course that we have long enjoyed the monumental advantage of voyaging in charted waters. Instruments as well have developed to the stage that electronic position systems have replaced the sextant and taffrail log, a chart plotter does away with obtaining fixes by plotting bearings with the compass, and the echo sounder succeeds the lead line. Nevertheless, all of these (with the exception of the electronic depth sounder) have only been in common use for the past twenty years or thereabouts, so when my early, inauspicious introduction led to a lifetime of venturing out onto that great "whale road" named Juan de Fuca, I could identify, just a little, with the British merchant mariners, the Yankee traders, the Spanish explorers, the Cooks, the Vancouvers, and the Broughtons of Barry Gough's latest tale.

In 1988, I was privileged to sail aboard the topsail schooner *Pacific Swift* as master on her maiden voyage to Australia and back with a crew of young men and women. Built at Expo '86 in Vancouver on the lines of the *Swift* of 1778, this new *Swift* would now provide an opportunity to ob-serve first-hand the sailing characteristics of a 200-year-old model. At 98 tons she was larger than the *Sutil* or the *Mexicana* but less than, say, Cook's *Discovery* of 1774, a small converted Yorkshire collier. With more than thirty aboard (including twenty-one trainees, five professional crew and our five daughters), the first lesson learned was how to co-exist in confined spaces. Another was that, in the right winds, her combination of square and fore-and-aft sails propelled her along in remarkable fashion. (With reefed main, foresail, and a forestaysail, she did several 200-mile-days, noon to noon, in the big seas south of New Zealand en route to Tahiti.)

Returning in the spring of the following year, we picked off our seem-ingly minuscule progress on the chart toward the entrance to the Strait of Juan de Fuca from Hawaii. How small the runs of twenty-four hours appear on a chart covering such an immense ocean! And then one evening my wife, Margaret, who was mate on that voyage, woke me and asked me to come on deck. Though Vancouver Island was a long way over the horizon, the unmistakable smells of land were borne on the night air—cedar boughs hanging low on the water, towering firs, fields of salal, wet ferns and damp soil. One can only imagine what the first, chartless visitors made of this heady aroma.

Fast forward twenty years, and Margaret and I are travelling from Mexico to South America on an unhurried five-month ramble. A conspicuous bulge in my backpack is Barry Gough's *Fortune's A River*. Having reviewed Barry's *Through Water, Ice and Fire* for Canwest Global (now Postmedia), the *Times Colonist* of Victoria asked me to do the same for his then latest tour de force. Promising I would file in Panama City, I had the leisure to pursue *Fortune's a River* in a calm and deliberate fashion, often using its generous displacement as a bulwark against over-zealous passengers on "chicken buses" or as an auxiliary pillow in ill-equipped guest houses.

Coming to the end and scanning the appendices, I noticed a brief but tantalizing mention of the Strait of Juan de Fuca and the report of an English consul in Venice that an old pilot in the employ of the Spanish had entered it in 1592. I wondered then if Apóstolos Valerianos had smelled some 300 years earlier the same things we did and marked "land" in his

Built in 1986 on the lines of her 1778 namesake, the *Pacific Swift* sails past the Olympic Mountains. JAMES MAYA

rutter. And I wondered whether anyone would tell the remarkable story of its discovery, and of the dramatis personae who first ventured onto the Salish Sea through this often-elusive portal, without playing fast and loose with the recorded facts.

The answer to the first rests with Juan de Fuca, the navigator. The story of Juan de Fuca, the strait, is in your hands. Meticulously researched and brought to life by Barry Gough's hallmark cast of characters—the brave, the unscrupulous; the wise, the foolish; the honest and the stretchers of truth—this book not only further cements the author's reputation as one of Canada's leading historians but also reintroduces us to Gough the mariner and a writer who combines history and sailorizing in an eminently readable fashion.

I recommend a long sea voyage or an extended road trip to do it justice.

MARTYN J. CLARK
Past Master, Schooners *Robertson II*, *Pacific Swift* and *Lynx*
Executive Director, Maritime Museum of British Columbia,
Victoria, BC

PREFACE

For the present work I have selected a charming theme long in need of elaboration and explanation. I have concentrated on one of the geographical postulations about a northwest passage in the region of 48° and 49° N latitude. Four such postulations were the subject of speculation in the eighteenth century, and in this regard the reader's attention is respectfully drawn to the appendix on this subject in *Fortune's a River*. Here, in this book, I have not sought to set one theoretical water passage against others but only to follow one—the primary one to my way of thinking: the strait reported by the aged Juan de Fuca to the Englishman Michael Lok in the closing years of the sixteenth century. The story takes us forward 200 years into the heated international rivalry that developed between Spain and Great Britain. That hot rivalry nearly resulted in war in consequence of the Nootka Sound crisis. That event, which began in a little-known harbour on west coast Vancouver Island, had repercussions around the world. It all began when a Spanish official inadvisably seized British ships and property at Nootka—an account, and its diplomatic results, I have narrated in my book *The Northwest Coast*. Here, as before, it is the personalities that come to the fore, appearing as it were from out of the fog banks of history.

In Part II we have the strange congruence of another unlikely duo, that of John Meares and Alexander Dalrymple, which almost mirrors the relationship between Juan de Fuca and Michael Lok. Merchant mariner John Meares haunts the margins of this book as a double-headed genius at business and a deceiver of geographical secrets. Alexander Dalrymple, former mariner and a rising force in hydrographical science and cartography, appears as a powerful agent accepting information supplied by Charles Duncan, former master in the Royal Navy, who, as we will see, found the Pillar of Juan de Fuca near the entrance to the fabled passageway. There was no vagueness to Duncan's efforts, for with the professional skills of his calling he drew the first surviving draft plan of the pillar, entitled "Sketch of the Entrance of the Strait of Juan de Fuca," and, an elevation drawing showing Pinnacle Rock (that is, Fuca's Pillar), Green Island (Tatoosh) and Cape Claaset (Flattery). The plan is complete with valuable ethnographic and geographic commentary. By this time, the late eighteenth century, British commerce and British hydrography had supplanted old Elizabethan schemes of trade and empire. And by this time, rivalry between Spain and Britain had become intense. They waged a high-stakes contest, the prize being control of the last unclaimed quarter of the temperate world.

Throughout, my objective has been to follow Ariadne's thread in and out of the maze of historical data and to bring all of the parts together in a workable and sensible whole. I must make it clear that this book is not a history of the maritime or sea-otter trade. Nor can it be regarded as a history of the Northwest Coast of this period. It is a story of a man who believed that he had discovered the strait that carries his name, and it is an account of how mariners in the age of sail pursued rumours to make their discoveries. The strait, such as they found it, proved different than advertised. And in the course of making their discoveries, they laid down markers of empire. They disclosed to the wider world one of the great passageways of the world, one which now sees the great ships pass and repass, to and from China, Korea and Japan, and elsewhere as well. All of this has happened within the span of a mere five centuries, and it began with Juan de Fuca's tale.

PROLOGUE

I like to think of Juan de Fuca and the search for his strait as a great sea venture tied up with piracy, political loyalty and betrayal, and bound up in a web of international intrigue. It is a story concerning dramatic shifts in foreign affairs and cross-national loyalties and aspirations. For me it has another abiding attraction: it goes deep into the sustained distrust and outright animosity of two empires, that of Philip II of Spain and Elizabeth I of England. It is, too, a chapter in global history, for it spans and connects the rocky, icy wastes of the Canadian Arctic, a hoped-for passage to fabled Cathay, some backroom dramas and machinations of London's commerce, and, above all, discoveries of the true nature of "the backside of America," as Elizabethans called the Pacific coast of North America.

And as if that were not enough, it is, too, a story of commercial aspirations not fully achieved, and of honour unfulfilled and unrecognized; a story of pilotage and navigation—and of what the Elizabethans called the haven-finding art. It takes us dervish-like into diplomatic records, narratives of explorers and commercial aspirants, legal affidavits and court records. This story takes us to the heart of a strange and unique correspondence between an old pilot, now, at last and regretfully, "on the beach," and a disenchanted English merchant, long at odds with his bosses and creditors, who was trying for one last grasp at commercial wealth in times when a connection with Asia seemed to afford the greatest prospect for advancement.

Then again, the participants in this story knew that risk was the hand-maiden of commercial enterprise, and that the stars would have to be in harmonious alignment to effect the grand design. Marine insurance was then in its infancy. Partners put up all the stakes in marine endeavours. Lloyd's of London had not yet arisen to spread the risk. In these pressed circumstances, crowned heads provided ships and shares for the mariners most capable of stating their case to the narrow-minded privy councillors who guarded the monarch's finances and credit. It says something for the high-spirited investors that they were often prepared to mortgage their manor houses and farms to take a chance on what they thought could yield abundant wealth and quick fortune. And once the Spanish had cornered the silver of Mexico and the gold of Peru, their rivals soon looked for their own easy motherlodes. More often than not, the paths to such wealth led to disappointment, disaster and even death.

The history of the world is frequently tied up with some combination of great personages: a hero and his sidekick, a king and his lord chancellor, a president and his general, a first lord of the Admiralty and a first sea lord—the professional head and the willing agent or accomplice. Mariners needed business fixers, persons to do the work at the seat of finance and empire. The charismatic courtier Sir Walter Raleigh had his kinsman William Sanderson as his merchant-treasurer. So it is with Juan de Fuca. His tale is inextricably entwined with the life story of Michael Lok. And from this tale flow others. Some are of intrigue and deception, the falsification of evidence and the hiding of secrets. Others recount aspects of nobler calling—of science and surveying. Still others tell of deeds of a more acquisitive and grasping nature—of planting flag-markers in distant quarters, carving out empire in the last unclaimed quadrant of the temperate zones, itself a vibrant native habitat colonized millennia ago from Asia and Siberia.

What Juan de Fuca told Michael Lok about a strait leading from the Pacific to the Atlantic, one he claimed he had navigated, must have seemed to Lok to be eminently feasible. Even if Juan de Fuca were telling a fib, his story had compelling attraction to Lok and to generations of Englishmen who followed. Given the English fixation on the advantageous prospects of a northwest passage, it is not surprising that Juan de Fuca's story refused to die. Many explorers on official business or merchant traders knew about the prospects of finding such a passage, and by 1792 the real truth about the Strait of Juan de Fuca was revealed to the wider world. Truth had supplanted Romance.

For the present we must turn to the essential and quizzical account, written by a well-educated Englishman who had no reason to falsify the details but rather every good cause to recount the particulars so that his betters and other partners would take seriously the commercial prospects that might unfold. He had to get them to open their purses, and that was quite different from telling an inflated account of some voyage through a mystical passage, a shortcut to the South Sea (the Pacific Ocean). This story of Michael Lok and Juan de Fuca necessarily takes us, crablike, into the lives of others of that remarkable and energetic time—Asian traveller Anthony Jenkinson, Francis Drake, his imitator Thomas Cavendish, the cosmologist and mystic Dr. John Dee, and Martin Frobisher, the privateer turned gold-seeker in the regions now known as the Canadian High Arctic. And in the background is that famed patron of seaborne trade and incipient empire, without whom nothing really could be accomplished of a lasting nature—Elizabeth I, Good Queen Bess.

The lands in question and the secret and dark strait that was the object of pursuit were known to the aboriginal inhabitants and provided an environment for cultural and political development and diversity. These peoples were known one unto another, were linked by clans and protocols of inter-clan unions, and had high concepts of property. They lived in general isolation from the wider world and its global connections. However, events were overtaking them swiftly, and by the mid- to late 1770s the general silence of the land and its vibrant occupation by indigenes was soon to be punctured by the sounds of a foreign culture brought from half a world away by sailing ships of the industrial age.

Almost two centuries before Juan Pérez of Spain and James Cook of Britain reached these shores in men-of-war, dreamers and schemers already had their eyes glued on this distant margin, this future empire of fortune. Our attention, therefore, is called back to the era of the Italian Renaissance and to that of the upstart English seadogs who were threatening to bring down the great edifice of Imperial Spain.

At the outset the supremacy was held by Spain, backed by papal prescription and Iberian administrative zeal. The English were the underdogs, the pretenders to empire. The chrysalis of the European world was being broken by explorers in armed sailing ships, and the wider world was drawing mariners out from the coasts and seas of northern Europe, testing their every skill in contests for supremacy and for fortune.

TIMELINE

1592   Voyage of Juan de Fuca as told to Michael Lok

1596   Michael Lok meets Juan de Fuca in Venice

1617   Acapulco, terminus of the Manila galleon and cross-Pacific trade, is fortified by Spanish

1625   Juan de Fuca's account of his voyage, undertaken for the viceroy of Mexico, is published by Samuel Purchas in London; sparks English northwest voyages of discovery

1741   Bering and Chirikov cross the Pacific from Kamchatka to Alaska

1768   Spanish build naval base at San Blas for northern maritime quests

1769   Spanish reach San Francisco Bay and erect a presidio

1778   Captain James Cook names Cape Flattery but misses the entrance to the Strait of Juan de Fuca and discounts the ancient mariner's story

1784   Russians erect a trading post on Kodiak Island

1785   British commence the sea-otter trade from Nootka and gain early mastery, with links to Canton and Macao

1787   Frances Barkley writes that her husband Charles, to the astonishment of all on board, has rediscovered the waterway and named it the Strait of Juan de Fuca

1788   Robert Duffin, in a longboat, under directions of John Meares, enters the strait but is driven back by Natives

Charles Duncan draws a plan of the entrance to the Strait of Juan de Fuca, giving a sketch of the land and Fuca's Pillar

Boston traders begin trade with the Makah at Cape Flattery, then winter at Nootka Sound

1789   Esteban Martínez, the first Spaniard ashore at Nootka, later commandant, seizes British ships, property and shore establishment at Nootka Sound, setting off the Nootka crisis

1790   Manuel Quimper explores the Strait of Juan de Fuca, examining many coastal indentations on both sides of the strait and taking formal possession for the king of Spain

1791   José María Narvaez, in company with Francisco Eliza, sails as far as Cape Lazo (Comox), visiting and naming various islands, including Saturna Island, in the Strait of Georgia

Captain George Vancouver is instructed to sail to Nootka Sound to implement the Nootka Convention and also to explore the waterway reputed to be that sailed by Juan de Fuca

1792   Captain Vancouver's ships on discovery encounter the Boston ship *Columbia Rediviva* near Cape Flattery

Vancouver explores Puget Sound; William Robert Broughton conducts a survey of the San Juan Islands; Vancouver and Broughton explore the Strait of Georgia

Spanish naval officers Alcalá Galiano and Cayetano Valdés, having voyaged north from Acapulco and then to Nootka, enter the strait

Captain Vancouver, by investigating each and every continental inlet to its disappointing head, disproves the existence of a northwest passage in these latitudes

Alcalá Galiano and Valdés complete the circumnavigation of Vancouver Island and arrive at Nootka Sound

Bodega y Quadra and Vancouver fail to agree at Nootka

1795 Spain and Britain enact the mutual abandonment of Nootka, ending Spanish activities there

1796 William Robert Broughton returns to Nootka and is greeted by Maquinna, now in sole possession

1812 Russian-American Company establishes a short-lived base at Fort Ross, Alta California

1819 United States acquires, by treaty, Spanish claims to sovereignty of New Spain

1846 Oregon Treaty sets the middle of the Strait of Juan de Fuca as the boundary between British and United States possessions, the continental division being set at the forty-ninth parallel, leaving Vancouver Island in British control and the ownership of the San Juan Islands in doubt

1859 San Juan Islands boundary dispute; in subsequent diplomacy the United States backs the claims of Juan de Fuca's voyage and discoveries

1867 Russia sells Alaska to the United States

1872 German Kaiser finds for the United States in its claims for the San Juan Islands; Haro Strait deemed the main channel

Introduction

NAVIGATING THE STRAIT
OF JUAN DE FUCA

The entrance to this important and fabled body of water lies on the Northwest Coast of North America between the parallels of 48° 23' N and 48° 36' N, on the meridian of 124° 45' W. It runs between the south coast of Vancouver Island and the mainland of Washington State and is the connecting channel between the Pacific Ocean and the inland passages extending southward to Puget Sound or northward to the inland waters of British Columbia and southeast Alaska. Earliest editions of the *British Columbia Pilot*, or sailing instructions, warned mariners that the strait was "liable to all those sudden vicissitudes of weather common to high northern latitudes; and in few parts of the world is caution and vigilance of the navigator more called into action than when entering it."[1]

At its entrance, the breadth of the strait between Cape Flattery, its southern point of entrance, and high and bold Bonilla Point on Vancouver Island, its northern, is 13 miles, while within these points it narrows to a breadth averaging 12 miles in an easterly direction for 60 miles. Eastward 50 miles from the entrance lie Race Rocks, near the Vancouver Island shore. Eastward again from Race Rocks it extends east-northeastward for 30 miles, broadening out and then connecting with Georgia Strait, to the north, through the channels that flow around and through the San Juan Islands, or connecting with Puget Sound to the southeast through

Admiralty Inlet. The waters lying northward eventually reach the Pacific near the northern extremity of Vancouver Island, while to the south they dead-end in a series of passages and canals that form an immense maze of land and water.

On a clear day, and in good sailing conditions, the entrance and strait exhibit every indication of regularity. "The depths, as a rule, are bold to within a short distance of the shore, with but few outlying dangers, most of which are in the eastern part," the *US Coast Pilot* advises. But it is well inside where the dangers lie, in and around the San Juan Islands, a rock-strewn barrier that separates the strait from Georgia Strait. Tide-rips, up-wellings and overfalls are the bane of the mariner and have been the cause of many a calamity.

Fogs are heavy near the western entrance to the strait, decreasing in density and frequency up the strait. Near the entrance, the fog sometimes stands like a wall or thick blanket, but vessels entering the strait commonly run out of it into clear, bright weather even before passing Tatoosh Island, just inside Cape Flattery. These fogs can extend a long way to seaward, and when they are combined with the smoke of forest fires, they can become exceptionally dense. Wind gradually works the fog into the strait, hugging the northern shore, occasionally to Sooke and at times to Race Rocks. Sometimes, however, the fog clings to the southern shore as far as Port Townsend.

As to winds, the following are observed: in the summer the prevailing northwesterly winds draw into the strait, increasing toward evening. (This wind enabled mariners on a journey of exploration in the age of sail to make their entrances into the strait, and I concluded years ago that it was invariably on such southwesterly passages on the Northwest Coast that the discoveries were made, not on voyages north along the coast from California.) In the winter, southeasterly winds draw out of the strait, caus-ing a confused cross sea off the entrance as the heavy southwesterly swell meets that coming out. The set of the sea inshore has always been toward the north, and thus the great majority of ship strandings that have oc-curred have been on the Vancouver Island shore.

A sailing vessel approaching the strait was warned to keep well off the mainland coast south of Cape Flattery unless working to windward against a fine northerly wind, which was often present in summertime. In such circumstances, sailors could approach to within three miles. Says one source: "At other times there is no inducement to hug the coast, on which a long rolling swell frequently sets, and this swell, meeting the southeasterly gales of winter, causes a confused sea."[2] Cape Flattery and its off-lying dangers deserve a wide berth. The same holds true on the Vancouver Island shore. In short, a vessel approaching the entrance in winter months, especially in November and December, and experiencing the easterlies or southeasterlies, should not enter the strait until an opportunity exists of getting well inside. Captain John Duntze of the forty-two–gun British frigate *Fisgard*, dispatched from Valparaiso in January 1846 to protect Hudson's Bay Company possessions in Vancouver Island and Puget Sound (the Oregon boundary then being a matter of serious moment to British interests in that remote quarter of the globe), recounted that they had not proceeded very far into the strait when all of a sudden a heavy squall threw the ship almost on her broadside. The men being at dinner, sail could not be shortened quick enough, though it lasted only a few minutes and no harm done. Here, therefore, was one trick a mariner needed to know in advance. The other was this: that once inside the entrance, a vessel might find the Vancouver Island coast a dangerous lee shore if an easterly wind were blowing out of the strait. But once inside safely, and with these matters taken into consideration, it was a fair sail up the broad and widening channel. It was easy for the Spanish to conclude in 1790 that the strait was a cul-de-sac, for ahead, or well into the strait, a wall of land, or islands, came into view, and beyond that was a broad band of snow-capped mountains stretching northwest to southeast, as far as the eye could see.

In fair weather, the dark forested outline of Vancouver Island is visible from the entrance to the north, with its sequence of coastal hills and mountains majestically rising beyond, some with snowy peaks, giving an indication that this is the continental mainland, which it is not. On the south is a characteristic benchland that hugs the shore, while inland a few miles the land rises into a great rampart stretching almost the entire length of what is called the Olympic Peninsula. This sensational grey mass, fringed year-round with glaciers and holding alpine meadows and hot springs, is the main geographical feature of this part of western Washington. Storms off the Pacific deliver abundant rainfall to this coast; Cape Flattery gets over 100 inches a year, although the rain shadow, as it is called, in the lee of the Olympic Mountain range, will get less than a quarter of that. On the north shore, Victoria, also in the lee of the Olympics, is similarly favoured, while Vancouver, which is inland and across Georgia Strait, receives about 50 inches of rain each year. In other words, the strait, from its entrance to its inward extent, is generally well protected from great storms and heavy seas. On occasion, however, this can change in a flash. Easterly or south-easterly winds, notably in winter, draw the air off the mainland and blow hard down the strait or up along what might be described as the spine of Vancouver Island.

In the days of George Vancouver and Dionisio Alcalá Galiano, argu-ably the most famous mariners to sail this strait, no aids to navigation existed. There was no reliable chart. There were no buoys or markers, no lighthouses, no wireless, no radar, no LORAN, and no Global Positioning System to guide them. Caution thus ruled their every proceeding. Using line and lead they sounded the depths, watching carefully for a sudden shortening of the line, which spelled danger. Mariners built up a statis-tical knowledge about the approach to Cape Flattery: they knew that if they made their first sounding in 100 fathoms, they were approaching the shore, though still at a safe distance, and they grew to expect that sooner or later they would reach another ledge closer to shore at about 50 fathoms. They now looked for changes in the sea indicating reefs, shoals or similar dangers. Men were posted in the foretop and rigging to call out early in-dication of changes. In narrow passages or unknown waters, a ship's boat would be sent ahead on reconnaissance. Sail was shortened or backed as required. What seemed to confuse these mariners most were the tides and currents, both strong in the strait and sometimes quite unpredictable. A case was noted in 1792 when Vancouver's two ships were near one another and at anchor, but each pointed in the opposite direction to the other ow-ing to the set of the current.

Putting up lighthouses was the first benefit to mariners after proper hydrographic surveys were undertaken. Cape Flattery was given a light-house early (on Tatoosh Island) and so were Swiftsure Bank and Umatilla Reef, both on the outside, where lightship vessels were positioned. At Cape Beale, Vancouver Island, a lighthouse was erected to mark the strait's en-trance, while inside, lighthouses at Pachena and Carmanah flashed out the warning. All of these had fog signals. There are other lights and horns inside, too. At Race Rocks, a circular tower decorated with black and white bands gives out a light for 18 miles or more, a sort of cousin to the light at Port Angeles, nearly opposite. On a clear night, standing by the foreshore, you can see one by one the progression of light sentinels inward from the broad Pacific, and you can imagine the careful mariner in the late 1800s, one eye glued to the chart and sailing directions, watching for the next light to come into view, perhaps around the next island or headland, and sure enough, it is there. Race Rocks and Fisgard lighthouses, the latter marking the entrance to Esquimalt, were erected in the late 1850s to encourage commerce and the colonial development of Vancouver Island and British Columbia.

When fog blanketed the straits, mariners used their hearing. Sailors, knowing the headlands, would sound their siren and wait for the echo, using the elapsed interval to compute their distance from the dangers of land. They also took soundings with lead and line. During World War I, the venerable Canadian light cruiser HMCS *Rainbow*, carrying the tsar's gold from near Bamfield, Vancouver Island, to the waiting railway cars in Vancouver, destined for Ottawa, sought passage into the dangerous First Narrows using just such a method. Commander Walter Hose, hearing the fog signal from Point Atkinson, decided to proceed dead slow for ten more minutes. If he had no confirming accurate bearing by then, he would return to the open gulf. Proceeding up the outer harbour for almost the full ten minutes, taking echoes all the way, Hose was favoured when the fog lifted and Prospect Point light, on the south side of the First Narrows, could be seen dead ahead.

Those were the days of less reliable navigational techniques and aids than exist nowadays. Still, errors do occur, often attributable to negligence on the bridge or even the licensed personnel engaging in some distracting embrace or quarrel. From the perspective of my years and our times, we can but wonder at how the "ancient mariners" did what they did with such an absence of electronic gear, tide tables and weather reports. They command our respect, and we could learn something from their powers of observation, which required a harmonious understanding of the seas, the shores and the ever-present dangers.

Large vessels with billows of canvas were seen in the strait even in the early years of the twentieth century. Lacking steam power, they had to pick up a tow at the western entrance. This was easy to do, as the tugboat captain looking for work would patiently ride the waves there until a four-masted schooner or a windjammer came into view and completed the contract formalities. Perhaps outward bound, in light airs, the same vessel could be seen working down the strait, tack for tack, but inasmuch as time meant money, the towing contract was often for a return passage. Nowadays, of course, pilots operate from Victoria's outer wharf and from Port Angeles, and all shipping is required to have a licensed pilot aboard. Lanes of passage are marked on the chart and rigidly followed, and coast guards on both sides of the strait, alerted by aerial units, can give aid in times of distress. But still nature throws up its surprises. Not too long ago a seasoned tugboat captain, with thirty or more years under the keel, found his tow, a great concrete barge, embarrassingly blown up on the rocks at the south end of Vancouver Island on New Year's Day. He had taken a shortcut inside Trial Island and was not mindful of the force of the winds outside, nor of the tides and currents that frolic in this particular marine playground.

The history of hydrographic surveying is a subject all to itself, and rates far more in importance than the attention it earns. Its findings were harbingers of commercial development and human progress in our own times. In the last analysis, the charts and sailing directions bequeathed to the world by the Admiralty's hydrographic office are the most lasting testament of the almost extinct British Empire. Yet it is interesting to note, in connection with the Strait of Juan de Fuca, that the lighthouses were erected at Race Rocks and the entrance to Esquimalt on the advice of Royal Navy hydrographers and on the recommendation of British admirals of the 1850s. Navigational aids were essential to the growth and prosperity of British Columbia, western Canada and the adjacent United States.

All of this lay far ahead of the years that are the subject of this book, and we are taken or called back in time to a simpler age and perhaps a more ignorant one, when shipwreck was a more common occurrence, when sailors lived short lives, and when hard-driving ship masters worked their vessels under royal instructions. Far away from dockyards and other places of repair, they lived by their wits and ingenuity.

Part One

THE TALE OF AN ANCIENT MARINER

Chapter 1

A CONVERSATION IN VENICE

Our scene is a steamy waterside bar or coffee house near the Grand Canal of Venice, a city that was the centre of a republic dubbed the Queen of the Adriatic. Venice ranked as the most powerful Christian state of the central and eastern Mediterranean. The novelist George Eliot described it as "a creature born with an imperial attitude," and true this was, for its wealth and treasures had been acquired by trade, war, conquest and pillage. There in its stunningly magnificent palaces, houses and piazzas, the vast outworks of empire enriched and gilded the imperial seat. Napoleon thought it the most elegant drawing room of Europe. Loot from Constantinople, captured in 1204, was everywhere on display. There had always been rivals to the pride of place of this seemingly floating city— Venice had to fend off Genoa in a contest for primacy, then fight against the resurgent Turks—but in the late sixteenth century, Venice still reigned supreme and was in its glorious prime. Even so, signs of decline and decadence that were to characterize its transformation over the next few centuries were presenting themselves.

Venice had not yet taken on the aura of "a ghost upon the sands of the sea," as John Ruskin described it in 1849, a little unhappily. No, Venice was a powerful maritime state still—Italian but, strangely, almost Oriental. It remained a vibrant and prosperous city state, confident in its oligarchic authority, sufficient unto itself but holding an eastern empire in fee. Some indication of this self-assuredness is given in the description penned by the French ambassador upon the occasion of his waterborne entry there in 1495:

> They placed me between these two ambassadors—in Italy it is considered an honour to sit in the middle—and led me along the great street which they call the Grand Canal, and a very wide street it is. Galleys can pass through it, and I have seen ships of a hundred tuns or more close to the houses: it is, I believe, the most beautiful and best built street in the world, and it runs the entire length of the city. The houses are large and tall, and made of fine stone, and the oldest ones are all painted; and the rest have been constructed within this last hundred years; which all have their fronts of white marble brought from Istria, a hundred miles away, and besides, many a large piece of porphyry and serpentine upon their fronts . . . It is the most triumphant city I have ever seen, and foreigners are entertained better there than anywhere else; it has the best government, and God is served most devoutly there: and while it may well have other faults, I think God favours its people for the reverence they bear to the service of the Church.[3]

Meanwhile, on the shores of the western Mediterranean, particularly in Spain and in Portugal—the latter "the western rim of Christendom"—fundamental changes were occurring that would revolutionize the world's affairs and vault the European maritime powers—Spain, Portugal, Holland, France and England—onto the global stage.

Our story stands on this threshold of history. Already the great shift outward from the Mediterranean was in train. In 1492 the "Admiral of the Ocean Sea," Christopher Columbus, sailing in the service of Ferdinand and Isabella of the combined crowns of Castile and Aragon, had made a landfall on a Caribbean island off a continent that came to be called America. After the death of Columbus, the Spanish extended their discoveries. All the coasts of the Caribbean Sea and the Gulf of Mexico, and the islands similarly, fell under Spanish influence if not sovereignty. Balboa crossed the Panama isthmus in 1513 and gazed upon the Pacific Ocean. The Spanish began the conquest of Mexico in 1519, the same year Magellan began his circumnavigation, and the conquest of Peru in 1532.

By the end of the century, and throughout almost all quarters of the world, European nations had spied out places for imperial acquisition or otherwise set up trading factories. The process of Europe's expansion overseas was rapid and its effects prodigious. As of 1596, Spain's star seemed in the ascendant everywhere in distant oceans save where the Dutch, Portuguese, French and English threatened, though never in combination. The Spanish had pioneered the use of the sea route via Magellan Strait; of that there was no doubt. The red and yellow banners of Spain, backed by the power of Roman Christendom, reached out across the sea lanes. These stretched from the Iberian peninsula westward round Cape Horn to the Philippines, holding all of Central and South America in sway save Portuguese-held Brazil, and with it, all the gold and silver of the New World on which to finance the empire at home and abroad. Every year, beginning in 1565, lofty "galleons of the Indian Guard" provided convoy support for the vast *flota* of vessels that annually brought to Spain the treasures of the New World. The Old World lived on the spoils of the New.

Like the Spanish, the Portuguese claimed for their own exclusive use the countries they discovered. During the fifteenth century they made the whole west coast of Africa a place for trade and, in so doing, laid foundations for sailing via Brazil round the Cape of Good Hope to India and beyond. Their discoveries left their mark on every shore of the eastern hemisphere. They were leaders in scientific navigation, and Prince Henry the Navigator founded a teaching centre for it. In 1511 the Portuguese reached the Moluccas or Spice Islands; in 1516, Canton; and in 1542, Japan. Apart from the Philippines and some other island clusters nearby, Portugal was as supreme in the eastern hemisphere as Spain in the western—that is, south of a line which, with the exception of Japan (where the Portuguese had an establishment for a century), coincided with the latitude of Gibraltar. Portugal excluded other nations with a jealousy equal to that of Spain's, though less effectually. At various places on the African coasts, the entrances of the Red Sea, and the straits of Malacca, Siam and Sumatra, their forts stood as entrepôts of trade, watchtowers of compressed power, visited by trading vessels year in and out.

All of this changed in 1581, when Spain took over the Portuguese court, and the exiled claimant to the throne, Don Antonio, waited vainly in hope that the English would come to his rescue. Drake, the most formidable of the seadogs of England, mounted, with military support, a

1589 expedition to capture Lisbon. But disease wracked the expedition, and a Portuguese rising in support failed to materialize. This attempt was not so utterly a failure as the Spanish Armada of the year previous—the "Enterprise of England," as the Spanish masterminds called it. Even so, at the time our story begins, King Philip II of Spain had a sway that Queen Elizabeth could only look on with envy matched by fear, for always the shadow of popery lay over the fragile court at Greenwich and Hampton Court. However, one thing the English had to a greater degree than the Spanish was commercial zeal, with that zealous know-how matched by exalted skills as shipbuilders and sailors. This was the trump card in the game of imperial stakes.

This, then, was the general state of global history in April 1596, when two outsiders to the Spanish empire and its oceanic enterprises met in Venice and engaged in rapid, animated conversation.[4] The inquisitive one in the discourse (for which we need to be reminded we have an attested record) was the questing Michael Lok. He then lived in Venice, in the house of Signor Lasaro Mercader Ingles, near the ferry of St. Thomas (now the San Tomà stop for the vaporetto).

The Englishman observed every formality in dealing with his new associate, addressing his opposite in glowing terms as "the Magnificent Señor Captain Juan de Fuca, Pilot of the Indies." But Juan de Fuca could turn a nice phrase in return compliment. He styled his friend, as subsequent correspondence noted, "the illustrious signor Michal Loch Ingles."

In their conversation, Juan de Fuca told the "illustrious signor" a fabulous tale of an inland sea, a potential passage from Pacific to Atlantic Ocean, that he had discovered while sailing for the Spanish viceroy of Mexico. Lok wrote in his account of the conversation that Juan de Fuca left Mexico in 1592 "with a small Caravela and a Pinnace, armed with Mariners only," in search of the "Straits of Anian, and the passage thereof, into the Sea which they call the North Sea, which is our North-west Sea. And that he followed his course in that Voyage West and North-west in the South Sea [Pacific Ocean], all alongst the coast of Nova Spania, and California, and the Indies, now called North America (all which Voyage hee signified to me in a great Map, and a Sea-card of mine owne, which I laied before him) until hee came to the Latitude of fortie seven degrees."[5] It was there that Juan de Fuca found the land trended North and Northeast, with "a broad Inlet of Sea, betweene 47. and 48. degrees of Latitude."[6] This he entered. He sailed therein for more than twenty days. Sometimes the land trended northwest and northeast and in other cases east and southeast. (All of this is suggestive of the waters of the Strait of Juan de Fuca, Puget Sound and the Strait of Georgia or Salish Sea.[7])

Juan de Fuca, said Lok, recounts a "very much broader Sea then [than] was at the said entrance"—perhaps the Strait of Georgia—"and that hee passed by divers I[s]lands in that sayling. And that at the entrance of this said Strait, there is on the North-west coast thereof, a great Hedland or Iland, with an exceeding high Pinnacle, or spired Rocke, like a piller thereupon."[8] He saw people clad in animal furs. He "went on Land in divers places" and said the land was fruitful, and "rich of gold, Silver, Pearle, and other things, like Nova Spania."[9]

Lok immediately saw the significance of this tale. Sailors had sought such a northwest passage for years, knowing it would cut the length of a voyage from the Pacific to Atlantic Ocean by weeks and avoid many of the dangers that attended the known routes.

The strangers, soon to become friends, had been brought together in one of those strange combinations upon which the events of history so often turn. They had come to this place and to this unusual encounter from two most different pasts. Opposites in so many ways, they were yet soon to be joined in common purpose, though nonetheless at the whims of fate.

Michael Lok had been born to a large family of the wealthy merchant Sir John Lok, alderman of the City of London, and commercial connections surrounded him from birth. "England's wealth by foreign trade" was the hallmark of this remarkable class of gentlemanly capitalists. It was quickly becoming the credo of the English nation. Commerce, not the law or the church, coursed through Michael Lok's veins. Like his father he was a mercer by calling—that is, a dealer in fine fabrics. We can imagine him as a young man to be beautifully attired in the elegant materials of the day. Ostentatious display was a characteristic of Elizabethan life among the political, professional and business segments of society, and flamboyant dress, decoration, colour and texture were marks of individuality and not conformity.

Lok family members had been among the earliest in the West African coastal trade, during the 1550s, where in Guinea they did business in gold, elephant ivory, pepper and slaves, who, it was said, were as remarkably tall as they were black. The Lok business interests did not carry slaves to the western hemisphere; that would come later, with the voyages of Sir John Hawkins.[10] The Lok family flourished in the expanding trade of those times and became well-to-do, and Michael Lok grew up in an era of high-risk merchant enterprises, one in which monopolies and special favours constituted the only safeguards against unbridled ruination. Various combinations of like-minded persons, interests and talents managed the commercial affairs of the Port of London. In addition, merchant companies formed to pursue trades in or toward specific geographical areas, such as Muscovy (Russia), the Levant (eastern Mediterranean) and Cathay (China).

Like any other commercial unit, family or otherwise, the Loks sought some sort of preferment from the Crown and the Privy Council, some sort of monopoly that would offset what they had had to risk personally in regards to capital, cargoes, ships and men. Without such preferment they would otherwise be ruined if faced with pestering, rival countrymen. In the days before the Board of Trade came to regulate these matters sensibly, the monarch and close advisors acted as gatekeepers of commerce and often as financiers of special projects regarded as advantageous to England's wealth and future. The nature of politics and commerce in the unfolding Elizabethan age favoured Lok's religious persuasion and fuelled his ambition.

Michael Lok remained under tutors until age thirteen. He was tutored in many languages and acquired knowledge of French, Spanish, Italian and Latin. But like many a young man of his station in life, he was sent abroad to enlarge his horizons: he served his apprenticeship as a merchant adventurer at Antwerp. There was another reason for his absence from London in these years. He was a Protestant, and to avoid the pressing requirements of the Roman Catholic Queen Mary, he had remained on the continent free from interference, returning to England only after Mary's reign ended in 1558. He turned exile to advantage and soon became a well-known traveller, conscientiously working all the towns and marts of Europe on family business.

Along the way he acquired antiquarian instincts important in later life, as we will see, and became conversant with matters cosmological and geographical: in due course he not only wrote a treatise on northern explorations to the Arctic but also compiled a map of these regions that is remarkable for its cartographic flourishes and appreciations of then current thinking and postulations about a part of the world that had not yet been explored. He had Latin and, later in life, made a distinguished contribution, in imitation of Richard Hakluyt, of translating accounts of voyages to the New World, notably those of the famous Italian historian Peter Martyr.[11] He had lived for a time in Portugal and Spain and built up extensive mercantile connections. There is no reason to doubt that he had an interest in cosmology, navigation and even alchemy—all then preoccupations of learned men and aspiring savants, and it seems probable that he met and knew Dr. John Dee, the noted scholar (of whom more presently).

On the personal side, Lok had sharp-edged characteristics more typical than not of the Elizabethans. He had an undoubted belief in his own capabilities and future, and his handwriting shows both the greatest care and the most abundant style, both flowing and artistic—and eminently readable to this day. That handwriting betrays lessons from a writing-master, and the style reflects not the cramped hand of native English origin but the taught and imported fair Italian hand, then so fashionable among the progressive segments of society, who were conscious of the renaissance of learning. He was also good with numbers, and he kept careful records. He had about him a slightly sad air, a rather sallow disposition, and seems to have been haunted by prospects of success not quite achieved. A colleague said that he longed for pre-eminence among his peers. He was not an insider, we judge from this, but stood on the margins of clusters of merchant adventurers who were moving forward the trade and empire of the Elizabethan expansion. Richard Madox, a fellow of All Souls Oxford and a valuable observer of the Elizabethans of 1582, summed up the man's character and style this way: "Lok . . . is [a] man of great wit and admirable honesty, as the master [Edward Fenton] reported to me, but unhappy."[12]

Lok had good reason for such unhappiness. He had a knack for raising credit for distant voyaging and saw himself as what we might call a fixer of oceanic enterprises. He therefore had every reason to believe that wealth and fame would soon attend his ventures. Perhaps he could become prominent, as were some of his contemporaries, in opening new avenues of trade to Persia and Central Asia. However, as will be related, many of his great prospects faded before he realized his visions of power, glory and wealth. Even so, he was the moving spirit behind Sir Martin Frobisher's three summertime voyages of 1576, 1577 and 1578 to the High Arctic of what is now Canada and the search for gold in that part of the world Lok called Meta Incognita.

Frobisher, to whom we now turn momentarily, was a Yorkshireman of no eminent lineage but endowed with superior mental qualifications. He had attended school in London under the care of a kinsman, Sir John Yorke, who, seeing his abilities, sent him on a voyage to Guinea. The youngster soon became acquainted with all the skills of navigation and gained a good knowledge of geography. His early career was as a privateer, and he grew rich on the profits of robbery at sea. He also became cocksure of his own abilities, much like Lok. Frobisher believed that he could accomplish his desires in the way of exploration and financial advancement. But others thought him not so gifted, and would-be investors among friends and acquaintances shied away from his wild projects. For fifteen years he tried to raise support, even pressing his schemes on the Earl of Warwick, who was a power at court. In the course of his solicitations he met Lok, who provided supplies and monies to begin the venture. The Muscovy Company, though chartered under patent to promote "new trades," actually thwarted the scheme, fearing rival interests. After Frobisher, Lok and their associates appealed to the Lord Treasurer, that company granted a licence in February 1574, under its seal, for the project to proceed. The discovery of the northwest passage, said Frobisher in 1576, seemed "the only thing of the worlde . . . yet undone, whereby a notable minde might be made famous and fortunate." With licensed authority at hand, Frobisher began to outfit his ships, his intention to reach Cathay and the lands of Kublai Khan.

Just at this moment, Dr. John Dee, the celebrated cosmologist who lived in a great riverside house at Mortlake near Richmond, Surrey, raised objections to the Frobisher scheme, but on different grounds than corporate ones. Likewise the son of a London mercer, Dee was educated at St. John's College Cambridge and was later a fellow of Trinity. He had travelled to Louvain and Paris, studying with the noted geographers Frisius and Mercator; wrote treatises on navigation and navigational instruments; coined the term "British Empire"; wrote the book *Sovereignty of the Sea;* and gained fame in mathematics, especially Euclidian algebra. His favour in court circles was due largely to his practice in judicial astronomy, for science was battling witchcraft and winning.

He had a reputation as a conjurer, which began when at Cambridge he produced a play in which extraordinary stage effects were used. It is said that he conjured a wedge of gold from a pool in Wales and found himself facing charges in the Court of Assizes. Children were frightened of his magic, which presumably included some chemistry experiments. Dee is supposedly the subject of inspiration for Ben Jonson, whose comedy *The Alchemist* hit the stage in 1610. Dee may have been a believer in the transmutability of metals, but it turns out that he was not alone in this line of work. A company was formed in London to put the process of "multiplying gold" into operation. Astrology flourished as an art even as astronomy was in the ascendant as a science—and it flourishes to this day.

In later years, however, John Dee tended toward the occult, the last of the medieval alchemists. His interest in alchemy and the search for the philosopher's stone led to gradual abandonment of other work, and eventually, in later years, he retreated into mysticism and psychic research. Dee's conversations on the secrets of the universe through the assistance of angelic spirits were bound to attract suspicion, and one critic, the learned Robert Hooke of Gresham College, London, was not alone in suspecting they were really intelligence reports in code.

Besides his many other strange pursuits, the good Dr. Dee was a student of history, and a noted antiquarian. For many years he had followed the history of exploration of northern waters and lands. In 1578, for instance, he inserted on a map of the North Atlantic some notations about the mystical expeditions of the Welshman Madoc and the Irishman St. Brendan, and to this he added remarks about how it was that Bristol merchants were the discoverers of Newfoundland in 1494—that is, before John Cabot. Historical scholarship does not now see reason to dethrone Cabot from primacy of discovery, but Dee obviously had access to unconfirmed data that is suggestive of earlier English encounters with the New World.[13]

As for Lok's and Frobisher's scheme, Dr. Dee expressed grave doubts respecting the voyage, but Lok was not to be deterred. In reply, he expounded his reasons with care and certitude. He showed Dee his portfolio of maps and charts, his books and memoranda, and "his cards and his instruments." Dee was won over by the cogency of Lok's arguments or, at least, he offered to give scientific aid. Just as the officers and men were assembling on the vessels in the Thames preparatory to sailing, the learned man arrived on the scene. Dee was tall and elegant, with pale skin and a long white beard that flowed over his artist's gown. He would have made quite a sight as he walked down to Frobisher's vessel.

Dee then "took great pains to instruct the masters and mariners in the rules of geometry, cosmography, the use of instruments in their voyage, and for casualties happening at sea, which did them service; whereby," Lok observed, "he deserveth just commendation." A draft of instructions framed in connection with this voyage, in Dee's handwriting, survives in the British Library.[14]

Frobisher sailed in the *Gabriell*, with other vessels in company. The Labrador coast was forbidding. There was, "so great store of ice all the coast along, so thick together, that hardly his boat could pass unto the shore. At length, after divers attempts, he commanded his company, if by any possible means they could get ashore, to bring him whatsoever thing they could first find, whether it were living or dead, stock or stone, in token of Christian possession . . . and some brought flowers."[15]

George Best, who sailed with Frobisher, remarked on the Baffin Island Inuit in 1578, when he wrote of the voyage: "These people I judge to be a kind of Tartar, or rather a kind of Samoed, of the same sort and condition of life that the Samoeds bee to the North-eastwards beyond Muscovy . . . eaters of themselves, and so the Russians their borderers doe name them. And by late conference with a friend of mine (with whom I did some travell in the parts of Muscovy) who had great experience of those Samoeds and people of the Northeast, I find that in all their manner of living, those people of the Northeast, and these of the Northwest are like." Such evidence is cited as laying to rest claims that the Inuit were not of Asian origin but of a new culture derived from the intermixture of the Icelanders and the Scraelings of the Norse sagas.[16]

Frobisher captured an Inuit and his kayak and decided to take them back with him to England, for it seemed that here was a representative of a people who resembled those of Cathay. The fur-clad men who shot arrows and darts at the intruders paddled through islands of ice in skin boats. How these people had adapted to northern lands and circumstances invited the admiration of the English. Frobisher's men saw the Inuit, as modern ethnologists do, as a circumpolar culture.

Best observed that the glowingly optimistic theory of discovery that the English carried forth with them met with harsh experience in these high latitudes. Heavy weather, tantalizing glimpses of gold, and edgy relations with apparently hostile Inuit obliged the English to think in new ways about their imperial ambitions.[17] It would have been odd if this were not so, for everywhere expectations clashed with realities.

Frobisher was back in London in the *Gabriell* on 9 October 1576. The ship's arrival was met with joy and admiration, not only because the ship was thought to have been lost but also, as Lok put it, because of the "strange man and his bote, which was such a wonder onto the whole city and to the rest of the realm." Lok had been promised the first thing found in the new land, and Frobisher gave him a piece of mineral. Three assayers had a look at it, at Lok's request, and pronounced it to be marcasite. But a fourth assayer, an Italian named Agnello, returned three tiny amounts of gold for three each of marcasite. Here was promising news. Lok asked Agnello how he had succeeded when others had failed. "It is necessary to know how to flatter nature," was the Italian's reply. With this assay, Frobisher's second and third voyages to the Arctic were born, although visions of the northwest passage were fading.

On these later trips, sailors were sent ashore to rockbound Baffin Island with pickaxes and shovels and by main force (some suffering terrible ruptures) hauled the ore down to the waiting vessels. Heavily laden, the ships made the long homeward voyage and unloaded their cargo not far from the Tower of London, where Lok's business partner, Sir William Winter, had set up his great furnace. The Saxon assayer Jonas Shutz, on loan from the Duke of Saxony, made every attempt with bellows and furnace to get gold and silver from the "fool's gold." He found the percentages were insufficient to make the whole thing a workable proposition. It was, in all, heartbreak. Some of Frobisher's "black ore" is visible at Dartford, Kent, where it was used in the reconstruction of the Priory walls—an oddity, a curious legacy of a northern empire vanished but not altogether forgotten.

Lok never sailed with Frobisher on these hazardous voyages. In fact, he heaped abuse on the seaman when the scheme went wrong. Lok's damning testimony against Frobisher for the horrors of his gold-hunting and empire-building project is printed in a close study of the third voyage.[18] James McDermott, who edited the account, puts it correctly when he says: "Clearly, Frobisher may only be regarded as substantially guilty of these charges if every misadventure to befall the three voyages, and the supremely flawed assumptions upon which they were dispatched, were entirely the result of his 'doinges.' Insofar as Lok himself was one of the principal movers

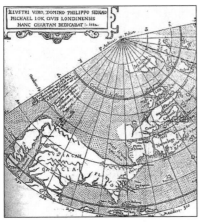

Eager to map the new world, Michael Lok's 1582 attempt was as much based on conjecture and rumour as it was on fact.
ARCHIVES CANADA

behind attempts to find value in the sample of ore returned from the first voyage, he must be regarded as at least as—and probably more—culpable than Frobisher himself for the expensive perpetuation of the enterprise beyond its failure to establish a sea-route to the East."[19] In the Lok–Frobisher disputation we have what a psychologist might call a case of comparative, differential projection of blame.

But, antiquarian and geographer that he was, in the mould of Dr. Dee, Lok compiled a good deal of information about these northern lands and seas. His 1582 engraved map of North America shows how incomplete was his knowledge, what a wild guess he might make about its true nature. On the map he placed some notes describing how the Portuguese had sailed from some western strait in the 1520s, the Spanish in the 1540s, and the English in 1580—all speculative and doubtless cribbed from other maps.

The Cathay Company, an unincorporated firm that Lok organized for this great Elizabethan-age venture to what is now Canada's northland, brought no promise of a northwest passage and certainly no financial benefit or even hope of such. He always seemed to be one step ahead of his bankers, but eventually he could not outrace them. As his creditors despaired of seeing returns on their investment, and as Lok's debts mounted, he was thrown into Fleet prison, London, for debts clearly related to Frobisher's ventures. There was much bad blood. Lok charged Frobisher with "evil victualling" of the ships sailing to Meta Incognita, which accords with other snippets of evidence we have of Frobisher from a later voyage—that he pocketed money intended for provisioning, shortchanged the specified number of tuns of beer, and added rye to the whole meal, thereby cheapening it and probably making it unusable.[20] Frobisher was a quarrelsome and angular fellow, and if popular with the sailors was pricklish when it came to dealing with other officers. Vilhjalmur Stefansson, among the first to study the Frobisher voyages, gave this useful assessment of Frobisher's character, a counterpart to the derogatory comments of some of his contemporaries: "Though he is frequently described as a hasty, choleric, or passionate man, this estimate appears to be based mainly on the abuse heaped upon him by his old friend Lok when schemes went wrong."[21]

Before we leave Frobisher altogether, it is noteworthy that in 1585, as a vice admiral under Drake, he did strike gold—on a privateering expedition to the Caribbean when he took £60,000 in booty. Knighted for distinguished services against the Spanish Armada, he died in 1594, at Plymouth, from a wound received while storming a fort held by the Spanish. In all, he lived a life that startles the historian with its varieties and multitude of fortunes and misfortunes.

As for Lok, the business promoter, good fortune smiled on him at last; when he explained that his fiscal accounts were clean, and that he had fifteen children as dependents, he was released from the Fleet prison.[22]

We have noted that Frobisher stated flamboyantly that the discovery of a northwest passage was the only thing of the world which was yet left undone. A few other Elizabethans thought similarly. Lok had taken to the idea, and with Sir Humphrey Gilbert he preached the doctrine of a northwest passage. The two of them were good at ransacking all manner of files, maps and records to prove what they thought others should believe. Dr. Dee, if not fully convinced, had listened and given support in the navigation line. He also later invested in the third Frobisher voyage. Gilbert, like Lok, had an equal interest in the wool and worsted trade to Russia and Persia. Meanwhile, and in the next few decades, all the pioneers in England's discovery of the East went about their business by the hard way, around the North Cape and into the Barents Sea in the search for Cathay. They never reached it by sea but penetrated to Persia and Central Asia, and eventually sought out India, the Spice Islands and Japan. They laid the foundations for English trade in the East, notably by establishing the East India Company in the earliest years of the next century, and by doing this they pointed the way to empire.

Lok had certain links with the traders to Russia and Persia known as the Muscovy Company. A pair of Londoners, Willoughby and Chancellor, had set out bravely and with high expectations but had come home with inconclusive results. In their wake had gone one of the giants of the Tudor age, Anthony Jenkinson. Gilbert, who knew him well, said he was "a man of rare virtue, great travails and experience." This intrepid traveller, to whom we now turn our attention, if briefly, was born in Leicestershire in 1529; his father was an inn owner with landed estates. The second son of the family, Jenkinson was sent to sea as a youth in 1546, travelling to the Levant for training in a mercantile career. He knew most of the countries and islands of the Mediterranean. In 1553 he was at Aleppo in Syria when Suleiman the Magnificent marched into that city with an army of three hundred thousand men and two hundred thousand camels, on his way to war against the Persians. From Suleiman, Jenkinson got a *firman* (safe conduct or privilege) to trade in Turkish ports with his ships without hindrance and with freedom from tolls. At Bokhara, his next stop, he was summoned before Abdullah Khan. "He presented his letters, explained his mission and with that uncanny ability to win the confidence of Muslims, which had twice previously saved his life, he became a favorite with this prince." There was something about Jenkinson that made an immediate impression on the khans—"some combination of pride and deference which held their respect."[23] His was a wonderful personal manner, which when combined with courage and dedication to task made him a formidable trader in foreign lands. On this expedition he failed to reach the land of the Great Khan but even so had found potential for English goods in the cities of South Persia and the basin of the Caspian. As an agent of Elizabethan commerce, he had no equal. In 1553, back in London, he was admitted as a member of the Mercers' Company, and in 1557, fresh with success, was appointed captain-general of four ships of the Muscovy Company sailing for Russia via northern seas.

Jenkinson made the passage, then left the ships and travelled to Moscow, where he was admitted to the presence of Ivan the Terrible. He dined with the tsar by candlelight. In April he travelled into the Caspian, then to Bokhara. He did not enter Persia as he had hoped, for obstacles presented themselves. He returned to Moscow with some freed Russians, thus enhancing his prestige with the tsar. He reached London in September 1564—"God be praysed," he breathed in relief and gratefulness—where he was well received by the company. The next year he went again to trade in the Transcaspian region, retracing his route but was again unable to visit Persia because of problems with the Turks.

After his return to England he addressed a memorial to the queen, dated 30 May 1565, urging the probability of a northeast passage to Cathay and offering to head up the expedition. He had his day in court, so to speak, for he debated the issue with Gilbert before the Privy Council that winter. Nothing came of it.

In 1576 we find him connected to Frobisher's second gold-hunting expedition in the Canadian High Arctic—Lok would have made the introduction—and in 1578 he sat on a commission struck to report on the ore, the "fool's gold," brought home by Frobisher. But Jenkinson's days of adventurous travel had ended. He obtained some royal assignments and acted as a commissioner for the King of Denmark regarding navigation rights beyond Norway. He married Judith March, daughter of a member of the Muscovy Company, and acquired Sywell Manor near Northampton. The queen granted him additional lands and favours. He again moved, to nearby Ashton. "And thus being wearie and growing old, I am content to take my rest in mine owne house, chiefly comforting my selfe in that my service hath bene honorably accepted and rewarded of her Majesty and the rest by whom I have been employed." In 1606 he died in the quiet of the countryside. In all, his was a remarkable story, significant to all Elizabethan doings in high latitudes and in the promotion of trade and navigation. One of his descendents, Charles Jenkinson, was a mastermind of British commercial policy in the late eighteenth century, and as the first Earl of Liverpool became prime minister.

Michael Lok therefore knew Anthony Jenkinson, who was his senior by some years. In 1571, Lok, as London agent of the Cathay Company, had an ear to the ground concerning trade developments near and far. Once out of the Fleet prison he had taken a new lease on life, establishing himself in the eastern Mediterranean and the waters leading to Constantinople.

In those days the principal trade of Europe flowed through two great channels from Asia. One was, as Jenkinson had promoted, through northern lands, waters and ports, from Novgorod in Russia through Riga, Bruges and Bergen and thence to London, with the Hanseatic League a contending force to be reckoned with in all English trade. The other connected through the eastern Mediterranean from the caravans of the Black Sea coasts and thence to Damascus and Aleppo and other Syrian cities or by Arab traders to Alexandria, where they came within range of the Christian traders and nations. Genoa and Venice had contended for the second of these routes, with Venice gaining the advantage. Spices and silks came that way, to which were added wine and foodstuffs from the eastern Mediterranean, manufactures from Genoa, then wines and fruits from Cadiz, Lisbon and Bordeaux and cloths from the Low Countries. In these days the English Crown always preferred profit in trade to considerations of settlement overseas, and thus a merchant class grew up with expansive interests in marine endeavours; the early origins of a merchant marine and even a royal navy make their appearance in the fifteenth century, if not before.

In this early swing of interests to the eastern Mediterranean, Lok was one of several Englishmen pursuing the lucrative business to Turkey in the late sixteenth century, and from his Muscovy Company connections he enlarged his network to yet another. As agent for the Company of Merchants of Turkey, otherwise known as the Levant Company, he was for a time the English consul at Aleppo. But he had withdrawn from Turkey to Venice, and for a time there was in a battle with the heads of the company, notably Sir John Spencer, for monies owed him as a pension for services rendered. Lok always seems to have been at odds with those he was in partnership with, and his tendency to advance services and monies without assurance of collecting what was his due seems to have been his Achilles heel. As with the Cathay Company, so, too, the Levant Company.

The Levant Company, established 1577, had a growing membership in the late sixteenth century, a mix of nobility and gentry adding to the purely mercantile segment from London and the key English ports. In 1580, London merchants Sir Edward Osborne and Richard Staper obtained a *firman* from Sultan Murad III granting full rights and privileges to English merchants within the Ottoman empire.[24] The company established a depot at Aleppo, Syria, where Lok was often based, and others at Damascus, Tunis and Alexandria. A few years later the Venetians followed the Levant Company into the eastern Mediterranean. In their commerce to the Levant, the English sailed their fast race-built ships; the Venetians kept to their stout, deep-waisted galleys. From the near east came peppers and other spices, fabrics and metal-wares, persons in human bondage (there was a trade in female slaves), and birds and animals. The story is told of a parrot destined for England who rode all the way on the tunic clothing his dead master's body.

The English and Venetians worked in alliance, and it was from Venice that Lok pressed his claim against the Company of Merchants of Turkey, obtaining an English court order (from the Lords of the Privy Council) to get partial compensation for money owing for services rendered. Lok, unhappily, had pegged his future on a fading star, for the trade that took English worsteds and tinware to the Levant in exchange for peppers, damasks and other rarities was a fragile and unstable business. But he knew the ships that ventured to and from Tripoli and the other ports near Aleppo, and he knew those that could carry messages to Juan de Fuca in later years, right up to the regrettable time when the correspondence between them came to a sudden end.

Lok had also come to Venice to meet Juan de Fuca, a meeting set up through the agency of a third party, another mariner, one John Dowglas, or Douglas. This person, of whom we sadly know so little, was said by Lok to be "an Englishman, a famous Mariner, ready coming for Venice, to Pilot a Venetian Ship, named *Ragasona* for England." The English master and pilot would make the intended passage through to London, there to unload cargo, probably of currants, and ship out independently back to Venice, a regular passage, possibly.[25]

For many other merchants, the tale of Juan de Fuca would have made no sense, but Lok immediately recognized that it might provide a real advantage in the quest for new trade and empire in the South Sea. We do not know Lok's age in 1596 but imagine him to be of middle years, and he was as well connected as he was determined to press any advantage that would give him benefit. He lived by guile and cunning, matching resourcefulness with determination.

As for Juan de Fuca, he had lately come out of Spain, had arrived first at Livorno, the port for Tuscany, and went thence to Florence. There he had found Dowglas. And together, as stated, they travelled in company to Venice. Juan de Fuca's ultimate destination may have been Greece—his native Kefallinia, or Cephalonia, the largest of the Ionian Islands along the Adriatic coast, held in fee by Venice.[26] Or, and this seems more likely given his reduced financial circumstances, he may have been in Venice in search of a ship for further work. We will never know, but it seems from the casual evidence that he was bound for Cephalonia and to the hearth of his family.

Juan de Fuca, says Lok with concern for accuracy, was named properly "Apóstolos Valerianos, of Nation, a Greek, born in the Island Cefalonia, of profession a Mariner, and an ancient Pilot of Shippes." Apóstolos Valerianos translates as "Gallant Messenger."[27] Lok put his acquaintance's age as three score, or sixty. That means Juan de Fuca would have been born in about 1536 and likely would have gone to sea at a young age. He missed that tumultuous climactic of Mediterranean history, the Battle of Lepanto, 1571, when the grand alliance of Christian states defeated the Turks at sea. At that time he would have been sailing as a hired pilot in a Spanish ship on the broad oceans of the Atlantic or Pacific. Michael Lok gives no physical description of the man, a shame, but we might imagine him as bronzed, heavy-set or stocky in body and limbs, bearded, and of moderate stature. Juan de Fuca gave testimony, not in English, for he seems not to have been fully conversant in it, but rather in Italian and Spanish. And it can be assumed, for reasons recounted below, that he was conversant in Portuguese. (Lok and Dowglas may have had similar multilingual capabilities, for men like these lived a well-travelled existence.)

Juan de Fuca was nominally a Venetian because at this time the Republic of Venice held the Ionian islands, including Cephalonia and Ithaca, as its own.[28] Venice had acquired Cephalonia in 1500, and although the Turks had taken many an island or outpost nearby—such as Kononi and Methoni and, closer to the time of the meeting of our conspirators in Venice, Naxos in the Cyclades and Cyprus—Cephalonia had remained part of the Venetian empire. The ruling power had always allowed its essential Greek culture, religion and tradition to continue unmolested, guarded as it were by the naval banners of Venice. Juan de Fuca was obviously Greek, a nation famously maritime, but he had moved out of Mediterranean bounds, passed westward through the Pillars of Hercules, and become a global mariner, an international citizen, one of the greatest voyagers of his time. More critically, his long employment in distant seas, voyaging for the king of Spain, had made him, for all intents and purposes, a Spanish subject.

What he did not know was that at the same time he was relaying his information about a strait leading from the Pacific to the Atlantic in a conversation with Michael Lok in Venice, the Parliament at Westminster was about to pass legislation saying that any person known to have been in the service of the king of Spain was to be regarded as an enemy of the English state.

Juan de Fuca talked freely with Michael Lok. He opened his testimony by saying he had been in the West Indies of Spain for forty years. By that he meant the Spanish continents, oceans and islands stretching westward across the Pacific to the Philippines, and he had sailed to and from many places thereof as mariner and pilot in the service of the Spaniards. He had sailed to the Philippines and China. But misfortune presented itself, for returning from those islands toward New Spain, the ship in which he sailed had been robbed and taken at Cape California by a Captain Cavendish, an Englishman, and he had lost 60,000 ducats of his own goods, his own consignment or share. The ship, we later learn, was the famed *Santa Ana*, with its own remarkable ending. We will come back to this and, in doing so, may be surprised to find how closely the details Juan de Fuca recounted square with the known record of events.

It is significant that Lok spoke of Juan de Fuca as mariner and pilot, just as he referred to Dowglas as a mariner and pilot. The two men were part of an international cadre with skills in navigation, pilotage and even command, abilities that made them the guiding lights of merchant voyaging and naval campaigns. Ship-handling was their domain; their duty, to set a vessel into position in time of combat or to wear away to safety as required by the commanding officer or fleet commander. The Elizabethans differentiated between a pilot and a master: "the Pilote is to looke carefully to the Sterridge of the Shippe, to be watchfull in taking the heights of Sunne and Starre; to note the way of his Shippe, with the augmenting and lessening of the winde." The office of the master was different: "For in matters of guide and disposing of the saylers, with the tacking of the Shipp, and the workes which belong thereunto, within board and without, all is to be committed to the master's charge."[29] A pilot in a Spanish vessel corresponded to a first mate of English and American ships; as second to the master in command over the seamen, he received twice the wage of a sailor and was recompensed equally with the master. One Spanish captain, García Palacio, declared that a pilot "should be a man of considerable age and experience, vigilant and weather-wise, knowing when to take in sail and acquainted with astronomy."

The pilots were experts at dead reckoning. In Columbus's time they knew no celestial navigation, and on his return, Columbus himself held to dead reckoning.[30] The lack of celestial navigational technique in those years invoked the ire of the Jewish-Portuguese mathematician Pedro Nunes (Nonnius), who asked in derisive tones, "Why do we put up with these pilots, with their bad language and barbarous manners; they know neither sun, moon nor stars, nor their courses, movements or declinations; or how they rise, how they set and to what part of the horizon they are inclined; neither latitude nor longitude of the places on the globe, nor astrolabes, quadrants, cross staffs or watches, nor years common or bissextile, equinoxes or solstices?"[31] Given this harsh indictment, one may wonder how their scientific capabilities had progressed by the time Juan de Fuca encountered Michael Lok.

As an experienced Mediterranean pilot, Juan de Fuca would likely have been more capable in the arts of navigation than some of the earlier Portuguese or Atlantic pilots. Mediterranean pilots lived in a sailors' world accustomed to plotting, pegging and coastal navigation; the culture of that sea gave them an advantage in capabilities over some who did straightforward oceanic transits by dead reckoning. Mediterranean pilots used a *Compasso da Navigare*, a chart based on coastwise compass bearings and distances between ports and prominent landmarks. From each of these reference points, radiating lines stretched across the chart, representing compass bearings. Placing a straight edge between departure and destination points, the mariner could calculate the distances along his chosen course using a distance scale and a pair of dividers, marking his position by pricking the parchment.

The Portuguese took this even further, making the first decisive steps from extended pilotage toward navigation proper, the "grand navigation" defined by the Fleming Michiel Cogniet in his treatise on the subject published in 1581. Spain had had a voracious need of pilots as commercial and imperial aspirations expanded, particularly after 1580 when the Portuguese kingdom came into Spanish possession. "Pilots were a versatile breed," wrote David Quinn. "In the discovery and exploration of eastern North America they were in great demand, more particularly if they were prepared to switch their expertise and possibly their allegiance from one power to another." One Portuguese pilot, Simon Fernández, had few scruples and greatly enjoyed robbery at sea, earning the distrust of many who sailed with him. He had considerable force of character and hated the Spanish, preferring the English. His instability of character discredited him with promoters, and the last that was heard of him was that he was in the English service against Spain in the Frobisher-Hawkins expedition of 1590. Sir Francis Walsingham, England's Secretary of State, who ran all sorts of intelligence and protection rackets, was prepared to forgive sea robbers if they helped against Spain.[32] He bore no malice toward the Portuguese, nor would he have toward a Greek such as Juan de Fuca.

Intriguing points, but ones to be put aside for now with the suggestion that Juan de Fuca might have been at the top of his capabilities in that line of work.

Chapter 2

PIRATES ON THEIR BEAT

*I*n 1579 Francis Drake made his dramatic assault on Spanish shipping, commerce and settlements beyond Cape Horn. In daring raids and ship captures he earned the enduring hatred of the Spanish. He caught them napping, for they had not invested in defences to their ports or their shipping, and what they had was no match for the furious and sudden onslaughts that were Drake's hallmark. The story has been told many times and needs no repetition here, except to say that the corsairing of the English was their special mode of warfare at the time, and these were the methods of the underdog. They relied on surprise and initiative duly taken when opportunity presented itself.

Nuño da Silva, a Portuguese pilot and native of Lisbon, who had been made a prisoner of the English on his voyage from Oporto to Brazil, provided to the Inquisition a deposition about Drake, the robberies he had committed, and many other particulars of Drake's voyage. He was a bit uncertain about Drake's northern voyage and his plans for returning to England. Even if Drake had told da Silva the details he recounts, it is entirely possible, given Drake's character, that what was supplied was disinformation.

Drake told da Silva that he intended to discover a northern strait that would take him back to England, and, failing that, that he was bound to return via China. Drake said he had to be home by August 1579. He also told the pilot that he had come to the Pacific for a much more important mission than seizing Spanish shipping; he left the pilot to guess what that was. Then da Silva recounts, "In Guatulco he took out a map and showed that he was bound to return by a strait that was situated in 66 degrs. and that if he did not find it, he was to return [home] by China. On the bronze cannon he carried in the pinnace, there was sculptured the globe of the world with a north star on it, passing over. He said that these were his arms and that the Queen had conferred them upon him, sending him to encompass the world."[33]

Drake missed the northwest passage and put the geographical difficulties this way:

> The Asian and American continents, if they be not fully joined, yet seem they to come very neere, from whose high and snow-covered mountains the north and north-west winds send abroad their frozen nimphes to the infecting of the whole air—hence comes it that in the middest of their summer, the snow hardly departeth from these hills at all; hence come those thicke mists and most stinking fogges—for these reasons we coiecture that either there is no passage at all through these Northerne coasts, which is most likely, or if there be, that [it] is unnavigable.[34]

In the wake of Drake, English mariners came not to find such a passage but for purposes of plunder. Our scene now shifts to Cabo San Lucas, Baja California, on 4 November 1587, a mere nine years before the Venice encounter of Michael Lok and Juan de Fuca. On this occasion, the pilot Juan de Fuca would encounter, and not by choice, an English mariner named Thomas Cavendish, or Candish, a young, headstrong squire from Trimley, Suffolk.[35]

Cavendish, like many an aspirant, had lingered at the English court seeking preferment. For a young man such as himself, the life of a swain or squire held no interest. More exciting fields beckoned than those on which sheep grazed. In London he had become acquainted with Sir Walter Raleigh, the colonial promoter and importer of tobacco. He met, too, some veterans of the sea who had gone with Sir Francis Drake on his voyage round the world and had come home again with rave reports. Cavendish was rightly fired with the prospect of emulating Drake's rapacious pirating

Called "The Navigator," Thomas Cavendish was the first to deliberately circumnavigate the earth in his attempt to imitate the exploits of Sir Francis Drake. By capturing the Spanish galleon *Santa Ana*, he was successful, and arrived back in London extravagantly wealthy. FROM *HERÓOLOGIA ANGLICA* BY HENRY HOLLAND

feat of circumnavigation and, above all, of returning a wealthy hero. He had little or no fighting experience. It is true that he had ventured to Virginia and the West Indies, but he had not prospered there and thus sought adventure farther afield, where rewards (commensurate with the risks) were known to exist. He obtained through the Lord High Chamberlain, his patron at court, a royal commission for his enterprise, and to finance it he mortgaged his estates to outfit three small vessels—*Content, Desire* and *Hugh Gallant*. His object, in imitation of Drake, was to prey on Spanish towns and shipping. The Spanish were largely defenceless, as Drake had proved.

Cavendish sailed from Plymouth in July 1586, and an agonizing seven months later entered the Pacific via the Straits of Magellan. He navigated along the coast of Chile, Peru and New Spain, burning and sinking nineteen ships, and burning towns and villages wherever he landed. He had made great spoils and could have taken greater quantities of treasure had he not been discovered on the coast by the Spanish. Still, there was work to do in the pirating line. Of greater value than the petty wealth gathered ashore and the pleasure of singeing the Spaniard's beard was a great prize. Drake had missed it; Cavendish intended it as his big catch. This was the Manila galleon.

From the beginning of Spanish trade in the seas of southeast Asia, China had commanded attention, for it was here that the greatest economic power was generated.[36] They wanted gold and silver, and the Americas provided what was insisted on: silver, or *plata*, from Mexico and gold, *oro*, from Peru. From the Philippines a new trade had developed with China when shipwrecked Chinese sailors had demonstrated the link by sea. Manila vaulted forward as a trading and shipping hub. The Spanish promised the precious metals, and the Chinese responded with oriental goods—costly silks, satins, silk stockings and porcelains, besides pearls, diamonds, topazes, carved ivory chests and intricate wood carvings. There was hardly anything the Chinese could not make in the decorative line. From Japan came suits of armour, amber, samurai swords, knives, saltpetre to make gunpowder, cabinetwork and more. The Spice Islands supplied cloves, cinnamon and pepper. Southeast Asia provided musk, civet, sandalwood, tin, ivory, rubies and sapphires.[37]

From 1573, and for two and a half centuries after, the Manila galleons or *naos de China*—"the ship of China"—departed Manila in June or by mid-July, sailed north to Japan, then turned east and kept that latitude, bound for northern California. Ships' pilots would recognize the nearness of land by signs on the ocean surface such as jellyfish, seals, reed rafts or kelp, and they would usually make a landfall near Cape Mendocino in latitude 40° 26' N. The last leg of this longest, most tedious and most dangerous voyage of all the seas was a coastwise one, southeasterly along the shore on the approach to Acapulco, the terminus and welcome resupply point.

How Cavendish came to take the 700-ton Manila galleon *Santa Ana* is a famous account of privateer lore, and in later years English freebooters and even Royal Navy commodores of the eighteenth century sought to emulate his feat. As ever, the Elizabethans gathered intelligence from foreign pilots about the prospects to be gained at sea. From a Provençal pilot, Cavendish had learned of the expected arrival of this vessel at Cabo San Lucas at the tip of Baja California. Cabo San Lucas was one of the waypoints where the pilots of the galleons could check their bearings before proceeding to Acapulco, which lay still a few weeks' sail away. Cavendish thus steered to a golden encounter.

On 14 October 1587 he reached Cabo San Lucas. He lingered here, almost on the Tropic of Cancer, in a bay close under the cape, a suitable lair or base of convenience from which he could patrol in search of the galleon.[38] On 4 November a lookout on the *Desire* shouted the news of a great vessel steering for the headland. A message was immediately passed to the *Content*, and the two corsairs sailed in fast pursuit. Official complacency dogged the Spanish administration of Pacific affairs. The galleon, though of 700 tons, was devoid of cannon, for the Spanish feared no rival in those seas. She was a towering presence, her decks encumbered by cargo, and the English vessels, though puny at 120 and 40 tons and mounting eighteen and ten guns respectively, wreaked havoc with their gunnery pieces. The Spaniards replied with a couple of arquebuses and muskets, lances, rapiers and even great stones brought up from ballast.

Francis Pretty, master of the *Desire*, takes up the story: "We now trimmed our sailes and fitted every man his furniture [arms and armour], and gave them a fresh encounter with our great ordinance and also with our small shot, raking them through and through, to the killing and maiming of many of their men."[39] For six hours the action continued unabated, the Spanish suffering heavy losses and the galleon taking on water speedily. At last the Spaniards hung out a flag of truce. The galleon lowered her sails, and a passenger was sent on board the *Desire* to parley.

The register of *Santa Ana*'s cargo listed 122,000 pesos of gold plus a rich cargo of silks, glossy sateen damasks, all sorts of choice conserves and foods, and sundry sorts of good wines. When opened, the chests gleamed at Cavendish, who exclaimed, "Now we are rich, for in the two years that we have been going we have found nothing like this."[40] The total value of the cargo was estimated at over two million pesos.[41] Cavendish took what he wanted and even signed for it, signifying to the Spaniard that he had left something to him, a nice touch in the impoverishing circumstances. Cavendish sent 190 Spaniards ashore and gave them food and handguns as protection against the local Indians. He hanged a priest, the canon of Manila, from the mizzen arm of the *Desire*, and then set fire to the galleon and turned her adrift. To those shipwrecked, now on shore, Cavendish sent food and wine, firewood, sailcloth for tents and planking for a boat.

Juan de Fuca, one of the galleon's pilots, was among those put ashore. With him went Sebastián Vizcaíno, one of Spain's most illustrious marine explorers, who later explored the California coast.[42] Vizcaíno was returning from Manila with 60,000 ducats invested in rich merchandise, all of which had been lost to Cavendish. Juan de Fuca claimed a similar amount of his own trading stock taken by the privateer.

"It was [Vizcaíno's] resourcefulness that now saved his companions who were marooned on the peninsula far from the Spanish settlements on the mainland and with little hope of an early rescue," writes William Schurz, historian of the Manila galleon. "As an off-shore wind blew the smoking galleon in towards the beach, Vizcaíno called on the most able-bodied of his fellows and with them went out through the surf to the hulk. They extinguished the flames in the hold and then, after the most strenuous efforts, succeeded in putting the ship in condition to cross the Gulf of California and finally to reach Acapulco on the seventh of January."[43] This is the stuff of legend and ought to rank as comparable with Bligh's boat voyage after the taking of the *Bounty*.

"Another survivor of the *Santa Ana* is said to have been the mendacious Greek pilot, Juan de Fuca."[44] This is Schurz's opinion of Juan de Fuca. We do not know how many Pacific transits Juan de Fuca had made on the Manila-Acapulco galleon. But he was a workaday fellow of the kind essential to Spain's worldwide empire: like many another pilot not of Spanish blood, he had brought global reach to the Iberian kingdom. We might conjecture that his was, oddly enough, a prosaic life, guiding ships from port to port, pegging out the imperial progress of a maritime empire. Now Cavendish had spoiled any prospects Juan de Fuca might have had to abandon that life for one of wealth through trading. Resentment burned deep in de Fuca and others who faced a similar fate at the hands of the dreaded English pirates.

As for Cavendish, he sailed westward to reach the Philippines where at Cavite, the port for Manila, news of his deeds and misdeeds caused consternation and anger. Every Manila merchant had reason to be saddened by the loss of investment in trade items. Cavendish was a brazen fellow, cocky and boastful. The bishop of Manila had the displeasure of receiving a visit from the cheeky young man, who, to his face, proclaimed his achievements. "The grief that afflicts me," His Grace recounted with undeniable sadness, "is not because this barbarian has robbed us of the ship . . . and destroyed the property . . . but because an English youth of about twenty-two, with a wretched little vessel . . . and forty or fifty companions, should dare to come to my own place of residence, defy us and boast of the damage that he had wrought. He went from our midst laughing, without anyone molesting or troubling him."[45]

Cavendish arrived back in the English Channel not long after the defeat of the Spanish Armada. It is true that he had missed a glorious naval action in which most of England's seadogs had achieved their finest hours. But he had won a victory all his own, and he staged a triumphal entry up the Thames. "Among other things the Queen said, 'We care nothing for the Spaniards. Their ships, loaded with gold and silver from the Indies, come hither after all'." Every man who sailed with Cavendish sported a gold chain round his neck, and the sails were of blue damask. The ship flew a standard of gold and blue silk. "It was as though Cleopatra were born again," wrote Francis Pretty. "The only thing wanting was that the rigging should have been of silken rope."[46] Cavendish gave a banquet for the queen on 5 November. The influx of precious metals induced a violent occurrence on the London money markets. The pirates spent with a profligacy unheard of in the capital. The value of Cavendish's booty shrank daily, observed the Spanish ambassador Bernardino de Mendoza, but the English still estimated it at 500,000 crowns. "Cavendish must have brought great riches," he noted, "for they are coining new broad-angels [English gold coins], and gold is cheaper here than it ever was."[47] Queen Elizabeth chose not to knight Cavendish, for his ostentatious display of captured riches did not endear him to her or to her subjects.[48]

In an attempt to put the best face on the great robbery at sea, a Spanish official airily brushed off the defenceless state of the galleon by explaining that "they have always sailed with as little fear from corsairs as if they were on the river of Seville."[49] Even so, a defensive mentality necessarily ruled the Spanish imperial system. Spanish mariners and administrators feared any English or Dutch passage from Atlantic to Pacific via the Straits of Magellan. The Spanish had made plans, never effected, to set up a base there. Sarmiento's history of the Spanish discoveries in the area recounts the work of the Portuguese pilots who followed Magellan, on the one hand, and, on the other, those who set out from the Philippines on a reverse voyage across the Pacific (it took four attempts before success came) to reach Mexico's west coast.

Portuguese and Greek pilots made possible the Spanish discoveries of the South Sea. Now they turned their attention to the coast of America. Vizcaíno made a great exploration of the California coast by order of the viceroy of Mexico, set up some temporary bases, and suggested the occupation of Monterey Bay as a northern base to check the English. He was well aware of the incursions of the Elizabethans into the Spanish reserve, and who knew when they might come again? His premonitions and fears were well founded. English mariners now dreamed of duplicating the seemingly easy feats of Drake and of Cavendish. Sir Richard Hawkins would go in 1593, only to be captured in Peru, and Sir John Narborough went to Chile in 1670, returning fruitlessly.

In Venice, meantime, Juan de Fuca recounted to Lok the long and sad tally of his losses to Cavendish. His future had depended on the private investments he shipped aboard the *Santa Ana*. The losses were grievous. With time passing, it seemed less and less probable that he would ever be able to recover from this robbery.

Juan de Fuca had other matters to disclose to Michael Lok, and they had implications for the future. He recounted two other expeditions of note. In the first, he said, he was pilot of three small ships sent out by the viceroy of Mexico, armed with one hundred men, soldiers, under a Spanish captain, to discover the Straits of Anian. A second aim of that mission was to build fortifications at key points along the shore in order to resist the passage and proceedings of the English nation, which they feared would send ships through those straits into the South Sea. However, "by reason of a mutinie which happened among the Soldiers, for the Sodomie of their captain, that Voyage was overthrown, and the Ships returned back from California coast to Nova Spania, without any effect of thing done in that Voyage. And that after their returne, the Captain was at Mexico punished by justice."[50] And so we have a sexual crime setting back northern discoveries. That voyage must have been in 1591, or close to it.

"Also," Lok noted in his account, "he said that shortly after the said Voyage was so ill ended, the said Viceroy of Mexico sent him out again Anno 1592, with a small Caravela and a Pinnace, armed with Mariners only, to follow the said Voyage, for discovery of the same Straits of Anian, and the passage thereof, into the Sea which they call the North Sea, which is our North-west Sea." It was on this voyage that he found the "broad Inlet of Sea, betweene 47. and 48. degrees of Latitude," with the "great Hedland or Iland, with an exceeding high Pinnacle, or spired Rocke, like a piller thereupon" at its entrance.[51]

Juan de Fuca considered that he had fulfilled his instructions from the viceroy. He had gone as far as the North Sea, which at the strait's entrance, he said, was 30 or 40 leagues wide. A league is of variable determination, but the usual measure is 3 miles, and 90 to 120 miles seems beyond comprehension as an estimate for the opening of the Strait of Juan de Fuca, which is actually about 14 miles wide. Was Juan de Fuca referring to the Strait of Georgia, as Muriel Wylie Blanchet maintains in *The Curve of Time*? This seems eminently possible. Perhaps he assumed that the Strait of Georgia was the northwest passage, and was prepared to close off his discoveries there in response to dwindling supplies, ravages of scurvy, and discontented and debilitated crews. We do know that he worried that his vessels were not sufficiently armed to deal with any native force encountered, a just disposition. Thus he sailed to Acapulco, in expectation of a viceroy's reward for services rendered.

From Acapulco he went to Mexico, where he was warmly received by the viceroy and promised great reward. He waited. Two years later he was still without the reward he hoped for. The viceroy eventually promised the mariner would be rewarded by the king himself in Spain. So with great hopes he sailed for Spain. Arriving expectantly at the royal court, presumably at the Escorial, he received great treatment during another long wait but could get no satisfaction. We can imagine that Juan de Fuca's claim counted for little with Philip II, whose administrative rituals consisted of reading vast stacks of in-letters and appeals one by one, judiciously setting them aside or acting on them as required.

Delays ensued. Juan de Fuca grew weary. He fretted. His losses to Cavendish rankled, and against this he had no record of his navigational achievement except his own recounting of events. No chaplain seems to have been aboard to take notes or keep records. Juan de Fuca kept no journal, or at least not one that has survived. Official records are silent on the matter. No other mariner of Spain speaks of the Greek pilot's derring-do. Thus, at length, Juan de Fuca "stole away out of Spain" and came to Italy. Aged and weary, he decided to go home, to retire. It was time to live among his own people on Cephalonia below a mountain named for eagles, near sea cliffs named for ravens. Odysseus too, after years with a crew he called his Cephalonians,[52] at last reached home on his own Ithaca.

Juan de Fuca claimed the reason the Spanish king paid no heed to his appeals for recompense was that the English threat had disappeared. After Frobisher's disastrous "fool's gold" ventures and other wild English attempts to discover a northwest passage, the English had set aside the project. So the Spanish need not fear the English penetration to the South Sea by that route. That was a logical deduction. But de Fuca believed that Elizabeth would compensate him for the loss of his goods captured by Cavendish. That was a vain hope. He even said he would gladly go to England and offer his services to the queen if she would furnish him with a ship of 40 tons and a pinnace, and he would perform a voyage from one end to the other of the straits in thirty days.

Thus it was that Juan de Fuca begged Lok to write to his friends in England—the Lord Treasurer Cecil (Burghley), the courtier and colonizer

Sir Walter Raleigh, and that famous cosmographer and literary promoter of empire and marine enterprise Master Richard Hakluyt. If given £100 recompense, Juan de Fuca said, he would gladly undertake the venture. Lok was ready to go to London to do the Greek pilot's bidding. He asked Juan de Fuca to go with him. But by this time Juan de Fuca was in Cephalonia and still awaiting Lok's promised money. At this stage, mere promises would not do. As late as 1596 the correspondence continued, and the messages became more irregular and did not always reach their recipient.

Lok received a message from Juan de Fuca on 1 August 1597, conveyed to him by an English merchant, Thomas Norden, living in London. Again Juan de Fuca promised to go with Lok to England to undertake the voyage for the discovery of a northwest passage into the South Sea. He would do so only if Lok would send him money for his charges according to his previous demands. Otherwise, without the money, he could not go, for "he said he was undone utterly, when he was in the Ship *Santa Anna*, which came from China, and was robbed in California."[53]

Lok wrote again and received an answer, Juan de Fuca's last. In this letter, dated 20 October 1598 and written in his native Greek, Juan de Fuca stated he was still agreeable to making the voyage into what he called the Strait of Nova Spain—"which he saith is but thirtie daies voyage in the streights"[54]—if and only if he could get the promised money. Lok's hands were tied. He had his own troubles and was still seeking recompense from the Company of Merchants of Turkey for his labours on their behalf as their consul at Aleppo. He had no money to offer the mariner for his promised services. "I had not yet recovered my pension owing mee by the Companie of Turkie . . . And so of long time I stayed from any further proceeding with him in this matter."[55]

Then, lo and behold, Lok came into his money from the Company of Turkey. Was it too late? He sent one last plaintive letter to his Greek friend. But as Lok later learned, the ancient mariner had been very sick and had died.[56] And with the death of Apóstolos Valerianos, Juan de Fuca, "the Pilot of the Indies," passed the last possible chance of the Greek mariner leading a voyage of English exploration to locate the elusive and fabled waterway to Cathay, the islands of Kublai Khan and the ports of the Celestial Kingdom of China.

Chapter 3

PURSUING THE LEGENDS, EXPLODING THE MYTHS

*D*ark shadows were gathering around many of the great personages of the age. Philip II died in 1598, leaving his son (in whom he had little confidence) the governance of the largest, most powerful and most complex empire in the world. After the Spanish Armada of 1588, two other armadas had been sent against England—in vain. Peace with the English came at last in 1604, by the Treaty of London. The Spanish, wracked by financial disasters, arranged a ceasefire with the Dutch in 1607 and sought other arrangements to bring peace in northern Europe, all the while retaining heavy defence commitments in the Mediterranean. They resorted to the debasement of their currency, and long after the Moors had been scattered abroad, the king began a campaign to expel the Moriscos from Spain. At home the Castilians, whose wealth rested in agriculture, groaned under the tax burden, and the shift in wealth-creation spread to the Americas, notably to the silver of Mexico and the trade of the Pacific.

Meanwhile, Drake died, as Hawkins had, of disease on board ship off Portobello, Panama, in 1595. The courtier Raleigh, the last of the Elizabethan adventurers, dreamer of empire in Virginia and the Orinoco, fell afoul of Elizabeth when he bedded and secretly wedded one of Elizabeth's ladies-in-waiting, thereby injuring the queen's pride, for she had closely favoured the adventurer. Queen Elizabeth died in 1603. When

James I came to the throne, Raleigh's hopes faded quickly. He came under suspicion for his supposed conniving with Spain. When he was released in order to undertake another search for El Dorado, he violated the king's trust by attacking the Spanish and creating another diplomatic incident. He brought home potatoes and tobacco, no small consideration, though the king penned a treatise condemning the dreaded weed and its foul and unhealthy smoke. On his return, Raleigh was again held in the Tower of London. There he worked away at his poems and his *History of the World* but the prosecutors finally could resist it no longer, and Raleigh was taken to Westminster, where he was beheaded in Old Palace Yard in 1618. It is true that Raleigh lived careless of his future, unmindful of consequences to his person. And as was said at his trial, he had indeed abused the permission to put to sea to find the gold mine in Guiana he said was there, and in doing so had violated the trust of King James I. "You have lived like a star," the Chief Justice reported in sentence, "and like a star you must fall when it troubles the firmament." As for William Sanderson, Raleigh's fixer, he fell on hard times, in no small measure because of his financial dealings with his kinsman.[57]

Even had Lok been able to get Juan de Fuca to England to make the case for a voyage to prove the existence of a strait to the Pacific and beyond to Cathay, there is no assurance the Greek would not have been arrested as a person detrimental to the security of the kingdom. Nests of Spanish suspects had been netted, seaport watches were strengthened to watch for spies, and directives were issued by privy councillors for "the apprehension of suspicious persons coming into England from beyond the sea." Justice in those days was not guided by statute law, criminal codes or defence of the realm acts. The work of national defence was undertaken by a small committee of six or seven men sitting with the queen at the Palace of Placentia in Greenwich. Rules and regulations were issued thick and fast. Foreigners lived under suspicion. An Irishman had to present himself to the Lord Mayor for examination as to his way of living and why he remained in England. And no person who had served the king of Spain was to be allowed to come into the realm. Unless there on permission, he was to be imprisoned and punished as an enemy. Such were the harsh and irrefutable laws of the land.[58] The ways of justice were swift, violent and effective in those spacious days. Against these, Juan de Fuca held no prospect. Employment under Queen Elizabeth was a vain hope.

The dream of the northwest passage never faded. In 1616 Robert Bylot and William Baffin explored Baffin Bay by way of Lancaster Sound but found it frozen and the passage elusive. As for a northeastern passage, it fell to the Russians to make the discoveries there. The Russian Dezhnev explored the strait between Asia and America in 1648, and eighty years later Vitus Bering, a Dane sailing for the tsar, made notable northern discoveries and with Chirikov is credited with having spied Alaska.

How did Juan de Fuca's tale come to light? In 1589 Richard Hakluyt, the great publicist of the voyages of the English nation, had put into print his remarkable, hot-selling compendium *Principal Voyages and Navigations*, a collection of voyage accounts and postulations about imperial expansion. Searching for a northwest passage was among the prominent themes; colonization and trade were others. Hakluyt was in touch with all the key players of this global expansion, and during his time in Paris, where he served as chaplain to the English ambassador, he gathered information about Spanish and French activities, "making diligent inquiries of such things as might yield light unto our western discovery of America." At Christ Church, Oxford, he lectured on geography and "shewed the old imperfectly composed, and the new lately reformed mappes, globes, spheres, and other instruments of this art." No man knew world developments better than Hakluyt, and his publication contains references to Lok alongside treatment of Drake, Cavendish, Frobisher, Davis and the rest who put North America more accurately on world maps. Lok's account was not published by Hakluyt, for reasons not known, but it is highly likely that Lok and Hakluyt discussed the story, and perhaps Hakluyt was awaiting confirming accounts of the amazing tale.

In any event, Hakluyt died in 1616, and Lok died in 1622, though even that date is uncertain. Lok's paper on Juan de Fuca's experiences in discovering a northwest passage in 1592 passed to the Reverend Samuel Purchas, as did other literary fragments of oceanic enterprise. They became the nucleus for a new work.[59] In fact, they fit the Purchas adage: "My purpose is not to steale Master Hakluyt's labours out of the World . . . I had rather giue you new things."[60]

When at last Juan de Fuca's account as told to Lok was made public by Purchas in the widely read *Hakluytus Posthumus; or, Purchas His Pilgrimes* in 1625, it formed much more than an idle tale. The story presented all sorts of possibilities to eager and inventive map-makers. It likewise had a considerable effect on the early cartography of western and northern America.

Hakluyt had no reason to hide Lok's story about Juan de Fuca and no reason, moreover, to falsify any of the accounts that he saw into print. Sam Bawlf, in *The Secret Voyage of Sir Frances Drake,* says that Hakluyt saw in de Fuca's story Drake's actual account of northern explorations. Bawlf has the famed editor of English navigations substituting the imagined latitudes of Drake for those of de Fuca. Thus, according to this mis-telling, Drake reaches the Northwest Coast in 54° N latitude, at the northwest tip of Haida Gwaii, sails south and east through narrow Clarence Strait and hazardous Johnstone Strait. He then passes miraculously through turbulent Seymour Narrows and Ripple Rock, reaches Georgia Strait, passes Pillar Rock when outward bound to the Pacific via the Strait of Juan de Fuca and proceeds homeward via the Pacific. It did not happen. It could not have happened without independent motive power (such as 250-horsepower outboard motors strapped to the transom of the *Golden Hind*). Bawlf has Drake unarmed so as to resist the First Nations that might be found in Georgia Strait, an oddity of logic given what the unvanquished Elizabethan warriors had done in a military way to Spanish soldiers and sailors.[61] There was no reason to falsify Juan de Fuca's tale so as to render it Drake's and then to drop it from publication altogether. Bawlf's chronology is woefully wrong. Drake met de Fuca before, not after, he sailed north to Nova Albion and his further courses north. De Fuca's voyage was in 1592; Drake's was in 1579.

As for a reported Strait of Anian as explored by Juan de Fuca, that too was of fading import. Another tale, by Maldonado, was in competition with it, and although some sort of strait was said to exist, the French enlarged upon it gleefully and blew it into a great sea of the west. De Fuca's tale and that of Maldonado did not die and, in fact, refused to go away. Thus Spanish and English explorers were led to enormous expense and effort to search for a seaway eastward from the entrance to de Fuca's strait by way of complex interior waterways, island clusters and river estuaries, and hitherto unimagined inlets and fjords.

English mariners continued to press on with the thought of finding a northwest passage to Japan by sailing from east to west. And so it was that in 1631 two rival projects, got up at exactly the same time, possibly in response to Purchas's recently published report about Juan de Fuca, prosecuted the very same scheme. This pitted upstart Yorkshire against experienced Bristol. Luke Fox—"North-west Fox," he's called—had a fruitless voyage and so did his great rival Thomas James, who had sailed from his native Bristol.

James, a barrister who had forsaken the bar for the sea and its opportunities, had been commissioned by the Bristol Society of Merchant Venturers to search for a passage to Asia. He said many highly disparaging things about those Portuguese pilots and their search for a passage from the west side of America. He was pointing a finger at Juan de Fuca, whose tale he knew. Like Fox, he had faced ice and rock in northern Hudson Bay. It gave him ice-cold pause. He wrote, with sardonic wit:

> What hath been long ago fabled by some Portuguese that should have come this way out of the South Sea, the meer shadows of whose mistaecken relations have come to us [Lok's account printed in *Purchas His Pilgrimes*], I leave to be confuted by their own vanity. These hopes have stirr'd up, from time to time, the more active spirits of this our kingdom, to research that merely imagin'd passage. For my own part, I give not credit to them at all, and as little to the vicious and abusive wits of later Portuguese and Spaniards, who never speak of any difficulties, as shoal water, ice, or sight of land; but as if they had been brought home in a dream or engine. And indeed their discourses are found absurd; and the maps, by which some of them have practis'd to deceive the world, meer falsities; making sea where there is known to be main land, and land where is nothing [but] sea.[62]

With the expeditions of James and Fox in 1631, the dream of a northwest passage leading out through Hudson Bay came to a dismal end for the time being. The hard west shore of the bay offered no seaway to Cathay; thus, the seamen concluded, if such existed it would have to be in higher latitudes. "Even if that merely imaginary passage did exist," recounted James with a certainty borne of grief and hardship, "it would be narrow, beset by ice, and longer than the route to the east by the Cape." But he noted that the shores of Hudson Bay were the home of many of the choicest fur-bearing animals in the world. Captain James was pointing toward the prospects of a trade in peltry, though it interested him not at all. That business would be left to wily traders and the support of government in the age of Charles

II—and the founding of The Gentlemen Adventurers of England Trading into Hudson's Bay, on 2 May 1670. In the meantime, James's account of his expedition took its place in the English literary world as a classic, and some consider that Coleridge drew on it when writing *The Rime of the Ancient Mariner*.

James, with undying conviction, declared that no passage existed south of 66° N latitude. In consequence, that illustrious mariner of the exquisite mind, William Dampier, pirate and naturalist, in 1686 thought it best to search for a northwest passage from the Pacific side.[63] Even so, nothing was done in this line. The true pickings, as the commercial statistics showed, lay in Chinese seas and those of southeast Asia. William Dampier and Woodes Rogers played havoc on Spanish galleons in the Pacific, but sometimes the Spanish were ready for them, and English greed backfired in at least one case off the tip of Cabo San Lucas.[64]

For the next century, at least, the quest for the passage was over, and although the search was revived in the mid-eighteenth century and led to no result via that eastern approach, there seemed always one or two self-appointed persons in politically powerful positions who could fan the flames of hope and keep the idea alive. Arthur Dobbs, MP, was one such; the Admiralty secretary, Sir John Barrow, another. Whether it was goading the Hudson's Bay Company into action or supplying a make-work scheme for the officers and men of the Royal Navy in the post-Napoleonic war period, the quest for the northwest passage from the eastern High Arctic continued. It was "the Arctic grail,"[65] and it led to the death of many officers and men, the loss of many a ship and, not least, the making of many widows.

Part Two

MYSTERIES OF THE
WATERWAY REVEALED

Chapter 4

BRITISH MERCHANT MARINERS ON DISCOVERY

The tale of Juan de Fuca refused to die. It passed from hand to hand, from one believer to another. Even so, those who doubted its authenticity abounded—and rightly so. In fact, so discredited was Juan de Fuca in the eyes of the new breed of explorers—those finely trained in scientific navigation with their *Nautical Almanacs*, sextants, chronometers and much else—that when Captain James Cook sailed by the entrance of the Strait of Juan de Fuca in March 1778, he seems to have bothered little with prosecuting the search for the passage in those latitudes. There is no doubt that his expedition was attempting a northern passage from the Pacific to the Atlantic but in far higher latitudes than what Juan de Fuca had proclaimed.

James Cook ranks among the top navigators of all time. A stolid Yorkshireman of controlled bearing and strict regimen, he had learned through hard-earned experience about the grey killer of the seas. By urging the use of a strange concoction called wort, a brew of malt, vinegar, sauerkraut and such other vegetables as were available, he had made long-distance voyaging safe and healthy for the crew. One watch on and two off was the routine so as to keep a ship's company sound. In two flawless voyages to the Pacific he had been to Tahiti, found Antarctica, coasted eastern Australia and cleared up many a puzzle about the lands and peoples of the Pacific. Now he had come again to the great ocean to spy out its northern limits and its Arctic seas and ice barriers.

He had left Plymouth, England, in July 1776, having two ships under his command, himself in the *Resolution* and Captain Charles Clerke in the *Discovery*. In December 1777 they were amid the familiar pleasures of Tahiti and all too soon on new fields of discovery, in January 1778, in the Sandwich (or Hawaiian) Islands. Cook quickly grasped the importance of the Hawaiian Islands; to his way of thinking they held a

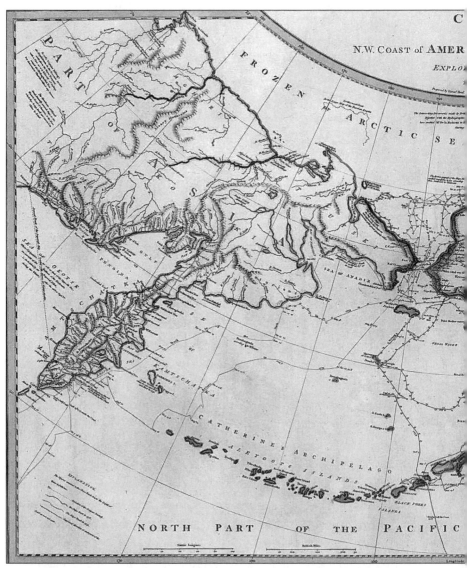

Detail from a "CHART of the N.W. COAST of AMERICA and the N.E. Coast of ASIA Explored in the Years 1778 and 1779. Prepared by Lieut. Heny. Roberts under the immediate Inspection of CAPT. COOK." Cook added considerably to Western

central position in the Pacific, offering a tempting prize in the imperial scramble. He warned that prior discovery by the Spanish would give Spain commercial advantages over other European nations, since ships sailing from the Philippines to Acapulco could use the islands as a mid-ocean place of resupply and refreshment. He rightly understood that the chief utility of the islands lay in their strategic location—a fact which

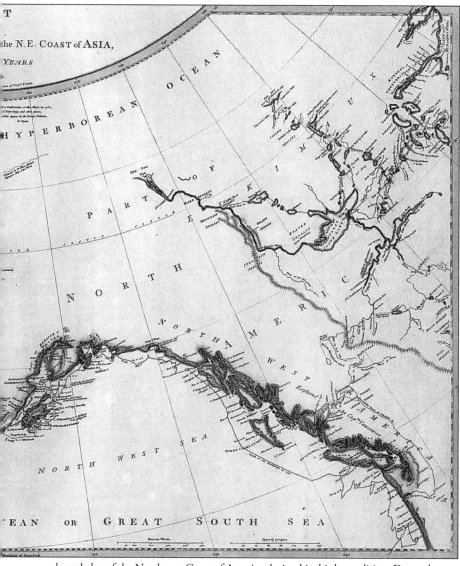

knowledge of the Northwest Coast of America during his third expedition. Due to heavy weather and poor visibility, he was obliged to seek safety well off shore, missing the entrance to the Juan de Fuca Strait. DAVID RUMSEY MAP COLLECTION

maritime fur traders in the next wave of voyaging in these seas later exploited to good effect.

Sailing before fair winds northeastward in an easy, quick passage to North America—from warm tropical isles to a grey, cold and unforgiving coast—Cook made a landfall on the morning of 7 March in latitude 44.5° N, where he came in sight of what Drake had called Nova Albion (now the coast of present-day Oregon, about 100 miles south of the mouth of the Columbia River). He was looking for a harbour for wood and water before continuing northward on his mission. "This Land is high and craggy & mostly covered with Snow. We saw prodigious large flocks of birds lying about. Having squally Wr. With fogs & frequent Showers of Snow, Hail and Sleet, which made it very dangerous to approach this unknown Coast too near where we knew of no Shelter, we were kept cruising off & on the Land till the 29th of this Month," wrote surgeon's mate David Samwell.[66]

The unfavourable winds and weather obliged Cook to keep well off the continental lee shore, discouraging any discoveries. "In times of the greatest danger," wrote Heinrich Zimmermann, a seaman in the *Discovery*, "his chief concern was to keep calmness and order on the ship. In this he was so successful that for the most part all eyes were fixed on him." Let us put our feet in the footsteps of the master mariner. It is easy to appreciate the difficulties of travelling under sail and "keeping the coast aboard" so as to satisfy the purposes of exploration and survey. Many years before, Cook had faced "the very jaws of destruction" when sailing in the Great Barrier Reef. He knew fully "the Vicissitudes [which] . . . must always attend an unknown Navigation." Cook had an uncanny sense, said those who sailed with him, of knowing where the dangerous shore was, even if he could not see it. He could smell a coast over the horizon. Five seasons surveying the Newfoundland shore had honed his skills of navigation in fog. Caution and discretion ruled, and this inspired the officers and men of the ships of discovery.[67]

In the circumstances, off the coast of Nova Albion, he stood well out to sea after making a landfall: heavy and contrary weather drove the ships as far south as 43° N. "And when we again made way northward, blowing and thick unsettled weather prevented our tracing a continuation of the coast, so that between a Cape in latitude 44° 55' N named by Captain Cook *Cape Foulweather*, and a point of land in 48° 15' N, which he named *Cape Flattery*, because the prospect of the land near it gave doubtful promise of a harbour, we obtained only now and then a glimpse of the land."[68] So wrote novelist Fanny Burney's brother James, the first lieutenant of the *Discovery*. Heavy weather dogged the explorers now. Nothing seemed to favour their explorations at this stage.[69]

Cook must have felt the frustration of having to be offshore so much of the time, unable to draw a clear indication of this coastline on a chart. He was the person who had written about himself "I who had Ambition not only to go further than any one had done before, but as far as it was possible for man to go." He also regarded it as unforgivable for a surveyor on exploration not to seek out the particulars of a new coastline. On 22 March he wrote in his journal that on shore "there appeared to be a small opening in the land that flattered us with hopes of finding a harbour." These hopes lessened as the ships drew nearer, "and at last we had some reason to think that this opening was closed by land."[70] He may not have been as far north as what Burney claims.

What Cook saw was what appeared to be a round hill of moderate height, standing over, as it were, the low cape, one ragged with evergreens. All the land in that part of the coast, he observed, was of a moderate height, seldom varying in that regard, well covered with wood and with a very pleasant and fertile appearance. In the growing darkness, when the ships were near but still south of Cape Flattery, Cook decided to tack off-shore to wait for daylight next day, intending to make a closer examination and to find the needed harbour. But that night a hard gale came on and with it rainy weather. Once again the ships were obliged to keep well off from the land. In the circumstances, a closer look at Cape Flattery proved impossible.

The British ships did not encounter the Makah—a pity, for had they done so, surely some ethnographic details would have been recorded by one or more of the inquisitive literary persons who were in the ships' companies. In any event, the Makah called themselves the Kwe-net-che-chat, that is, the Cape People, the people who live on a point of land projecting into the sea. (An alternative spelling is Qwidwidiccait, with the similar meaning of "People of the Cape.") The tribes on the western coast of Vancouver Island called them the "Klas-set" (now Classet, or Claaset), and the peoples who lived south of them, toward the Columbia River, knew them as the "Kwe-net-sat'h." The website of the Makah Nation on the Olympic Peninsula adds: "We call ourselves Kwih-dich-chuh-ahtx, or 'People who

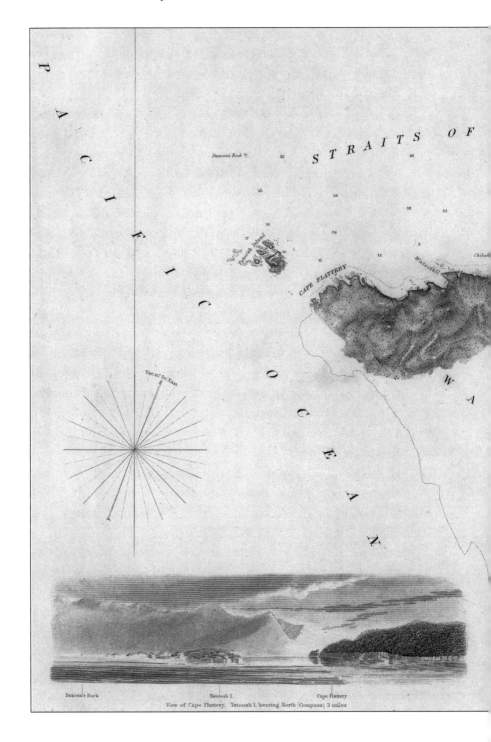

View of Cape Flattery, Tatoosh I. bearing North (Compass) 3 miles

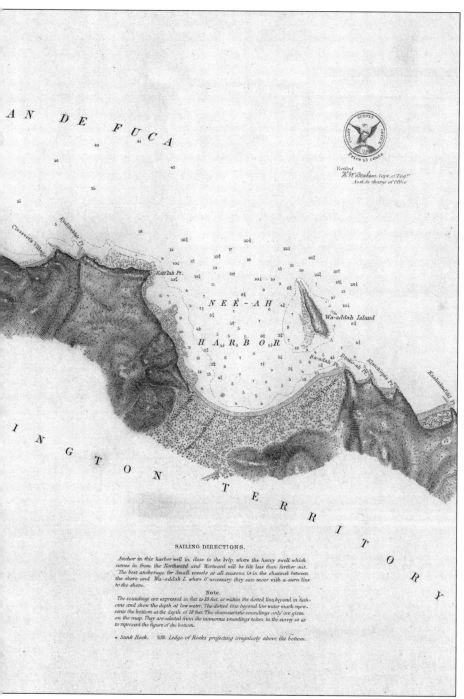

As this 1853 US Coast Survey chart illustrates, Cape Flattery was the first signpost for the Juan de Fuca Strait for those approaching from the south, though in physical terms it was both elusive and underwhelming. DAVID RUMSEY MAP COLLECTION

live by the rocks and seagulls.' The name 'Makah,' or 'Generous with food,' was given to us by our neighbouring tribes."[71]

The lands the Makah called their own stretched east along the shore of the strait for about 15 miles and a similar distance south on the Pacific shore.[72] The nation also claimed Tatoosh Island, that is "the thunderbird," where at one time they had a stockade. There is another claimant to that island. Tatoosh was originally occupied by the Ditidaht, who moved to Vancouver Island after a battle with the Makah. They first settled around Jordan River and then moved north to Pacheedaht territory.[73] Archaeologists found signs of the occupation of Tatoosh to around AD 950. A census of the Makah taken in 1863 gave a total population of 663, and as of that date their relative isolation had saved them from the ravages of smallpox and spirituous liquor, a temporary reprieve as it turned out. They had intermarried with tribes north and south, practised polygamy, and gave potlatches as did other coast tribes. They drew their food mainly from the sea and shore. The California gray whale passed conveniently nearby in its migrations and was an attractive catch. Other whales hunted by the Makah were the humpback, right, sperm, gray and blue whales, and to this day the nation maintains a right to hunt whales.[74] Their villages were few in number, and one of them, Ozette, was buried in 1700 as a result of an earthquake-generated tsunami. The new European settlements at Astoria on the Columbia River and Fort Victoria on southern Vancouver Island changed somewhat the voyaging patterns of the Makah, who usually voyaged north and south. They engaged in raids and captured slaves and took advantage of the persons and property of shipwrecked sailors.

Transplanted New Englander and US Customs collector James Gilchrist Swan, who lacked any skills as an ethnographer, nonetheless tried to write down the history of the Makah, with whom he lived for some time. He wrote in despair, "The history of this tribe, as far as their knowledge extends, is a confused mass of fables, legends, myths, and allegories. Nothing that they can state prior to the existence of a few generations back is clear or wholly to be relied upon. There are a few prominent events that have been remembered as having occurred; but the details [are] confused, and it is very rare that two Indians tell the same story alike, unless it may be some wild and improbable legend, like the fairy tales related in nurseries, which are remembered in after life." Swan cited the various accounts of the Spanish settlement attempted by Lieutenant Manuel Quimper at nearby Neah Bay in 1790. None of the accounts squared with any other. The Makah remembered hearing about more recent events, such as the murder of the crew of the *Boston* in 1803 and of the *Tonquin* in 1811, and the captivity of the *Boston*'s blacksmith, John Jewitt, among the Nootka. As to their early history, Swan was convinced that as the events receded in years, the details became obscured with legends and fables, "so that the truth is exceedingly difficult to discover." Nowadays, however, ethnohistorians have been able to reconstitute, at least in writing, the ways and traits of the Makah.[75] In short, then, Swan's testimony tells us a good deal about himself and, sadly, insupportable observations about the Makah. Only ninety years before he compiled his *The Indians of Cape Flattery, at the Entrance to the Strait of Fuca, Washington Territory* (1870), Cook had passed this way, and so much had transpired in the meantime.

In 1852 a smallpox epidemic decimated the Makah and eradicated one of the ancient villages. Amidst this devastation of the population, the policies of the United States were being exerted—to "improve" the Indians off their land. In 1855, by what is called the Treaty of Neah Bay, a reservation was set aside for the Makah. It was a constrained portion of the cape, from Neah Bay to Waatch Creek on the Pacific side, both points being about equally distant from Tatoosh Island, about six miles each way. Heavy brush and low-lying land separated the rugged inland Olympic Peninsula from Cape Flattery, giving the Makah very little arable land, suitable only for growing potatoes. Like the cape, a projection of a last wilderness at the northwest corner of the continental forty-eight states, they were as yet an isolated people but fast becoming fenced in by historical forces.

Cape Flattery is no great bluff or headland. It is no sentinel of the Northwest Coast, no Rock of Gibraltar. It is, rather, the reverse. The Makah told Swan that at one time, "but not at a very remote period," the sea rose steeply and passed around Cape Flattery, making it an island, then flowed outward and north toward Nootka, a four-day cycle. These remarks accord perfectly with a documented tsunami caused by a magnitude 9.0 earthquake dated to 26 January 1700. The tsunami destroyed Oregon tribal villages in low-lying coastal estuaries and caused damage as far away as Japan.[76]

The area was *terra incognita* to the Europeans. The marine corporal John Ledyard, born in Connecticut and sailing with Captain Cook in 1778, was stirred by the thought that he was at the back door of his own

America. "Though more than 2000 miles from the nearest part of New England," he wrote in his journal, "I felt myself plainly affected. It soothed a homesick heart and rendered me very tolerably happy."[77] "The grandeur of the scenery about Cape Flattery," wrote James Gilchrist Swan seventy years later, in the mid-1850s, "and the strange contortions and fantastic shapes into which its cliffs have been thrown by some former convulsions of nature, or worn or abraded by the ceaseless surge of the waves; the wild and varied sounds which fill the air, from the dash of water into the caverns and fissures of the rocks, mingled with the living cries of innumerable fowl . . . all combined, present an accumulation of sights and sounds sufficient to fill a less superstitious beholder than the Indian with mysterious awe." The writer Ivan Doig, inspired by Swan's life, and desirous to spend a season at the edge of America, speaks of the strong feel of Cape Flattery as "an everlasting precipice of existence."[78]

The Makah have their own explanation about their origins, recorded by Swan for the Smithsonian Institution: "The legend respecting their own origin is that they were created on the Cape. First, animals were produced, and from the union of some of these with a star which fell from heaven, came the first men, and from them sprang all the race of Nittinats, Clyoquotes, and Makahs." History has strange twists, and Swan ruminated on the thought that because the early explorers and traders had so much to do with Maquinna and the Nootka, the language family has been designated "Nootkan." Swan believed that the Makah were part of the Nitinat family rather than the Nootkan or Clayoquot; he was pointing to the similarity of the Makah with the peoples of the southwestern portion of Vancouver Island. That having been said, he was content with this generality: "I have not been able to prepare vocabularies of all these tribes, but their language, so far as I can judge from hearing them speak, is sufficiently alike to be recognized, and to leave no doubt that it was originally the same in all . . . The Makahs believe in a Supreme Being . . . the Great Chief who resides above." The name of the divine being was never spoken, except by those who had been initiated into the sacred rites.[79]

Leaving the Makah, we return to the cabin of James Cook, sailing aboard His Majesty's vessel *Resolution*, with the *Discovery* in company. Off the storm-tossed coast of Oregon and what is now Washington State, the heavy weather continued unrelentingly for almost a week. The pleasures of

Hawaii were now an ever-fading memory. It was not until the afternoon of 29 March that the ships again made land. But this time they were well north of Cape Flattery and the entrance to the Strait of Juan de Fuca, in 49° 28' N. Now a new sense of urgency existed aboard ship, for Cook was looking for a place to wood and water and repair the lower rigging. They chanced upon the southern entrance of Nootka Sound. (I say "chanced" because slightly different circumstances of wind and weather could have brought them into, say, Clayoquot Sound or Barkley Sound or Kyuquot Sound, and one of these rather than Nootka Sound would have found itself on the pages of charts and world history.) In any event, they entered the southern entrance of Nootka Sound, found a snug place to moor their vessels, then shifted to a safer anchorage near the Native village of Yuquot, on Nootka Island, and remained there in comfort for a month, making repairs, wooding and watering, before continuing their far northern exploration up into Bering Strait and Sea.

Cook did not know that what he called Cape Flattery marked the southern entrance to the Strait of Juan de Fuca. As to the possibility of such a strait in those latitudes that Juan de Fuca spoke of—47 and 48 degrees north—Cook seems strangely, at first sight, to have been indifferent. He made note of this in his journal. "It is in this very latitude where we now were, that geographers have placed the pretended *Strait of Juan de Fuca*. We saw nothing like it; nor is there the least probability that ever such thing existed."[80]

But perhaps, after all, it is not Cook's fault. Among the reasons Cook dismissed the possibility of Juan de Fuca's strait is the fact that the Lords of the Admiralty, in issuing their secret instructions dated 6 July 1776, called for him to press his search "to find out a Northern Passage by sea from the Pacific to the Atlantic" in the vicinity of 65° N—a high latitude indeed. He was not to dawdle and examine the coast as the opportunity presented itself; in fact, he was to avoid contact with any part of the Spanish dominions on the continent unless driven there by some unavoidable accident. He was to examine rivers and inlets appearing to lead to Hudson Bay and to inquire from the Natives concerning the possibility of a passage. If he were to find such a waterway, he was to proceed in one or both of his ships and make the passage. The Admiralty had equipped the ships with two small vessels in frame, so that if the fabled passageway appeared narrow they could be constructed and outfitted for the exploration. The Admiralty left nothing to chance. Cook had his orders, and he followed them to the letter. Thus it seems his biographer Beaglehole, and other historians, have been unduly and carelessly guilty of attacking Cook for missing the entrance to the strait.

The publication of Cook's voyage account, and his dismissal of the possibilities of a northwest passage where Juan de Fuca had said it existed, took British geopolitical thinking off the track for almost twenty years, and it had a good deal of influence on his acolyte, George Vancouver, of whom more presently.

Pursuant to orders, Cook sailed north from Nootka to Alaska, then to the Aleutians and to Bering Strait, examining the American and Siberian shorelines. Navigation in those cold high latitudes was demanding, and the voyage confirmed the esteem in which Cook had always held Vitus Bering. Late in arriving in the Bering Sea (because of the loss of a month's time at Nootka to make repairs), Cook had to stop his eastward progress at well-named Icy Cape. He planned for an earlier attempt to discover the northwest passage the next year, and a return to London by the passage in these latitudes. Then he went to Kamchatka and south to Hawaii, where he was killed.

At Nootka and in Alaska, he and his ships' companies had discovered the prospects of a trade in sea-otter pelts. News of this reached all quarters of the world, and by 1785 expeditions by sea were being launched from India and Macao. That story lies elsewhere.[81] The merchants of Boston soon entered the business in highly successful fashion and in keen competition with the British, as told in the next chapter. But here it is significant to observe that the historian John Reinhold Forster, closely connected to Cook's voyages, produced a history called *Voyages and Discoveries in the North*. That book, remarkable for its time, presenting as it did all sorts of hitherto-kept secrets, was first printed in German; the London edition appeared in 1786, just as the sea-otter trade of the North Pacific became an active and rich field of commerce.

For those of us engaged in historical sleuthing, here is the most significant item: Forster's work advertised Juan de Fuca's voyages and claims. Further, it not only cited Lok's testimony but also added details from the voyage account of Luke Fox, who cribbed Lok's story. Juan de Fuca, discredited and all but forgotten, had been given a new lease on life.

Our story now shifts to London and to Alexander Dalrymple, of ancient Scottish lineage and distinction. He was the seventh son of a Scottish baronet, and as such had little to expect from the family patrimony. Indeed, his parents apprenticed him as a clerk to the East India Company. At age fifteen he was sent to Madras to take up a "writership," there to make his way in the world. He spent thirteen years in India, the

The only known portrait of Alexander Dalrymple was likely painted after his return from his thirteen years in eastern seas in the service of the East India Company. A great collector of information that would serve the British Empire and its economic interests, Dalrymple was appointed the Admiralty's first hydrographer, in charge of chart making.
NATIONAL MUSEUMS SCOTLAND

Philippines, Borneo and Sulu. He displayed many of the characteristics of Dr. John Dee, namely, inquisitiveness, antiquarian instincts, historical consciousness, and mathematical and scientific knowledge. Like Dee, he was an imperialist for Britain, particularly in the advancement of trade, the lifeblood of the kingdom. Unlike Dee, he had no truck with astrology: Dalrymple was a man of the scientific age of the Enlightenment.

His passionate interest in geography and history dated from his youth, and as time passed he acquired a vast assemblage of charts, maps and voyage accounts. His knowledge and his collection made him an authority to be reckoned with in regards to any future discoveries or possibilities of finding straits, continents, islands and passages. Good at administration and arranging, he decided to create a hydrographic department for the East India Company, an empire all on its own, headquartered in Leadenhall Street, the City of London, and dominant in the realm of knowledge concerning British trade from the Indian subcontinent to China. He was, too, at least in early years, a mariner, and had five years in command, principally on board the schooner *Cuddalore* in the employ of the East India Company. He proved his skill in navigation, cartography and surveying. Moreover, he acquired an encyclopedic knowledge of previous voyages to the Pacific, including Spanish, Portuguese and French accounts as well as British. He had a good deal of Scottish thistle in him, which scratched against many an English human skin.[82] In any event, he was an authority to be reckoned with, for not much of importance passed him by without notice.

Had he been an officer in the Royal Navy, he probably would have been appointed to command His Majesty's bark *Endeavour*, sent in 1768 to observe the transit of Venus at Tahiti and to seek out the rumoured Terra Australis, a Great Southern Continent. However, that appointment could not be approved. One member of the Admiralty, Sir Edward Hawke, said he would rather cut off his right hand than sign a naval commission for a civilian. Passing on Dalrymple, the board chose James Cook, a known and trusted master in the Royal Navy. Dalrymple, as said, had become the examiner of charts of the East India Company in London, and given his global interests and inquisitiveness had followed the activities of the three component factors in this emerging equation: Canadian fur traders exploring west from Hudson Bay and the Great Lakes, sea-otter traders like John Meares and James Colnett making their passages to and from China, and the Spanish sailing northward from Acapulco and San Blas, Mexico.

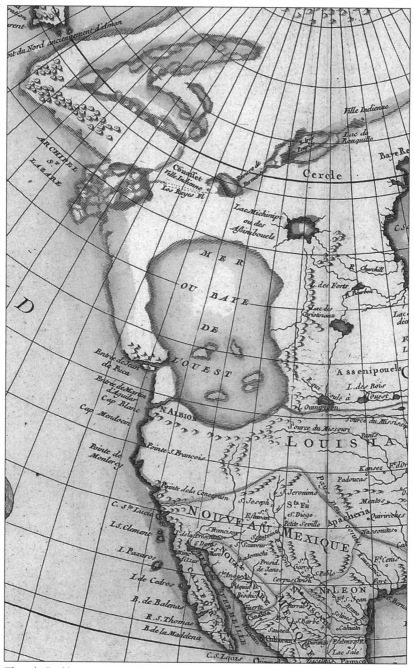

Though Cook's voyage seemed to disprove the existence of Juan de Fuca Strait, a multitude of map makers (as seen in this detail from *Atlas moderne ou collection de cartes sur toutes les parties de globe terrestre, 1762, no. 33*) still persisted with their fantastical imaginings of a giant inland sea or link to Hudson Bay. FROM *BRITISH COLUMBIA: A NEW HISTORICAL ATLAS*, COURTESY OF DEREK HAYES

Dalrymple was an advocate of a commercial link between the East India Company and that other great chartered firm, the Hudson's Bay Company, founded 1670. He himself had been at Canton, where he had observed that "not only the Climate, but the Habits of China, make it the great mart for Furs of all denominations, and their own Country and Coasts are too well inhabited to afford an asylum to animals, which abound only in wastes and wilds." He also knew that the Chinese permitted trade in furs only by way of Kiatka, on the Amur River, and only through Russian hands there. But, with an eye to a new possibility, that of a link between India and Canada, he advanced a new scheme for trading with the Chinese. Hence he wrote in 1789 his *Plan for Promoting the Fur-Trade and Securing It to This Country by Uniting the Operations of the East India and Hudson's Bay Companies*. That scheme, as wild in its financial design of a great corporate merger as it was impossible to bring about, necessarily brought him to become an advocate of a northwest passage.[83]

Dalrymple knew about Juan de Fuca, Thomas James, and John Reinhold Forster. Thus, not surprisingly, he was intrigued by the prospect of a northwest passage in latitude 47° and 48° N. He knew that James Cook had dismissed the prospect, all too off-handedly. What was needed was on-the-spot proof. Dalrymple was shortly to be appointed the first hydrographer of the Admiralty and was already in a position to give the British ministry advice about the recent developments of discovery on the Northwest Coast.

The story of Juan de Fuca and the possibilities of a passage particularly interested Dalrymple. And he gathered jewels of information from mariners who had been doing business in the sea-otter trade on the Northwest Coast, from Cape Blanco north to the Gulf of Alaska. At Canton and Macao they sold their lustrous furs to wealthy mandarins. There, they also took on supplies, refitted their ships, passed information among themselves, planned corporate deals and mergers, and gingerly plotted how to circumvent the rules and regulations of the East India Company, which had the monopoly of trade between Cape Horn and the Cape of Good Hope. British ships sailing those seas also had to fulfill the obligations imposed by the restrictions of the South Sea Company. In Canton, John Henry Cox, a consul, was the fixer for the maritime traders who were working around these British monopolies. He had key connections to London and the government of the day, which wished to limit the monopolistic power of the

East India and South Sea Companies, and necessarily worked in concert with them. As a result, the Cox syndicate grew powerful under the trading influence and success of such traders as James Hanna, the pioneer, John Meares, James Colnett and others. Some resorted to a flag of convenience, the Portuguese flag, in order to circumvent British regulations. Naturally, the Spanish objected to seeing a Portuguese flag waving from a masthead in Nootka Sound, and they were quick to take affront at this when British maritime fur traders arrived there under those colours.

As late as 1786, maritime fur traders working the Northwest Coast gave no credence to the possibility of a Strait of Juan de Fuca. How do we know this? Instructions that year to Nathaniel Portlock and George Dixon, sailing for the London syndicate King George's Sound Company (and with close connections to the British government), make no mention of the possibility while giving specific directions about sailing on that shore. But others who came in their wake, perhaps influenced by French cartographic work that was often based on Russian postulations, were on the lookout for a passage—and dreams soon became realities. In consequence, at this turning point, the much maligned Juan de Fuca suddenly took on a new persona, one larger than life. No longer was he looked on as some sort of trickster or a magician of geographical details. He had pointed to particulars, given the details to Michael Lok, some two hundred years before. The mariners were on the hunt for the strait, the entrance and Pillar or Pinnacle Rock. All the while, in London, Dalrymple awaited news of discoveries.

It was in these odd circumstances that the long-hidden Strait of Juan de Fuca was disclosed to outside eyes. Credit for rediscovering the entrance goes to Captain Charles William Barkley in the 400-ton ship *Imperial Eagle* (originally the *Loudon)*, a London ship and former East Indiaman mounting twenty guns, but sailing under the double eagle of the Emperor of Austria, departing from Ostend. The whole arrangement smacked of subterfuge so as to get around the octopus-like character of the East India Company.

Romance stalked the quarterdeck and the captain's cabin. Barkley first went to sea at age eleven with his father, a commander in the East India Company shipping service. Now he had his own command. With him sailed his young bride, Frances Hornby Trevor, an English lady. She was the daughter of the English cleric the Rev. Dr. John Trevor, and she

Cutting a romantic figure, in large part due to his equally adventurous wife, Frances, Charles Barkley won the honour of rediscovering the Juan de Fuca Strait while trading for otter pelts. He was surprised to find the waterway, heretofore thought a literary invention or fabrication. ROGER PARKER, COURTESY OF CATHY CONVERSE

had been born in Bridgewater, Somerset. Her mother had died, and she and her three sisters had to cope with their father's remarriage and four half-brothers. Going to sea may have been a relief. In any event, the prospects of this happy couple sailing the briny deep has enchanted many a writer. This is what a writer in the *Western Home Monthly* of July 1929 had to say: "Captain Barkley, a dashing, showy fellow—already at twenty-five in charge of a large trading vessel, and outward-bound on an incredibly dangerous venture, must have seemed to sixteen-year-old Frances the very figure of romance; and one concludes after reading her chronicle that their hasty marriage was never a matter of repentance to either of them; that they remained steadfast lovers to the end of their days."

Together they faced storms in the Bay of Biscay, the doldrums of the equator, the perils of dreaded Cape Horn, his worrying rheumatic fever, her defences against the unwanted amorous attentions forced on her by the first and second mates, and much else. But at the end there was the happy arrival at Nootka Sound in mid-June 1787. He did a booming business there: "He engrossed the whole trade & ruined ours," complained a rival English trader, James Colnett, who had the misfortune to arrive after Barkley. At Colnett's request, Barkley sent over considerable quantities of wine and brandy, then had the good grace to defer payment until they should meet later in China. Barkley's behaviour was "as humane & generous as ever I met with, and I am sorry his Busyness so clash'd with mine that I was oblig'd to behave in the distant manner I did."[84] On 24 July the *Imperial Eagle* sailed from Nootka Sound.

Working south a day or two later, Captain Barkley brought his ship into Clayoquot Sound, which Barkley named Wickaninnish's Sound, "the name given it being that of a chief who seemed to be quite as powerful a potentate as Maquilla [Maquinna] at King George's Sound," said Frances. The trading had been fine—"this part of the Coast proved a rich harvest of Furs," Frances Barkley recounted. They did well in Clayoquot Sound, where they were anchored in a snug port. Then they sailed south to another very large sound, Barkley, which the captain named after himself.

Again our correspondent waxes eloquently about Frances: "Can you not just see young Frances, on those warm days, standing on the deck of the *Imperial Eagle* and watching with interested eye all that took place; marveling at the barbarous [sic] natives in their primitive garb, maneuvering their canoes to the side of the big ship; admiring the prowess of her clever husband; gazing at the wild beauty of the rugged coast-line. Then when they left the shelter of a bay, and encountered the Pacific rollers that pound unceasingly against the rocky shores, she would be forced to forsake the decks and would perhaps sit and watch her husband working on his charts, or bringing his journals up to date, and help him decide on names for the islands, straits or bays he was continually discovering. Frances Island and Hornby Peak were named after herself, Hornby being her second name."[85]

The long coast of Vancouver Island had many bays, inlets and islands but nothing promising a strait to the Atlantic. The officers and men held no great expectation of a strait in these latitudes. The *Imperial Eagle* anchored in Effingham Bay, on the west side of Effingham Island in Barkley Sound, which Captain Barkley made a plan of (and which Meares copied for his *Voyages*). Sailing south from Barkley Sound (the exact day in July 1787 does not survive), the discovery of the Strait of Juan de Fuca was made—or as those who believe in the exploits of Juan de Fuca will have it, the "rediscovery."

Barkley steered for Cape Flattery, and a new coastline came into view. A segment of Frances Barkley's diary miraculously survived fires and other dislocations. She takes up the story: "In the afternoon, to our great astonishment, we arrived off a large opening extending to the eastward, the entrance of which appeared to be about four leagues wide, and remained about that width as far as the eye could see, with a clear westerly horizon, which my husband immediately recognized as the long lost strait of Juan de Fuca, and to which he gave the name of the original discoverer, my husband placing it on his chart."[86]

He spied a conspicuous pinnacle and gave its latitude as 47° 47'. He put the southern point of De Fuca's Entrance at 48° 26' and provided many other details of longitude and latitude (see page 95). The latitude of the strait's entrance squared perfectly with Juan de Fuca's. That was not all: the strait fitted exactly with what Juan de Fuca said was a "broad Inlet of the Sea."

To Barkley, then, goes full credit for the rediscovery, no small achievement. But tragedy awaited him just south of the strait. He could not have known that thirteen years previous the Spanish had found these dangerous waters for going ashore. On 14 July 1775, the Spanish captain Juan Francisco de la Bodega y Quadra anchored the *Sonora* at a small island about a league to the south of Point Grenville. He sent seven men ashore to refill water casks, cut a replacement mast and obtain firewood. All were ambushed and murdered at the hands of the Quinault and their allies, leaving the Spaniard to christen the island Isla de Dolores, "Island of Sorrows," and the point, which we know as Grenville, Punta de los Mártires, "Point of the Martyrs."[87]

Barkley similarly sent a crew ashore to examine the Hoh River. All six of his boat's crew, including the man in charge, the second mate, Mr. Moore, one of Frances's suitors and one she was not unattracted to, were killed by Indians. In sadness, Captain Barkley gave the stream the name Destruction River. But in time the river was named the Hoh, after the people living at its mouth, and the term "destruction" was affixed to the island. Barkley then sailed for China with 800 furs in his hold. There he fell into difficulties with the agents of the *Imperial Eagle* and ultimately left his ship. An arbitration board of merchants awarded him £5,000 for the loss of his appointment. Barkley had invested £3,000 in the scheme and spent a fortune on good navigational instruments, so his loss was great, even with this compensation. Frances Barkley wrote bitterly about her husband's mistreatment, including the fact that agents in Canton had confiscated his charts, journals and private stores without any remuneration. "Capt. Meares got possession of my husband's Journal and plans from the persons in China to whom he was bound under a penalty of £5,000 to give them up for a certain time for, as these persons stated, mercantile objects, they not wishing the knowledge of the [Northwest] Coast to be published."[88] The quarrel proved a long and bitter one, quite typical of the imbroglios that Meares found himself in with other traders. Likely he obtained the journals and charts through the agents of the *Imperial Eagle*.[89]

It is not clear when details of Barkley's discovery became known in London, but Dalrymple got word of them in surprisingly quick time and began to place more credence on the discoveries of fur traders than heretofore. He took note of Barkley's chart of the Northwest Coast, from Nootka southeastward, and also of his all-too-brief journal (which came to him courtesy of Mr. John Henry Cox in Canton). Barkley provided some crucially important positions, south to north (only latitudes listed here): Point Fear, in 47° 9' N, Destruction (probably Quillayute) River in 47° 43', Pinnacle (Rock) in 47° 47', Cape Flattery in 48° 8', and Center of Talouck Island, in 48° 24'. He placed the southern point of De Fuca's Entrance in 48° 26' and the north point of the same in 48° 33'. To these were added the southern point of Barkley Sound in 48° 50' and the west point of the same in 49° N. "The most important Discoveries in this Voyage seem to have been made in the boat, when detached, but there are no circumstantial details of her trip," observed Dalrymple with regret.[90] It is a great pity that Barkley's chart has not survived. But Dalrymple had the sense to write down the details.

What we do know is that the next mariner to arrive on the scene, whose more complete findings also reached Dalrymple, did get the attention he deserved. Dalrymple, we can see, was keen to receive further confirming evidence of Juan de Fuca's claim. In his view, the search was narrowing, closing in on the final particulars. Barkley had pointed out the Pinnacle and the Entrance. Confirming details would put all doubt out of the question.

Meares claims to have been instrumental in the discovery of the strait. The reasons are not hard to discover, though it was not he who penetrated its waters. Meares says that he sent Duffin in a longboat from Effingham Bay, on 13 July 1788. "You will take possession of this strait, and the lands adjoining, in the name of the King and Crown of Britain," Meares had instructed Duffin, adding that he should "instill into the minds of the inhabitants that you will return shortly to fulfill any treaties of commerce or amity that you may make with them, and for which you have my authority." Lieutenant Peter Puget, who sailed here with George Vancouver in 1792, knew of Duffin's explorations. Puget thought Duffin had come as far east as today's Port Townsend. There, canoes of Indians came out to sell halibut to Puget, who wrote that "the People however notwithstanding their present pacific dispositions must be of the same Tribe that attacked Mr. Mears longboat under the direction of Mr. Duffin." Admiral Bern Anderson, one of Vancouver's biographers and editor of Puget's journal, adds: "Mr. Duffin was one of Meares' officers . . . He made a boat trip into the Strait of Juan de Fuca and turned back when he was attacked by natives. Meares, believing this to be the opening of de Fuca's story, gave it its present name, and Duffin's party were the first Europeans known for certain to have entered it."[91]

The sublimely beautiful weather of that delightful summer belied the difficulties faced by Duffin and his men in the open boat. The boat crew was preparing to land, perhaps to trade or take on water, when set upon by Indians who had come out in canoes to meet them. The Indians were well armed with clubs, barbed arrows and stone "bludgeons." It was a sharp engagement, typical of so many encounters of the late 1780s and early 1790s. Duffin managed to return to Effingham Bay, reaching it 20 July, with several of his men badly wounded and the boat pierced "in a thousand places with arrows," another Meares exaggeration.

John Meares's testimony moved the British government to threaten war against Spain over freedom of navigation. A wily trader not above sailing under false papers and making self-advantageous claims, Meares helped spark the Nootka Crisis by voyaging and trading in waters claimed exclusively by Spain. IMAGE PDP 05179 COURTESY OF ROYAL BC MUSEUM, BC ARCHIVES

As to the distance up the strait that Duffin had gone, Meares says it was 30 leagues—that is, about 90 nautical miles—which would put them close to Port Townsend. This too can be doubted, however, and Port San Juan on Vancouver Island is a possible site for the encounter. In any event, Duffin's explorations had been cut short by the Indians, pointing to a certain difficulty that would face all voyagers on these waters in those days.[92] Meares was off Cape Flattery in 1788, and to him may be given credit for a connection with the Makah, though no specific details are given.

Three weeks after Duffin's penetration of the strait, on 7 August, the sea-otter trader Captain Charles Duncan, in command of the stout little 61-ton sloop *Princess Royal,* arrived off Nootka Island. Thick and misty weather had been nature's greeting there, and from time to time John Meares in the *Felice* had caught sight of the sloop. Before long, the crews of the two ships at anchor were in animated conversation.

As the two vessels rose and fell with the roll of the sea, the captains exchanged information and news. They worked in the same syndicate, or grand alliance, of traders, and of this, Meares was the key merchant mariner, representing the "Merchant Proprietors," as they called themselves, based in India. In opposition to this came the ships of the King George's Sound Company, of London, with strong government backing. This latter group was headed up by Richard Cadman Etches, with powerful influence in the City of London. The syndicate's ships, *King George* and *Queen Charlotte*, strongly outfitted, rounded Cape Horn. The *Prince of Wales* and the *Princess Royal* followed. The arrival of these vessels in the Pacific made an alliance necessary, for there were also other British rivals and, for the first time, formidable competition from the United States in the trade to China. Meares and the Etches syndicate entered into an arrangement that was not a merger, only the placing of vessels in joint account. In this way, Meares came under the umbrella of the permits held by the King George's Sound Company and, artful dodger that he was, benefitted most from the arrangement. He even became the self-appointed representative of wronged British merchants, ship owners, captains and crews who suffered at Spanish hands at Nootka Sound.

Duncan had sailed from the Thames River in the *Princess Royal* at the same time as James Colnett in the *Prince of Wales*. By the time Meares met him, Duncan had already been once to Nootka Sound, then sailed north directly to lucrative Haida Gwaii, the Queen Charlotte Islands, where on southeasterly shores he made a good trade. He crossed to the mainland and back again, then shaped a course southeast, first to Milbanke Sound and Cape Caution before crossing a water that became known as Dixon Entrance. After that he rounded the Scott Islands and sailed south to Nootka. He had been looking for Colnett but his partner was still sailing northern waters.

Following the encounter with Meares, Duncan steered southward, entered Clayoquot Sound south of Flores Island, passed through Brabant

Channel and anchored off Blunden Island. On 8 August he sailed south to Ahousat, a known place of promise, traded there until the 13th, passed the entrance of Barkley Sound, Cape Beale and Pachena Bay, and then crossed to Cape Flattery. On the 15th he anchored before the village of Claaset. He had made, as he put it, "the south side of the Straits of Juan de Fuca, in the latitude of 48° 30'." In doing so he had marked the strait's northern and southern entrances.[93]

Duncan was conscious of a great tide setting against him, one that flowed out of the strait, and of high land covered with snow on the south

A 1794 illustration from a French edition of Meares's account shows Meares, holding steady at the entrance to the Juan de Fuca Strait, with Robert Duffin in a longboat going in to

shore. On the north was land of a moderate height rising gradually from the sea shore and covered all over with fir trees. The uniqueness of this geographical locale did not escape him. Solitary splendour ruled every aesthetic appreciation, the tiny sloop dwarfed by the landscape and the vastness of sea and the motions of tides and currents. He tacked back and forth off Tatoosh Island and Cape Flattery, finally coming to anchor just within the strait's entrance.

If Barkley was in a hurry to get to Macao and Canton to sell his furs, Duncan had a sense of presence, one matched with more than a lick of

claim the land for the British—where they were not welcomed by the Natives. COURTESY OF BARRY LAWRENCE RUDERMAN ANTIQUE MAPS (WWW.RAREMAPS.COM)

curiosity. He held the rank of master in the Royal Navy and was rightly proud of his important vocation in life, on which the safe navigation of shipping depended. He likely knew that the illustrious James Cook had passed this way and given Cape Flattery a derisive notation in his voyage account. Duncan made his observations. Then he drew a plan of the entrance and strait, showing the tendencies of the shore and the strait's notorious currents (the bane of competing yachtsmen to this day). He put as his heading *Sketch of the Entrance of the Strait of Juan de Fuca*, and below it "Lat. 48°. 37' N long. 124°. 54' W. Variation Observed 19°. 14' E. is allowed."

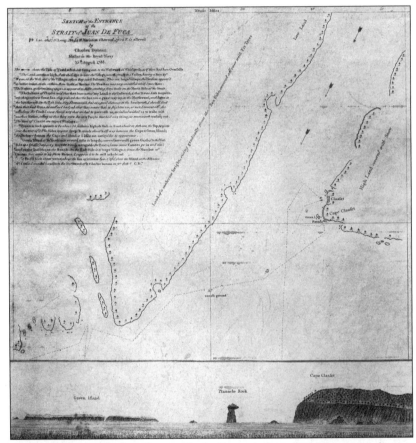

Revealed to the world at last: Captain Charles Duncan's chart of 15 August 1788 shows the pinnacle described in Juan de Fuca's account. This is the first clear depiction of the entrance to the Juan de Fuca Strait, along with notes about tides, currents and the local Natives, and shows places of occupation. Green Island (Tatoosh) and Cape Claaset (Flattery) mark the northwestern tip of Washington State. Engraving issued by Alexander Dalrymple, 1790. IMAGE CM/A442 COURTESY OF ROYAL BC MUSEUM, BC ARCHIVES

Duncan dated his plan 15 August 1788. It constitutes the first reliable sketch to show the southern separation of Vancouver Island from the mainland. It also showed Duncan's anchorage to the west of Neah Bay. But Duncan was not there just on a voyage of exploration, for the profit motive ruled his movements. For two days he traded with the Claaset Indians, the Makah. It was an important encounter with this famous whale-hunting people, whose kin at Nitinat, Clayoquot, Ahousat and Nootka shared much the same language (though there are differences) and certainly the same history.

Duncan also drew a profile of the entrance to the fabled waterway. On the south side, midway between Green Island and Cape Claaset, he depicted a pinnacle which he presumed was what Juan de Fuca had seen. Barkley had seen it the year before. "This is substantially correct," says Captain Walbran, who probably spied out the location in his Canadian coast guard and hydrographic vessel more than a hundred years later. Its position is invariably connected to that of Tatoosh Island, at the entrance of the strait. George Davidson, in the service of the US Coast Guard, made a survey of it in 1852 and recommended a lighthouse be placed there. The light, with its powerful beam, was dedicated in 1857, and a similarly powerful foghorn sounds out its call of danger. Walbran testifies: "The island is Tatooche, and the spired rock, now known as De Fuca's pillar, 150 feet high, stands in solitary grandeur, a little off shore, about two miles southwards of Tatooche Island."[94] "It is still there today, between Cape Flattery and Tatoosh Island, clearly visible from both ocean and strait as one approaches from the south," comments historian Warren L. Cook.[95] The pinnacle looks different today, its top hat having disappeared, perhaps in consequence of some seismic shift of the tectonic plate that bears the name, appropriately, of Juan de Fuca. Duncan portrayed all these features in his excellent drawing.

His sketch also carried a descriptive note that speaks of information gathered from the Natives of Claaset, who told Duncan that the sea ran a great way up to the northward and down to the southward—the latter an indication of that vast cluster of passages and inlets known as Puget Sound. He provides the first description of the Indian villages there at that time. The lengthy caption, which Dalrymple had the sense to reproduce when the plan went into published form, reads:

The [arrow pointing northwest] shows the tide of flood which sets strong out, to the westward in whirlpools, as if there had been overfalls. The land continues high, from the Cape to near the village which stands in a valley, having a run of water, at the west end of the village, where they catch salmon. This is a large village, the houses appear'd in better order on the outside than those at Nootka. The weather was very unsettled when I was here. The natives spoke two languages, & appear to differ something from those on the north side of the strait.

The Indians of Classet said that they knew not of any land to the Eastward and that it was A'as toopulfe—which signifies a Great Sea, they pointed that the sea ran a great way up to the northward and down to the southward. On the East Side, they likewise said, that a good distance to the Southward, I should find men that had guns as well as I had. Whether they meant that to frighten me or not I cannot tell for all along the coast I never found any that wished to part us or indeed wished us to trade with another nation, telling us that they were the only people that had anything or were worth trading with. The men of Classet are expert whalers.

Pinnacle Rock appears to be about 34 fathoms high, its base in front about 10 fathoms. The top projects over the rest of it. The sides appear steep. It stands about half way between the Cape & Green Island. The distance between the Cape and Island is fi[ve] mile not navigable in appearance. Green Island or to Touches is about 1/4 mile in length, covered over with green grass. On the east side is a small cove, very narrow and only navigable for boats. I saw some canoes go in and out and many Indians on the beach. On the east side is a large village and from the number of canoes that came to us from thence, I suppose it to be well inhabited.

A small rock above water, about the size of a canoe lies N 19° E from the island to a distance of 1 1/2 mile. I sounded 1/2 mile to the northward of it and had no bottom at 90 fath[om]s.

—C[harles] D[uncan]

The *US Coast Pilot* has this to say: "Cape Flattery, a bold, rocky head with cliffs 120 feet high, rises to nearly 1,500 feet about 2 miles back from the beach. From southward it looks like an island because of the low land in the valley of the Waatch River."

We are reminded here of what Juan de Fuca told Michael Lok: "And that at the entrance of this said Strait, there is on the North-west coast thereof, a great Hedland or Island, with an exceeding high Pinacle, or spired Rocke, like a piller thereupon." The *Coast Pilot* states that the pillar called Fuca Pillar, or Fuca Rock, lies 0.2 miles due south of the western point of Cape Flattery, 150 yards from the shore, and it is most prominent from the north. It is a rocky column 157 feet high and 60 feet in diameter. Juan de Fuca's statement says that the pillar was on the cape. Likely, because he gave notice of the pillar, he had sailed close to the shore, say a quarter of a mile or so, and coming up from the south the pillar would have appeared superimposed on Cape Flattery, with its 157-foot height rising above the 120-foot-high westernmost end of the cape.

To the pilot, long on the search for conspicuous geographical features, this headland to his strait with its distinguishing pillar was an important landmark to be remembered as an aid to navigation. Duncan was looking for it. Duncan had found it. Now it was time to sail for Canton, and on 17 August Duncan weighed from his last anchorage, bound first for Hawaii and a rendezvous with Colnett. Then it was on to Canton, where he would link up with the Meares and Etches group. As for the *Princess Royal*, Thomas Hudson was given command of her and sailed her to Nootka, only to have her captured by the Spaniards, who subsequently used the newly named *Princesa Real* as their own vessel of discovery. We meet her again later.

Duncan was back in England in August 1789, where he charged the Etches concern with sending him out in a vessel that was deficient in necessities. It was at this stage that he met Dalrymple, who verified the particulars. The stunningly important information Duncan brought home, largely geographical but also ethnological, was critical to the data provided to George Vancouver for his forthcoming expedition of national discovery.[96] And British fur traders also shared the newfound secrets: the entrance of the Strait of Juan de Fuca had been placed on the chart for all time. This was Duncan's achievement. Even today he lives in the shadow of the great mariners, but in his discovery he pointed a finger of destiny. His drawing of the entrance to the Strait of Juan de Fuca is a charter document in the history of the State of Washington, and it likewise has important implications for British Columbia's development.

Dalrymple was immediately attracted to Duncan's first-hand observation and his enticing plan of the strait with its telltale signs of de Fuca's discoveries. Losing no time, he had the plan engraved as a chart dated January 1790, then set about announcing that Juan de Fuca's strait had been rediscovered. The year before, we might note, in his *Plan for Promoting the Fur-Trade,* Dalrymple had written of an alleged Spanish discovery of the entrance to a strait, in longitude 47° 45' N, which brought them to the vicinity of Hudson Bay after a twenty-seven-day journey. "This Latitude exactly corresponds to the ancient Relation of Juan de Fuca, the Greek Pilot, in 1592, who sailed into a broad Inlet between 47° and 48° which led him into a far broader Sea, wherein he sailed above 20 days, there being at the Entrance, on the NW Coast, a great Head Land or Island, with an exceeding High Pinnacle, or spired Rock, like a Pillar thereupon."[97] Duncan had given him the proof he was looking for, and swept away all doubts and uncertainties.[98]

All of a sudden the entrenched Admiralty calculations about Juan de Fuca's humbug, which dated from James Cook's time, had to be thrown out the window. Complementary information came to London from the Governor General of India, Sir John Macpherson. He had been told at the Cape of Good Hope that Spaniards had recently found an entrance on the Northwest Coast in 47° 45' N, "which in 27 days' course, brought them to the vicinity of Hudson's Bay."[99] If this were true, all the old disbeliefs would have to be set aside. A new chapter in the Anglo-Spanish rivalry dawned.

Chapter 5

BOSTON TRADERS AND THE STRAIT: THE LINKS TO CHINA

Although Captain Cook had missed sighting Cape Flattery in appallingly heavy March weather in 1778, he soon thereafter placed Nootka Sound on the map of the world, and knowledge of this place and its inhabitants and the sea otters that lived there and along the coast brought Europeans and Americans in ever-increasing numbers. He gave its entrance a latitude and longitude and described its long-held secrets to the global audience, aided by the publication of French and German translations of his 1784 voyages. Any reader hungry to know about the famed mariner's death in Kealakekua Bay in 1779 could also read about his explorations in the North Pacific, including Nootka Sound. In reading his journals today, and those of his officers, we are even now witnesses to the unfolding of history, a turning point in human affairs, for the texts seem to draw open the blinds on a world never before seen from the outside.

In his depiction of Nootka Sound, Cook described its residents as a fine, handsome people who valued property above all else. They were commercially minded and were keen traders. He found them also quick to take offence. He was there a month and thus had a good chance to observe them first-hand. These people of Nootka Sound, he said, were keen to trade pelts of the sea otter for which they would accept items of metal.

For the several peoples of the west coast of Vancouver Island (and for their kin nearby and at Cape Flattery), the sea-otter pelt—5 feet in length and 24 to 30 inches wide—was their principal export as long as that remarkable mammal continued to exist by the hundreds and thousands on the littoral of the North Pacific Ocean. And Nootka Sound was an advantageous place for the First Nations to carry on their trade, though it was not the only location of commercial prominence—the coast of southeastern Alaska, Haida Gwaii and two great sounds south of Nootka, Clayoquot and Barkley, were also excellent places to trade, along with the southern entrance to the Strait of Juan de Fuca, in and around Cape Claaset and Cape Flattery, and south toward California.

The sea otter is a creature of outer islands and shores, where abalone and sea urchins provide good food, and kelp beds or rafts provide shelter. The pelt is delicate, thick and soft to touch and mysteriously luminous in appearance. Recounting his four voyages in pursuit of sea otter, William Sturgis said "that it would give him more pleasure to look at a splendid sea-otter skin, than to examine half the pictures that are stuck up for exhibition, and puffed up by pretended connoisseurs. In fact, excepting a beautiful woman and a lovely infant, he regarded them as among the most attractive natural objects that can be placed before him."[100] Sturgis was not alone. The naturalist Georg Steller, sailing with the Russian Columbus Bering, held the sea otter to be a beautiful and pleasing animal, cunning and amusing in its habits, and at the same time ingratiating and amorous.

At the time of Cook's visit to Nootka Sound, the British sailors had no idea of the pelts' real value. The skins they purchased had been worn by the First Nations; the sailors used them for bedclothes when the ships made their voyage into frigid High Arctic waters, via Bering Strait. Captain James King, who completed the text of Cook's account and made it ready for the press, is quite clear that they had underestimated the commercial prospects of a trade in sea-otter pelts with the Chinese. When the British ships called at the port of Petropavlovsk in Kamchatka, the Russians were keen to buy the furs, for they could peddle them to the Chinese overland via Kiatka, a border town of the Chinese empire.

However, when Cook's account appeared in print in 1784, the commercial prospects of the sea otter were revealed as a means of opening a trade with wondrous China in tea, porcelain, nankeens (pale buff cotton cloth) and much else. Any merchant company of Europe or America with a good ship, able officers and crew, and sufficient supplies and provisions for a voyage of two or three years might make a killing in this infant trade. Even so, the prospects of trade were based on a number of wild assumptions—that the Chinese would allow the trade on an enlarged basis, that the market would not become flooded with pelts—and other vagaries, including arrangements with the Russians in the north and the Spanish at Manila (with both of whom the Chinese had odd forms of indirect trade). These obstacles were not sufficient to kill the trade. It was high risk but yielded phenomenal profits to the successful. The merchant traders of Boston unlocked its secrets, and year by year they came to dominate the trade until the sea otter was hunted to extinction. They, more than any others, opened the interchange between Orient and Occident, brought Vancouver Island and the Northwest Coast into contact with Canton and China, and induced changes on both sides of the Pacific that reverberate down to our own times. We find Chinese workers building ships at Nootka, Hawaiians or Kanakas shipping aboard fur-trading vessels, and coastal peoples being drawn relentlessly into a worldwide web.

Captain Cook, as we have noted, put Nootka Sound on the chart, and the waterway on the inside of Nootka he called King George's Sound in honour of the king (the sound subsequently lent its name to the trading company headed up by Richard Cadman Etches). William Bligh, there with Cook and later famous in the mutiny on the *Bounty*, drew the first plan of the harbour. Just within the entrance, on the port side and guarded from surf and storms of the open Pacific, was a Native village known as Yuquot. Not only did the whole provide a safe, large and convenient harbour, but good anchoring was possible close in, which aided communication with the shore. Nearby, too, or farther up the channel leading northward toward the permanent or winter villages of the Natives, tides and shores were perfect for the essential careening of ships. Everything a ship's carpenter needed for repair in the way of wood was there.

Yuquot, "where the wind blows," is the name of the summer village of the people of whom Maquinna was chief. It is situated on what was later called Friendly Cove, which boasts a semicircular shore and wide stretch of white sea-sand. From prehistoric days it had been a village site. "We still don't know how long people have lived on the West Coast, or where they came from," writes John Dewhirst, the distinguished authority on these matters. "The Nootkans maintain that they have always lived on the West Coast, and strongly resent any suggestion that they might have ultimately come from Asia. It is now known that people have been living on the West Coast for at least 4,200 years, and probably longer—which is almost like 'always'."[101] These people were whalers, and proud of it, but their position also gave them access to fishing grounds. Here in the lee of the island they had safety for their canoes, and there was abundant fresh water for drinking.

In this class-conscious society, there were chiefs and there were commoners, plus slaves who formed less than 10 percent of the whole. The chiefs constituted true nobility. They had grown rich on trade and warfare. The anthropologist Philip Drucker tells us that they had an authority and prestige

The sea-otter chiefs and aristocrats of the Northwest Coast: Callicum (left) and Maquinna, brothers and chiefs of Nootka Sound. Callicum was later killed in a dispute with the Spanish explorer Martínez, while Maquinna was well known for his interaction with, and occasional enslavement of, Europeans. FROM *BRITISH COLUMBIA: A PICTORIAL RECORD, 1778–1891*

equalled by few other Native Americans. In the history of conquest and ruthless domination that had made the Nuu-chah-nulth the Native lords of this coast, they had equally dominated the affairs of their own tribe and the confederacy. Maquinna, Callicum, Wickaninnish and others who were less important but of the same hereditary peerages, who had been masters of the whale hunt and were now the sea-otter chiefs, arranged the privileges of land and sea as suited their purposes. They dispensed favours and showed their power by means of the potlatch. By giving away their collected wealth, they demonstrated conspicuous consumption, and in doing so they blatantly dared others to compete in this world of property acquisition and disposal.[102]

The sea-otter trade brought the chiefs wealth and enhanced station. Everything flowed from Europe and eastern North America to make the trade function. In the ships' holds were copper in large sheets and long bars of iron. There were woolens, blue baize, greatcoats, beads and bells, fish hooks and spear points, cereals and molasses, but it was metal that was most in demand. Accordingly, and answering to local tastes, the ship's blacksmith or armourer would be put to work cutting up the iron bars into a chisel weighing a quarter of a pound, the preferred size. Or a small sheet of copper about the size of a hand's width, or stretched fingers, would suit the customer. In certain locales an iron collar would be the requirement; in another, a copper collar. Rum was another essential import, and not to be forgotten were muskets and ammunition, highly prized and in much demand.

In 1792 one Boston trader, John Hoskins, with instincts of cost-benefit analysis, prepared a memo in which he described the going rates of trade and the commodities wanted on the spot. It is a telling point to see how at Cape Flattery and Cape Claaset certain items had certain value, and how the sea otter could be purchased more cheaply here than at the mecca of Nootka Sound or, for that matter, at Clayoquot or in the ports of Haida Gwaii.[103]

For this reason the mariners, especially those out of Boston, came time and time again to the southern entrance of the Strait of Juan de Fuca, although they did not penetrate far into the strait. The sea-otter habitat did not extend much inland, perhaps no farther than 30 or 40 miles. Besides, for navigation purposes, the mariners hated getting inside the strait, with its treacherous tides and currents, and then having to work out of it in enveloping fog banks or against the winds, being always reminded that they were working on a lee shore, with the dangerous coast of Vancouver Island not very far distant.

So back and forth across the strait's entrance the brigantines, schooners and others flitted, coming first down from Nootka Sound to Clayoquot, Barkley Sound and then, finally, to Nitinat if the weather was fine. Then, leaving Vancouver Island shores and ports behind, they would shoot across the strait to Cape Flattery, trade in that area east and south, then raise sail and make a quick passage up to Haida Gwaii and return south again before finding a winter haven or sailing for China via the Hawaiian Islands.

Seldom did the fur-seekers stay long in any one place, only enough to transact the exchange, by trade if possible and by force if necessary. And thus it was that the traders were the transients on this coast, the agents of change. All the while the First Nations had to be the suppliers and producers of the natural wealth in their local seas, and they often were obliged to put up with the indignities that were brought to them by the here-today-and-gone-tomorrow mariners. Here was a unique collision of civilizations, revolutionary in its impact on the First Nations and hugely profitable to the mariners. The sea-otter chiefs grew rich on the trade and were vaulted onto the world's stage.

Into this scenario the British had first sailed—Hanna, Guise, Strange, Meares and others since 1785—crossing the Pacific from China and even distant Bombay, all under the watchful eye of the East India Company, which feared interlopers but acceded to the pressures of independent

"country traders." Then London traders, by special arrangement, sent out Portlock and Dixon. James Colnett and Charles Duncan followed in a new global consortium linking London and Macao, in which Meares was the leading director in Chinese waters. Barkley, as we saw in the previous chapter, sailed from Ostend under a flag of convenience. In short, the first and formative phase was a British enterprise.

An engraved view of the Native dwellings in Nootka Sound by John Webber. Webber accompanied James Cook on his third voyage of exploration. DAVID RUMSEY MAP COLLECTION

But it was to the Americans that the next and most prominent phase belongs. It commands our attention because they sailed into a multilingual world, faced the challenges of the British, finessed the officialdom of the Spanish (with which they were sympathetic), and sooner or later made arrangements to partner with the Russians in distant southeastern Alaska.

They were a tough people, these Bostonians who commanded the trade, and they had vivid memories of the Boston Tea Party and the Battle of Bunker Hill less than two decades previous, their national baptism of fire against their old British masters and King George. With the sea at their doorstep, the merchant trades to Europe and the West Indies had enriched them, boosted their own industrial economy, and extended their trades in fish, timber and rum. They cared not a fig for the East India Company monopoly in the coastal trade of Asia; in fact, they were fond of pulling the lion's tail. Boston specialized in sea otter just as Nantucket did in whales, Salem in peppers and nutmegs, and nearby Stonington, Connecticut, in seals from the Falkland Islands. The Northwest trade was funded by tightly controlled family entities or partnerships, each and every one a rival of the others. They would not pass messages from ship to ship for fear of revealing trading secrets and ship movements. The sons and nephews of captains, partners in the enterprise, shipped as junior mates, then rose to the top. Many great Boston mansions were built on the profits of the trade and the labour and exchange of the Northwest Coast Indians.

Ship of American destiny: the *Columbia Rediviva*, captained by Robert Gray and belonging to Boston, successfully crossed the treacherous Columbia River bar in its second attempt, making the first entry into the great river of the West. OREGON HISTORICAL SOCIETY, ORHI 91188

In 1787 a syndicate of six partners investing $50,000 sent the *Columbia Rediviva*, Captain John Kendrick, and the *Lady Washington*, Captain Robert Gray, on the first approach to the Northwest Coast. They sailed from Boston on 30 September 1787 and arrived at Nootka Sound the following September. Kendrick wintered well up in Nootka Sound in 1788–1789 at Kendrick's Cove. Their trade began in earnest the next spring.

Here's what Robert Haswell, aboard the *Lady Washington*, recounted for Saturday, 28 March 1789: "at meridion I observed in Latitude 48° 44' North and at this time we saw a cape or Headland which I suppose to be cape Flattery bearing SE b E but to the eastward of this no land could be seen as we proceeded E b S as the coast trended I fully concluded we were in the straits of Juan de Fuca."[104]

The weather was horrible, dreary and wet. "[On the Tuesday] as soon as we came within 1/2 a Mile of the South shore of the Straits we bore up and went along shore in an ESE direction . . . we saw a large canoe cuming off their was at this time a tumultious sea caused by the meeting of the wind and tide we hove too to wate for the Canoe and the Sea made fare breaches over us they had no skins and told us their were none up the Straits but that the Chief Tatooth of Clahaset had purchased them all they offer'd their own manufactored blankets which weir realy curious . . . their was so disagreable a chop of a Sea."

And again, showing how, at every circumstance of these early days of April, the weather determined the vessels' actions and dictated the opportunities for trade and, indeed, every action of the solid men of Boston: "To have run farther up these Straits at this boisterous season of the Year without aney knoledge where we were going or with what difficu[l]ties we might meet in this unknown Sea would have been the hight of imprudence espesialy as the wind was situated so we could not return at pleasure. the weather was coald with heavy Squalls of Rain wind and Sleet all night much hail and Wind. the morning was pleasant and Clear but a very great sea out."

On Friday, 3 April, they were trading at Neah Bay. A large swell had set on the sea, and the wild white horses (the great waves) were racing up the strait, a powerful surf pounding the shore. A number of Natives came alongside with good skins, and so the vessel anchored to complete the exchange. The mates began to worry: "but our situation was so dangerous that Mr. Coolidge and Myself advised Captain Gray to weigh imediately we hove too and purchaced a number of good sea otter skins they told us the village abrest of which we anchored was named Nee-ah." There was now "a strong tide setting out of the Straits and a Wind blowing strong from the Eastward at 1 oclock PM we bore away and run out of the Straits."

To the Bostonians the coast hereabouts seemed to abound with Natives as well as good sea-otter skins, "but at this season of the year it is attended with the most eminent danger to cruze this part of the Coast and the advantages that may accrew from so great a hazard are by no meens equivelent for when we came along this shore Last sumer when the weather was mild and pleasant fue of the natives came off tho' we were day after day close in with the Land." They found it surprising that the Indians would venture off from the land when it was almost blowing a gale-force wind and the sea was running to a mountainous height. On 5 April the weather was changeable, with alternate squalls of wind and rain making it too precarious to venture in near the land. Early the next morning the gale increased in violence, and Gray determined to bear away deeper into the Strait of Juan de Fuca in hopes of gaining shelter in Clallam Bay, which the Bostonians called Poverty Cove, there being little trade there. When a break came and the weather cleared, Gray steered out toward open ocean for Clayoquot Sound.

On 10 April the *Lady Washington* was riding safely at anchor near Ahousat, Clayoquot Sound. The crew was abuzz with talk of a whale captured. Haswell had heard that Wickaninnish had taken a whale, and everyone aboard ship was curious about this. Haswell takes up the story, worthy of repeating here in full:

> My Friend Hanna [Captain Hanna, the chief of the village of Ahousat] . . . told me Wickananish had struck a Whale and that all the Villagers where going to his asistance.
>
> I was curious to se them kill this large fish with such simple impliments and went in a canoe accompaneyed by Mr. Treet to be spectators on our arrival at the place of action I found the whal was laying at this time unmolested waiting the return of the Chief who was in pursute of another but immediately on his return he gave the order for the atack his mandate was answered by a low but universal acclaimation the next brother to the Chief [Tatoochcosettle] invited me into his canoe this I rediely complied with . . .
>
> We were paddled up to the fish with great speed and he gave him a deadly pearce and the enormious creature instantly expired they fastened a number of Bois on the Fish and took it in tow to the Village.

I had maney invitations to visate and partake with them but with this I did not comply on my Return onboard I made particular inquieries relative to their customs in whaling.

They told me the first Whale that was killed in a season it was their custom to make a sacrefise of one of their slaves the corps they lay besid a large pece of the Whales head adorned with eagles feathers after it has lay'd their a sertain time they put it in a Box as usual they say it is particularly pleasing to their Deaty to adorn a Whale with Eagles fethers for they suppose thunder is caused in conflicts between that Bird and fish that an Egle of enormious size takes the Whale high in the air and when it falls causes the noise Thunder.

On their Whaling excurtions they frequently cut their tongues and paint themselvs with the blud that the Whale may not be afraid of them and run from them or they afraid of it they have maney other superstisious Id[e]as relative to this fish to consider the imperfection of their utentils musel shell harpoons and lances with Roaps we must allow them expurt Whalemen.[105]

Back the vessel sailed for Cape Flattery, for another trawl. "Friday 17th [April 1789] . . . and being out of danger we bore up for the Straits of Juan de Fuca." They expected a good trade. They sailed eastward and close to shore at Cape Flattery. Several canoes now came off from the shore. "Of these people we purchased several good sea Otter Skins at 5 Chizels each . . . we lay too off this place where there is a village . . . having purchaced all their skins we made sail for the Southward . . . but on Monday we found we were only 4 Miles to the Southward of Chandee or Tatooche's Island." Once again canoes came off from shore toward the ship, this time with the chief, who "sold upwards of 20 prime Skins and they departed well pleased with receiving 5 Chizels each and promised to bring a great number more the next day."

Once again the navigation proved hazardous. So strong did the current set that although it was calm almost all the succeeding night, they "were huried into the Straits." Daylight saw several canoes come off "and upwards of 30 Sea otter skins were purchased"—but here's the rub: "we had the Mortification to see them carey off near 70 Others all of excellent quality for want of Chizels to purchace them and they repeetedly told us they had left great abundance onshore."

On 21 April they made sail for Nootka Sound, with a passing call at Nitinat, where the traders once again had no stock to exchange for about two hundred sea-otter skins on offer. They sailed northwest yet again, facing heavy gales and rain that lasted all night before they reached the peace and shelter of Kendrick's Cove, Nootka Sound. The blacksmiths were ordered to make more chisels, sails were repaired, wood and water were taken aboard, and the vessel was made ready for another trading cruise on the coast.

Kendrick continued his trade in the nimble *Lady Washington* (he had converted this vessel from a schooner to a brigantine—the latter had a square sail suitable for "backing" or halting forward progress when required—a perfect sea boat for inshore navigation in preference to the hard-to-handle *Columbia*) and eventually sent Gray to China in the *Columbia* with furs, with mixed results there. The *Columbia* returned home to Boston with teas, porcelain of the blue-and-white willow pattern, fine silk fabrics and eastern oddities, the first vessel to circumnavigate the globe under the Stars and Stripes. The whole venture was not financially ruinous, and the owners hoped the *Lady Washington* would gather the profits that would make the whole matter worth their while. Meanwhile, the partners, still buoyed by the prospects, sent out the *Columbia* once more. And so it was that we find her collecting sea-otter pelts whenever and wherever they could be gathered.

Sailing from Boston in the *Columbia* on the second voyage, as fifth mate, was fifteen-year-old John Boit. He was brother-in-law of the ship owner and merchant Crowell Hatch, a principal in the enterprise. A lad of good judgment and acute observation, unique for his years, he made many fine observations about places visited. Through his eyes we have a sense of adventure, indeed even of wonder, at how the ship, and others like it, seemingly flitted about the Northwest Coast, north and south as required, and all under canvas or being pulled by ships' boats.

The three-masted *Columbia* had sailed from Boston on 28 September 1790, been refitted in the Falkland Islands, doubled dreaded Cape Horn and arrived at Clayoquot Sound on Vancouver Island with about a quarter of the crew off duty with scurvy. Boit was struck by the intricate cluster of islands, inlets and passages that is dominated by Lone Cone of Meares Island and other mountains. He wrote, "This Harbour is made remarkable by three remarkable round Hills, abreast the entrance. Hannah, Chief of the village Ahhoussett, came on board and appear'd friendly . . . We tarry'd in this harbour until the 16th June, landed the sick immediately on our arrival and pitch'd a tent for their reception, and although there was ten of them in the last stage of the Scurvy, still they soon recover'd, upon smelling the turf, and eating greens of various kinds."[106] A brisk trade ensued, with sea-otter skins exchanged for copper and blue cloth. There being no further business there, the Bostonians sailed south.

On 20 June 1791, they arrived at Chicleset in Barkley Sound and anchored in a small cove that they named after the ship. Young Boit recounts that they got many sea-otter and land furs in exchange for copper, iron and cloth as well as beads, fish hooks and "such small stuff." The local First Nations kept the ship supplied with various kinds of fish and greens, and also a few deer. Boit comments that "their Women were more Chaste than those we had lately left. But still they were not all Dianas . . . They dry their fish in the Sun, and then pack it in Neat wooden boxes. Necessity is the mother of invention."[107]

A week later Boit writes, "26 June. This day left Columbia's Cove, and stood along shore towards the Straits of Juan de Fuca. Crew all well." They steered south and then eastward. "This is an Iron bound Coast with high land back," he observed, referring to the hard shore of Vancouver Island here (along which the West Coast Trail now runs). On the 28th, they "Enter'd the Straits of Juan De Fuca and Hove too abrest the Village of Nittenatt found strong tides. Vast many Natives off with Sea Otter, and other Furs which we purchas'd with the same articles as before. 'Twas evident that these Natives had been visited by that scourge of mankind the Smallpox. The Spaniards as the natives say brought it amoung them."[108]

A fine trade was kept up here, and for about a week, until 3 July, the *Columbia* "kept beating about the entrance of De fuca Straits." Off a small island called "Tatooch" they collected many sea-otter skins, with the Natives there showing a preference for copper. Fine halibut and salmon were procured in abundance, and "Nails, Beads etc. serv'd for this traffic. This Chief at Tatooch's Isle offered to sell us some young Children they had taken in War." His offer was declined. They left the strait at 6 p.m. on the evening of the 3rd, young Boit making note of where Cape Flattery, as named by Captain Cook, was lying southeast by east on the horizon at a distance of 8 leagues, the land about 12 leagues. He mentioned seeing many whales in the vicinity. By 8 July the *Columbia* was up in the south-east part of Haida Gwaii, in Houston Stewart Channel, where they stayed until the 17th and completed good trade in sea-otter and other furs. Then they cut eastward into Hecate Strait, still rumoured to be the Straits of Admiral de Fonte, where they bought furs and lots of halibut (a board nail would buy you a halibut). Then it was south again in another search for sea-otter pelts at Juan de Fuca Strait.

The 11th of September found them once again abreast of Cape Flattery. Boit's journal gives some idea of the difficulty of navigation in these tide-swept waters. Excessively strong tides swept the vessel between some ledges and Tatoosh Island. "At daylight thick fog, saw the Rocks ahead within pistol shot, with high breakers. Out all Boats, and just towed the Ship clear." The weather came on difficult and miserable, with a good deal of fog, and Boit commented, "Our situation was truly alarming, but we had no business so near the land in thick weather." Good luck prevailed, and an offshore breeze sprang up, enabling them to stretch out clear of danger. The next day was much the same, and the surf pounding on the opposite side of the strait could be heard from the deck of the *Columbia*. "The Captain, at length, was frightened, and proceeded with the Ship to a good offing (this ought to have been done long before) thick foggy weather, with a moderate breeze."

First American circumnavigator: Robert Gray, an American captain and trader, discovered and named the Columbia River after his ship. OREGON HISTORICAL SOCIETY, BAO17994

Captain Gray did not invite admiration as a navigator, and he seems to have taken more than his share of chances. This was young Boit's first experience of working close in to shore aboard *Columbia*, but it is likely that others in the vessel had doubts about Gray's technique and his judgment. They worked the fogbound shore, searching out their customers. It was a hazardous business. Back and forth they tacked, in daredevil fashion, and we can almost hear the captain, or one of the mates, yelling out "away tacks and sheets," "hard alee" and then "haul, haul" as the vessel came back on another course. It was mind-bending work, too.

Boit now seethed with anger and disbelief at the tom-foolishness of this pelt-hunting cruise. On the 12th, still in foggy weather, they heard "the roaring of Breakers, foggy, haul'd more offshore. At 3 PM saw a rock about stone's throw distance, and narrowly excaped being dashed upon itt. Damn nonsense to keep beating about among rocks in foggy weather."[109] When the fog cleared, Cape Flattery came into view, and Boit thought it possible that a passage opened between Cape Flattery and this "Isle of Tatooche." "It appears about 2 miles wide, however cou'd see breakers between them, and currents are excessive strong, as we cou'd discern them to foam in that narrow pass. Many Natives came off, and we purchas'd a few skins and plenty Halibut. Weigh'd and came to sail towards evening, bound to Cloquot."

On the 20th, the *Columbia* was towed by the boats into winter quarters at a place they called Adventure Cove on Meares Island. Mooring lines were run ashore to the great trees and they prepared for another trading season, one that would again take them back to the Strait of Juan de Fuca. The sound of axes and hammers reverberated throughout the forest there under the shadow of Lone Cone and Mount Colnett. A small vessel, the sloop *Adventure*, was built on the ways. Wickaninnish, the chief, and his people paid a visit and carried on a trade. On 2 April 1792 the *Columbia* and *Adventure* sailed together, with the *Adventure* proceeding on coastal business and the *Columbia* sailing out and south so as to make a northern voyage along the coast from Cape Mendocino.

By this time other syndicates in Boston were outfitting ships for the trade. The 70-ton brig *Hope* sailed on 16 September 1790 under Joseph Ingraham, one of the more literate skippers. He was a vigorous and talented fellow, with excellent navigational skills. He had been in the *Columbia*, and Thomas Handasyd Perkins, who had gone out as a supercargo to trade in China, decided that here was a talent he should poach. Ingraham agreed, and at age twenty-eight he was anxious for a new adventure. Even so, he later recalled a little sadly that all his life had been "a series of storms, dangers and troubles."[110] No expedition of high adventure and fun, this—only difficulties along the way and, as it turned out at the end, not much profit either. He made only one Northwest Coast voyage, and his account helps us to understand further the connections then developing between the Bostonians and the Spanish, who were now setting up their imperial outpost at Nootka Sound.

On 1 June 1791, Ingraham took the *Hope* into the islands of Haida Gwaii, his first stop, and that summer and the next he traded between these islands and the main, all the while collecting information on geography, natural history, languages, manners and customs of the inhabitants, the details of which fill his interesting journal. (His observations about Nootka Sound are of great importance.) He, too, made an approach to the entrance of the Strait of Juan de Fuca. His journal is enriched by enchanting maps, none drawn with any scientific accuracy. On one of them Ingraham drew in "Streights of de Fuca" to show the waterway that continued eastward into unfamiliar waters. It is a wonderfully flamboyant chart showing ports south from Nootka—Clayoquot, Barkley Sound and Poverty Cove on the Vancouver Island shore and Cape Claaset and Neah Bay on the mainland—and to the north, Cape Scott and Lance Islands with snowy mountains and other details. Ingraham had no use for Meares's geography as given in his book. He was sure that John Kendrick had never passed through this channel in the *Lady Washington* as supposed by Meares. In fact, he specifically refers to the map that George Dixon said resembled nothing so much as a "good old wife's butter pat."[111]

On 29 July 1792, Ingraham approached Nootka Sound and anchored on the outside in light airs. He remained there for just over a week, sailing on 7 August for the Strait of Juan de Fuca, where he continued his trade at Cape Flattery and near Neah Bay, and then crossed the Pacific. He reached China in January 1793, then headed home on this his last cruise.

After weeks or months among the dark-forested Northwest Coast and the bright palm-fringed Hawaiian Islands, the river leading to Canton (now Guangzhou), known to the English as the Pearl, presented a unique prospect to the visitor—and an entirely different human world. "I scarcely believed I was fortunate as really to be in China," wrote the Scot John Nicol, cooper aboard Portlock's *King George*, there in 1788. "The immense number of buildings that extended as far as the eye could reach, their fantastic shapes and gaudy colours, their trees and flowers so like their paintings, and the myriads of floating vessels, and above all the fanciful dresses and gaudy colours of their clothes—all serve to fix the mind of a stranger upon his first arrival." Barbers, washerwomen, rice and vegetable sellers, plus beggars and thieves, all made for an animated, noisy scene. Neptune, the ship's great Newfoundland dog, made nightly sport by catching rats and "laid them down when dead at the tent door. In the morning the Chinese gave vegetables for them and were as well pleased as I was at the exchange."[112] So much for petty commerce.

On closer inspection, Nicol was shocked by the great human misery he saw, which "gradually undoes the grand ideas he has formed of this strange people." The Mandarins kept all doors locked tight against trade with the *gwei lo*, the foreign devils, and they would allow no stranger to enter the city.

In contrast to the locals at Nootka Sound, who were open and agreeable to commercial trade, the Chinese did things their own way and insisted that others stay out. No foreign power had any rights of trade in China. Everything had to be done with the most careful diplomacy and always on Chinese terms. A mindset that safely guarded the Celestial Kingdom put up every barrier to the outsider. In those distant days, and in all their commercial transactions, they insisted on gold or silver coin, or cash as they called it; they rejected paper money and would not allow European commodities and merchandise in trade. As we saw in Chapter 2, Spain had sought access to the China market and Spanish brought gold and silver from the Americas to exchange for Chinese silk, satin, porcelain and the like. Juan de Fuca, when pilot of the *Santa Ana*, had been to China and, like others then and there, knew of the luxurious items being carried to the New World.

The Americans, too, had to live by the rules, but they were artful in breaching officialdom and undertaking commercial transactions. The *Empress of China*, from New York, was the first American ship to trade to China, in 1785, and on that occasion it brought ginseng, a tuber with medicinal properties that was dug from the soil of eastern North America. Here was a commodity the Chinese would accept in trade as a substitute for cash. But ginseng was in short supply, and the sea-otter pelt came forward as another kind of suitable commodity for which the Chinese would trade. Fashion ruled. This ermine of Asia made handsome detail on a greatcoat and was highly prized, particularly among the official classes of the Chinese empire.

John Meares wanted more ports for trade, especially in northern China, Korea and Japan. He knew the Chinese and Russians controlled the sea-otter trade through Kiatka, and he sought to divert the fur trade out of Russian hands. What the British mariners wanted was direct access by sea. As well, there was an insatiable desire in Britain for things Chinese, especially tea, porcelain and silk. The East India Company held a monopoly on trade with India and China, and China managed that trade through one port and one port only, Canton. (The Portuguese were similarly placed at Macao.) Canton was an impermanent destination, for the Chinese would allow only a five months' stay to the "foreign devils." The Hong or Cohong and the Collector of Customs, the powerful Hoppo, managed the trade, exacting tribute as required. The British desperately wanted to open this trade. It would take them almost half a century to do so, at the cannon's mouth.[113]

In September 1792, the British government sent Lord Macartney to Peking with instructions to help the expansion of British merchant trading to China. Macartney's embassy consisted of three ships and seven hundred men—diplomats, scholars, botanists, painters, musicians and servants plus others, including two Chinese interpreters. He also took with him presents—Wedgwood china, clocks, a planetarium and a hot-air balloon—designed to crack open the Imperial Kingdom for British commerce and diplomacy. These presents from George III to Emperor Qianlong, "Son of Heaven," many of them sophisticated mechanical contraptions, were unimportant to the Chinese, who dismissed them as toys. Macartney was sent away as a mere "bearer of tribute."

The Chinese could not conceive that another state might be an equal to theirs. They were self-assured in their own system of governance and rule, and thus received the British just as they received other missions from Burma, Vietnam, Korea and Tibet—with inscrutable, bemused detachment. The cultural differences were intense when it came to the demands for the kowtow, the act of self-abasement in the form of kneeling three times and knocking the head on the floor nine times. As emissary of an equally proud nation, Macartney refused to do this, despite Chinese officials' appeals that he comply. The British did not accept subjugation; it has never been their style.

Thus did the attempt at official recognition come to a crashing halt, leaving smuggling as a way of life. In Lark's Bay, Macao, a regular haunt of Northwest Coast trading vessels, a pair of old English vessels lay at anchor, forming a floating depot for opium shipped from India, the drug destined to disappear somewhere up in the Pearl River above Whampoa, where the foreigners' summer trading houses were. Eventually the Chinese gave up their attempted long-range policing and allowed the opium traders right into the Pearl River. But they never abandoned political control or trade jurisdiction. The same was true in Japan, where the Dutch were the only ones allowed to trade, and even then in restricted numbers at Deshima, in Nagasaki harbour. The British, and other Europeans, were there on sufferance.

The sea-otter traders, however, had found something for which the Chinese would trade. And so it was that the pelts went in, and the teas, porcelains, nankeens and oriental productions came out. Traders often resorted to subversion, with customs officers turning a blind eye as intermediaries made the necessary arrangements. Sea-otter pelts thereby escaped duty.

The mariners from Boston, working their golden round, with a paying cargo on each leg, unlocked the secrets of profitable trade. With their swift vessels of economical size and with suitably small crews, they connected Nootka Sound and the Strait of Juan de Fuca with the Celestial Kingdom. This was no small achievement. For with it began the trans-Pacific trade linking societies on both sides of the great ocean, drawing North America toward Asia and subverting the insularity of the Chinese kingdom. From these early beginnings came momentous legacies in the centuries ahead.

Chapter 6

THE SPANISH PRESS SOUTH FROM NOOTKA

On 29 July 1792, Joseph Ingraham in the *Hope* approached Nootka Sound and anchored on the outside in light airs. A canoe came alongside, and Ingraham inquired as to how many ships were in Friendly Cove. He was in for a surprise: there were two Spanish, two English and one American, the *Columbia*, under the command of his old associate Captain Gray.[114]

Next, boats towed the *Hope* inside and she dropped anchor in Friendly Cove. A Spanish launch approached in which was *primer pilota* Gonzalo López de Haro. Ingraham was acquainted with the Spaniard, and though he knew the waters and wanted no pilot to guide him in, he indulged his opposite and allowed him the courtesy. Haro took him ashore, showed him the gardens; the village of sixteen houses, including the one for the commodore, Bodega y Quadra; and various storehouses, blockhouses, a hospital, and much else. Haro told him that the uncertainty of their keeping the place had obliged them to build houses merely for comfort and convenience and "without any attention to beauty or regularity." Cattle, sheep, hogs and poultry the Spanish had in abundance. To Ingraham, the Spanish village, no matter how temporary, had made a promising beginning. He added, with a note of regret as to what might transpire given the winds of change in the relations of Spain and Britain, "It seeemed a pity to disturb people in so fair a way to establish a good settlement and who to me seemed above any best calculated for such purposes."[115]

The Spanish imperial tide was flowing strongly now, and from Haro the American captain learned that the Spanish had three frigates, a brigantine and two schooners on the coast. The day previous, a frigate of forty guns had sailed for San Blas, taking away with it part of the garrison and supplies from the Nootka settlement. In fact, the Spanish were now expecting to evacuate the place shortly. They had another vessel stationed at their settlement in the Strait of Juan de Fuca, and a third, with the two schooners, exploring the coast. Ingraham noted that "the brigantine remained in Friendly Cove with the commodore's pennant, to answer salutes, etc."[116]

Three years earlier, Nootka Sound had been aflame with accusations and counter-accusations, with the Spanish gaining the upper hand when they seized the British vessels *Argonaut* and *Princess Royal* and imprisoned the *Argonaut*'s captain, James Colnett. Ingraham must have known how irritated James Colnett was when seized by the Spanish, for Colnett first came to Nootka at a time when no Spaniard was there, no Spanish guns bristled down from Hog Island, and no Spanish frigate or corvette lay at anchor in the harbour. No Spanish establishment had existed anywhere north of San Francisco in 1786, when Colnett had first been on the coast. He was no fool, and was regarded by many as cool and competent, and his encounters with the Nuu-chah-nulth are matters of great importance to us, but how he became the subject of controversy and how it connects to the exploration of the Strait of Juan de Fuca is our theme, so the details need recounting here.

In 1789 the viceroy of New Spain, Manuel Antonio Flores, had sent Esteban José Martínez north to Nootka Sound. Martínez took formal possession of the place in 1789 and established a post he named Santa Cruz de Nutka. He is a central and controversial character in the Nootka crisis, and no account of that affair or its aftermath can skip his important part in it, for he was largely responsible for the events as they unfolded. What might be called the back stories are of interest.

A Sevillano, Martínez joined the navy at the tender age of thirteen and began service as second pilot at the naval department of San Blas at age thirty-one. He sailed north with Juan Pérez to Nootka in 1774 and would have gone again, with Bruno de Hezeta, the following year had not

Pérez, no model himself, found Martínez wanting in navigation and seamanship. For twelve years he patiently ran supply ships between San Blas and Monterey, Alta California—a tedious existence for such an ambitious man. Somehow, perhaps because of seniority, he finally caught the attention of the new viceroy, Bucareli, as a competent and able officer. This was an administrative oversight on the viceroy's part, for such an opinion ran counter to Pérez's assessment. Indeed, in view of Martínez's subsequent conduct during his 1788 Alaska voyage (which provoked the wrath of his fellow officers) and his high-handed actions at Nootka (which, the British argued, precipitated the crisis), Pérez's report of incompetence seems the more reliable assessment.

On that 1788 expedition, the Spaniards found Russians solidly entrenched on many islands and inlets east of the Aleutians. The number of Russian occupants in the six posts was estimated at between 462 and 5,000, either total considerable in view of the obstacles of distance and environment. How many might soon follow these Russian pioneers? This was cause for anxiety, and Martínez was the right person to be a courier of alarms. If Russians coming southeast out of the fogs and mists of Alaska were not enough, Martínez also learned that the British were establishing a convict settlement in New South Wales, that Boston mariners were already coming to the coast in search of sea-otter pelts, that Americans were rumoured to be coming overland across the continent, and that other rivals were surely to arrive before long. In all, a worrying scenario presented itself to the nervous Martínez.[117] He reported these frightening revelations to the viceroy and recommended that Nootka be occupied. Based on his visit there with Pérez, and also from what he had read in accounts of Cook's voyage, Martínez believed Nootka offered an ideal location for a small naval base, with a garrison and what he imagined ought to be a sizeable settlement. When Martínez arrived at Nootka on 5 May, the British were already there, with another piece of upsetting news: more trading vessels would soon appear.

Into this heady mix sailed Colnett in the *Argonaut*, fresh from Hawaii and Canton. He was a partner in a steadily enlarging syndicate headed up by Meares, with most of the corporate backing arranged by Richard Cadman Etches' King George's Sound Company. Colnett was firm in resolution. He had sailed with the great Cook. He had been at Nootka previously in the *Prince of Wales* and without let or hindrance had gone about

The Nootka Crisis was touched off by actions of the intemperate or exasperated Estebàn José Martínez, who arrested James Colnett, a British trader and erstwhile Royal Navy officer, and seized Colnett's ship, the *Argonaut*, for violations of Spanish claims to exclusive trade. This illustration was created to enflame those tensions. FROM *BRITISH COLUMBIA: A PICTORIAL RECORD, 1778–1891*

his business. Now he found Martínez interfering with his expansive plans to establish at Nootka a great emporium of trade and possibly settlement.

To Martínez, in turn, true servant of the king and the viceroy, these were intolerable intrusions. Colnett's ships were seized, and Colnett himself was taken by ship to San Blas, though he was soon released and survived to make other great voyages.

Events moved quickly, with cataclysmic results. The full details do not belong here and are amply told elsewhere.[118] Suffice it to say that British shipping was interfered with, British captains complained vociferously, and the Boston trader there at the time, Kendrick, became complicit in the actions against the British. Colnett found Martínez's actions an insult to the British flag, and when news of Colnett's incarceration and Martínez's seizure of the *Argonaut* and another vessel, the *Princess Royal*, reached Meares while he was in China, intelligence of this was sent to London.

Meares himself went straight to London as soon as he could. He produced for Parliament a Memorial, dated 30 April 1790, which contained particulars respecting the capture of vessels in Nootka Sound, estimating the actual losses at 155,000 Spanish dollars, with probable losses of up to half a million of the same currency. The result of this testimony, backed by cries of outrage in the press, coffee houses and Parliament, was that the British ministry of the day raised what is known as "the Spanish armament" and threatened war against Spain unless recompense was given and a new arrangement entered into.

What are we to make of all of this? Quite simply, the period of quietude had ended. The isolation of the coast was breached. The aboriginal preserve was facing an onslaught. The rush for the sea otter was in the ascendant. The self-conscious Spanish, seemingly outflanked in their own zone of claimed sovereignty, needed to chart what they had so long claimed. This became the task of Quimper, Eliza, Narváez, Carasco and the rest of their young colleagues.

The Spanish had no clue as to what existed behind the "backside" of Vancouver Island or, at first, even that it was an island. Had Juan de Fuca been there? If they knew, it was a locked-up secret. Charles William Barkley found the strait. Charles Duncan, also on the hunt, found Fuca's Pillar near Cape Flattery on 15 August 1788. He charted and sketched it before leaving the coast. John Meares had talked about the strait in his famous book *Voyages Made in the Years 1788–1789, from China to the Northwest Coast*, published in London in 1790, which had included his "Observations on the Probable Existence of a Northwest Passage; and Some Account of the Trade Between the Northwest Coast and China." Yankee mariners in search of the sea otter were working that coast aggressively. As we have seen, they were frequently anchoring along the outer shores of Vancouver Island at Nootka, Clayoquot Sound and other inlets, and they were consistent presences in higher latitudes, in Haida Gwaii. Boston traders under Robert Gray wintered in 1791–92 at a secure and pleasant cove on Meares Island, put up a blockhouse called Fort Defiance, built the sloop *Adventure* and continued their trade early the next season.

Spain's overland quest for empire ended just north of the bay its explorers first charted in 1775, before they established their presidio or the mission San Francisco de Asís, and all efforts beyond this had to be done as maritime operations. The Spanish responded to the challenge and invested mightily in coastal infrastructure such as marine yards and docks—and in ships, the essence of maritime history. They built many fine vessels for work on the North Pacific littoral.[119] These needed to be able to endure long passages in open ocean, but too cumbersome a vessel could be useless inshore. Sheer tonnage, particularly too deep a draft, was also a deterrent to coastal exploration. And with the drive for exploration and the continuing need to supply not only the missions of Alta California but also any new posts of the North Pacific, even the older ships had to be used to full capacity.

By the time that workhorse of the Spanish marine, the *San Carlos* (alias *El Filipino*), sailed the Strait of Juan de Fuca, for instance, she had been twenty-eight years in service. Built in Manila, she was a sixteen-gun vessel described as a packet boat of 196 tons. Among her first assignments was her 1775 survey and supply duty in San Francisco Bay. Then in 1788 we find her in Alaskan waters, reporting on Russian activities and encroachments. In 1789 the *San Carlos* sailed into Nootka Sound and then departed north for Alaska yet again. Returning to Nootka Sound in 1791, mainly to help in the building of the garrison, she was soon designated an essential vessel and used in exploring Juan de Fuca's waterway. Survey crews rowing her longboats carried out much of the close examination of coast and islands. In 1793–95 she was again at Nootka Sound, with a new assignment: to take off from the shore the dismantled Spanish base under the terms of the Nootka Sound Convention. In all, this one ship's story is a remarkable history, little known in the aggregate. She was the largest naval vessel in Northwest Coast waters until Vancouver's *Discovery* arrived in 1792.

And what about the frigate *Favorita*, alias *Nuestra Señora de los Remedios*? She was built at Guayaquil, Mexico, in 1778, measured 193 tons, and came to Nootka in 1789. Then there was the *Princesa* (not the *Princesa Real* of immortal memory), more correctly named *Nuestra Señora del Rosario*. Built at San Blas, she was 189 tons and appeared on the Northwest Coast in eight different years between 1779 and 1794.

Yet another vessel of prominence was the *Nuestra Señora de Aránzazu*, also a frigate but larger, this time of 205 tons, another workhorse of the northern quest for empire. The frigates were ship-rigged—three-masted. Smaller was the schooner *Activa*, built at San Blas in 1791 and re-rigged as brigantine *Activo*, concluding service in 1795. (Although we are anticipating our narrative, it is useful to note here that along with the *San Carlos*, with which we began this inventory, the *Activo* had the sadder duty of closing the Spanish base at Nootka and hauling away anything useful to imperial purposes. They were the undertakers, so to speak.)

The *Princesa Real*, already mentioned, was an English-built sloop of about 61 tons. As the *Princess Royal*, she sailed to the Northwest Coast from China under the command of Thomas Hudson, in company with James Colnett and the *Argonaut*. Among the fascinating features of her history is the fact that after she was seized by the Spanish at Nootka Sound in 1789, she had a new career as exploration vessel for the Spanish discovery of the Strait of Juan de Fuca. History has many curious twists, and this is one of them.

Connected to the seizure of the *Princess Royal* (*Princesa Real*) was the building of a small schooner at Nootka by the Spanish. We know her as the *Santa Saturnina*. Hers is another fascinating history, particularly regarding origins, and it has taken much sleuthing to piece together her story. To do this we need to retrace our steps. We are reminded that James Colnett's command, the *Argonaut*, was seized by Martínez in Nootka Sound and was subsequently sailed to San Blas (with the irate if resigned Colnett and other Britons aboard as unhappy passengers). In the hold of the *Argonaut* was a vessel "in frame." The intention was to call that vessel, appropriately, the *Jason*. In the Mexican port, Colnett negotiated his release, and in doing so sold the materials for his schooner to the Spanish. These were transferred to the *Concepcion*, which ship then sailed to Nootka, where the erstwhile *Jason* was built and given the name *Santa Saturnina*. Launched 26 September 1790, she was the second vessel built at Nootka. Her importance in the exploration of the Strait of Juan de Fuca and Georgia Strait is second to none. It is estimated that she was 36 feet, 6 inches, on deck, with a 12-foot beam. The report of Spanish captain Francisco de Eliza indicates that she was a small vessel drawing very little water and had a deck on which she sported three four-pounders. Apparently, she was structured in such a way that her crew could be safe from attack by Indians. On survey voyages she had a complement of twenty-two men plus supplies for three weeks.[120] She was entirely suited for inshore waters, able to sail through narrow channels and shallow waters. Her sailing rig was such that she could be called "a handy vessel," easy of change of course, and requiring a smaller ship's company than

The launching of the *North West America*, 20 September 1788, built by John Meares in Friendly Cove, Nootka Sound. This vessel, of about 40 tons, constructed mainly by Chinese labour, was the first European-style vessel built on the Northwest Coast, and was soon confiscated by the Spanish. IMAGE A-02688 COURTESY OF ROYAL BC MUSEUM, BC ARCHIVES

a brig, brigantine or frigate with their large topsails. A schooner could largely be worked by sailors from the deck. This therefore allowed for smaller crews.

Next is Meares's *North West America*, built at Nootka, largely with Asian artisans and under the direction of English carpenters working to their own design. The vessel had been planned to be about 50 tons and turned out to be about 40. She entered the water at Nootka, from Meares Cove, where he had a little factory (in agreement with Maquinna). She was confiscated by the Spanish on 9 June 1789 and rechristened *Santa Gertrudis la Magna*,[121] was enlarged in 1789, reassembled in 1790 and was on the coast again in 1791. She is a key vessel in our maritime history. Captain Steve Mayo's painting of her is reproduced in Jim McDowell's *Narváez*.[122] Another vessel built was the *Adventure*, constructed by Bostonians at a cove on Meares Island. She was acquired by the Spanish in 1792 as a means of enlarging their already overtaxed marine capacity along the eastern Pacific coast.

The last two vessels requiring our attention are the twin schooners *Sutil* and *Mexicana,* built in San Blas in 1791. Designed for coastal supply work, these shallow-draft vessels were of identical dimensions: 50 feet

3 inches in length, 13 feet 3 inches beam, with a depth of hold on the main deck of 8 feet 7 inches. Mexican records state that they were 46 tons burden.[123] Reconstructed in Acapulco in early 1792, they then sailed for Nootka. The prospect of discovering a strait where Juan de Fuca had indicated vaulted these schooners into long-range voyaging—something never imagined by Juan Francisco de la Bodega y Quadra, their supervising

constructor at San Blas. That they completed these voyages, circumnavigated Vancouver Island and returned to Acapulco is, as we will see, a testament to their commanders and the hard work of their crews. Their voyage, as of yet undiscovered by Hollywood, is one for the ages.

Ships on discovery, or any other extensive navigation, needed to be well provisioned and supplied. The Spanish shipped bread, dried fruits

An engraving by José Cardero, from a drawing by Morata, shows Cala de los Amigos, a short-lived Spanish settlement in Nootka Sound. DAVID RUMSEY MAP COLLECTION

and vegetables and, in larger vessels, cattle and other livestock. They were well stocked with wines and brandy, but perishable food and liquids were always in limited supply. Moreover, they were often bulky commodities, taking up great space in the small vessels in comparison to space used for work or sleeping by members of the crew. Fresh water could be easily acquired ashore, the drinking water in these parts being invariably safe to drink.

Scurvy was a constant problem to the Spanish, as it was to all seafaring peoples; specifically, it limited Eliza's discoveries in the inland reaches of Juan de Fuca waters. The course from Acapulco, San Blas or Monterey to Nootka consumed usually four weeks and was by way of a westering track, sometimes out toward and near to the Hawaiian Islands. In some cases, high latitudes had to be reached, in the Gulf of Alaska, and the journals kept by the Spanish reveal that most discoveries on the Northwest Coast were accomplished on passages south from the Gulf of Alaska, not north from California and Nova Albion, as Drake called it. The British likewise made most of their discoveries on passages southward, as winds, tides and currents dictated the generality of sailing opportunities and possibilities.

The Spanish, fresh from enrichment with silver and gold, Indian slavery or conquest, the triumphs of the Inquisition, with sword and cross marching hand in hand, were now exerting the great example of imperial overstretch: a garrison and fortification at Nootka—which they called Cala de los Amigos (a translation of Friendly Cove, the name given by the trader James Charles Stuart Strange in 1786), in complement to the Moachat and Muchalat. There in 1791, according to an engraving by José Cardero from a drawing by Morata, we find the outpost's hospital, observatory, houses, gardens and freshwater well. A battery guarding the cove sits atop St. Michael Island.

Nootka Sound gave the Spanish a base from which to either mount sea expeditions of local discovery or supply and refit ships for more distant inquiries. Nootka served their every need, a handsome and secure port, well garrisoned and defended, but even so, in the main, dependent on food supplies that must come from distant California and Mexico. Try as they might to be self-sufficient at Nootka, the Spanish were reliant on seaborne links to their greater ports of call in Mexico.

From Nootka Sound the expeditions of discovery were usually sent south into the Strait of Juan de Fuca. The Spanish explorers take pride of place for identifying and naming many places in Vancouver Island's history—San Juan, Port Renfrew, Royal Roads, Gonzales Point and Hill, Haro Strait, Cordova Bay and many others. The place-names history of these waters has enchanted many a yachtsman and student of history, and rightfully so.[124] That some place names have been changed and obliterated should not be a surprise; one could say the same for the First Nations place names, perhaps moreso. If you consult an appendix in Henry Raup Wagner's mighty *Cartography of the Northwest Coast,* you will see that there are literally hundreds of Spanish place names on this coast that have disappeared and are only a matter of historical and antiquarian record. John Walbran did a good job at salvage, and we need more of his kind to do likewise.

The Spanish seldom named places after their ships; they preferred saints or administrative or naval bosses, and not a few of the place names are owing to George Vancouver's sensibilities, who wanted to save the Spanish record of achievement for posterity. Saturna Island, for which I have particular affection, is pleasantly named after a Spanish vessel, the *Santa Saturnina.*

But to return to our main theme. There can be no doubt of the influence of Juan de Fuca's tale on subsequent explorations. That influence was felt strongly during the years of the rivalry for the Northwest Coast between Spain and Great Britain, and, as we now note, underscored the very rationale for maritime exploration in these lands, seas and straits. But the findings of the maritime fur traders, British and American, could not long be kept secret. The Russians were reputedly moving south from Alaska toward Vancouver Island, and the Nootka crisis had changed everything. These encroachments, real and imagined, made the Spanish nervous, and they now sought to make explorations of their own so as to extend their geographical knowledge and their local influence. Such advances would possibly have diplomatic value at a later time. But were they too late? Had they waited too long?

Already a defensive shell was beginning to surround the Spanish empire in these seas. It is true that the Spanish search for the northwest passage lay behind their desire to explore these waters, but it was foreign incursions that prodded them to action. The state of foreign affairs had always driven British policies of trade and navigation and spurred them on to imperial feats; now the Spanish acted similarly. When the Nootka Sound crisis alerted them to British impingement on what they regarded as their proscribed reserve of trade and empire, they selected a commandant for Nootka to rebuild the establishment and make a muscular demonstration against their rivals. The task fell to a naval officer sent from Spain.

Forty-year-old Francisco de Eliza, a frigate captain in the Spanish navy and a recent arrival in Mexico, was picked by the Spanish viceroy in Mexico, the conte de Revillagigedo, and the commandant at the Spanish naval base of San Blas in Mexico, Juan Francisco de la Bodega y Quadra, to reestablish the Spanish fort and garrison at Nootka in 1790. He was to do so while the Anglo-Spanish dispute still lingered unresolved. Martínez had abandoned Friendly Cove in Nootka Sound the previous fall for reasons that are not exactly clear, but perhaps simply because of shipping inadequacies and logistics difficulties, now apparently overcome by administrative commitment, which made the necessary resources available. Eliza was also ordered to expand Spanish geographical knowledge of the Northwest Coast as far as the Gulf of Alaska and into the interior waters of Vancouver Island and beyond. It was a heady assignment, one of those multipurpose projects that European mariners sent to the Pacific on imperial purposes often shouldered. Poor George Vancouver faced something similar.

Eliza seems to have been of a stiff breed of naval officer, more narrow in his perspectives on what he saw on the Northwest Coast. He may have looked on two rainy winters at Nootka as assignments of exile, far from the pleasures of Mexico, Cuba or Spain—an imperial outpost on the distant margins with no horseback riding, no zarzuelas and no lively Spanish ladies. This was not an assignment for the faint of heart. There was much work to do. But he was anxious to serve his masters.

He brought with him to Nootka the makings of what might be described as a fist in the wilderness. The Spanish intended to stay. He was their agent. All prevarications of the Martínez era were set aside. With Eliza came a company of blue-coated soldiers of the Catalonian Volunteers under Pedro de Alberni. Gardens were begun, fortifications thrown up and guns positioned. A guard ship tugged at anchor off the village; it served as storehouse and barracks. The old Native village of Yuquot was eradicated in this explosion of energy released from the ships, and in its stead rose a series of buildings, a sort of rancheria, along with a place for the astronomers to make their observations, an infirmary or hospital, and a place for ceremonial purposes, where the cross and the flag were in near proximity. Maquinna no longer had a summer residence. He was, if not banished, escaped into exile, and was found later in the land of Wickaninnish, Clayoquot Sound, with no chance of a return for well over a decade.[125] For all the kind words that have been said about Spain's relations with the Northwest Coast peoples, the fact is that they took over Yuquot, renamed the whole Cala de los Amigos and set in for an indeterminate period.

Eliza's responsibilities were as numerous as they were complicated. Not only was he to fortify and settle Nootka, but he was also to report on its potential usefulness to Spain. He was to engage in the fur trade, because the Spanish had realized, though much too late, that the international rivalry pressing them hereabouts was driven almost solely by that trade. Fur trading was not the customary style of these Spanish mariners; most of them were born of the soil or of landed backgrounds—from a Spanish way of life so dissimilar to the English or the American navigators who were their rivals in these seas. In any event, the Spanish had learned that the Natives would trade their sea-otter pelts for sheets of copper, and the ships under Eliza's command had brought a goodly supply from Mexico. Scientific inquiry fell under Eliza's purview too. He was to report on the climate, flora and fauna, and mineral deposits. Not least in importance was observing the customs and nature of the Native people.

Francisco de Eliza possessed orders from the viceroy of New Spain to investigate the Strait of Juan de Fuca. The authorities were acting on garbled information regarding Juan de Fuca's voyage, but, more than that, they were pursuing the recommendation of Martínez, who, when at Nootka, and having taken possession of that harbour in the name of the king of Spain, related that in 1774, on his return from the Pérez expedition to the north, he sighted what appeared to be a very wide sound at 48° 20' N latitude. Thinking that this might well be the waterway discovered by Juan de Fuca, Martínez sent a second pilot, José María Narváez, in command of the schooner *Santa Gertrudis la Magna*, to find out if the strait existed.

Leaving aside Martínez's claim to priority of discovery of the Strait of Juan de Fuca—a dubious one according to Judge F.W. Howay, that diligent scholar who went searching for confirming evidence and found that not one of the four pilots on the expedition said anything about a strait—we do know that according to an 1802 resumé recounting Spanish explorations, the pilot of the *Santa Gertrudis la Magna* returned with a report that he had found a 21-mile-broad entry, the midpoint of which was at 48° 30' N.[126] Mention was made of a division in the strait, with one of the passages, the southern one, having a communication with the Mississippi River toward the east-southeast. These early gleanings and, truth to say, imaginings formed the preliminaries to subsequent explorations made in the following summers. All of these prospects had to be followed up.

Eliza ordered a young officer, one junior to him, to make a detailed examination of the entry. This was Manuel Quimper, *alferez de navio* in the king of Spain's navy—that is, an ensign or a sub-lieutenant—who sailed south from Nootka to make a comprehensive reconnaissance of the outer reaches of the Strait of Juan de Fuca. He commanded the *Princesa Real*, formerly *Princess Royal*, the British sloop that Martínez had seized at Nootka. A stoutly built but small vessel, the *Princesa Real* carried a bulging and probably uncomfortable complement of forty-one men and nine soldiers. Quimper sailed from Nootka on 31 May 1790. After lingering in Clayoquot for trade and diplomacy with Wickaninnish, he shaped a course southeast, entered the strait at Cape Beale and passed Puerto de San Juan (near Port Renfrew), where José María Narváez had been in 1789.

Quimper dropped anchor in Port San Juan on 11 June and stayed there until the 15th. On leaving it, he noted in his journal, "I made sail continuing my course for the inside of the strait, towing the longboat and two large canoes which I purchased with the king's copper, having in view their usefulness in the exploration, as they would serve as efficacious adjuncts in the indispensable tasks which were to be expected."[127] He applied to the landscape a number of place names that have happily survived, scattering the names of fellow officers, his pilots, his viceroy and, occasionally, the saints as required. En route he gave the Spanish names of Bonilla Point (Punta de Bonilla), Port San Juan (Puerto de San Juan), Sombrio River and Jordan River (Río Jordan). Other names do not appear on the current charts. They are lost to history, layered under the sequence of renamings: Sheringham Point, Otter Point, Pedder Bay, Parry Bay and Royal Roads. Rivers of fresh, sweet water were found.

On 16 June Quimper entered what we now call Sooke Harbour, named after the Sooke, "stickleback," who lived around the basin. Quimper took no notice of that; he called it "Puerto de Revillagigedo" after the powerful viceroy of New Spain. (In 1846 Captain Henry Kellett surveyed the harbour for the Admiralty, and in doing so reestablished the Native name of the place.) Here the Natives posed no difficulty. They were as agreeable as they were numerous. These people differed from those at Nootka and Clayoquot, Quimper noted. For one thing, they spoke a different language, now known as Northern Straits Salish. For another, he found "no superior chief" among them. Walbran, expert on place-names history, says that an early settler there, John Muir, learned that the Sooke, or Soke, were "a most warlike and hardy race, and that none of the largest tribes on the coast would attack them unaided, but that about the year 1848 the Cowichans, Clallums and Nitinats combined, attacked the Soke tribe and nearly annihilated them."[128] All that lay in the future; during his discoveries, Quimper encountered no resistance.

Sooke is blessed with a temperate climate, and the Sooke River drains into the harbour, forming a natural spit which divides the outer from the inner harbour. For mariners the whole presents a tightly guarded entrance, for a reef of rocks extends from the west shore to mid-channel at the Whiffin Spit extremity. These impediments to marine progress put Sooke Harbour out of bounds for great ships, but Quimper and the *Princesa Real* had no problem in making the entrance. He and his men found themselves in a delicious amphitheatre of nature. Surrounding the inner water were dense forests of hemlock, fir, cedar and spruce, with smaller evergreens, impenetrable salal, Oregon grape and ferns abounding. Logging the larger trees would sustain the earliest settlers, who arrived half a century after Quimper. There were trout-bearing streams nearby and shellfish on the shore for the taking, giving credence to the adage hereabouts that when the tide is out, the table is set.

On 23 June he carried out the ritual of taking possession for the King of Spain, though without the religious rites that were customary, in view of the fact that there was no chaplain present. The Holy Cross was planted in the name of His Catholic Majesty Carlos IV. Salutes of musketry were fired as was a twenty-one-gun salute from his vessel. The Spanish had laid claim to the north shore of the Strait of Juan de Fuca and to this part of Vancouver Island.

On 30 June Quimper, pressing eastward now in the longboat, arrived in Royal Roads, where again he took possession in the name of his king. He called the Roads the "Rada de Valdés y Bazan" after the minister of the Spanish Marine, Antonio Valdés y Bazan. "At 4 in the afternoon I took possession, planted the cross, buried the bottle with all the ceremonies which the instructions prescribe and fired repeated salutes. The Holy Cross was placed on a mesa which consists of a piece of land without any trees and bears W 08° N (of the compass) from the point at the entrance to the roadstead. The bottle is buried at the back of the Holy Cross at the foot of a pine tree on which a cross was formed by cutting off the bark. This will distinguish it from five others close to it and the only ones in the neighborhood."[129]

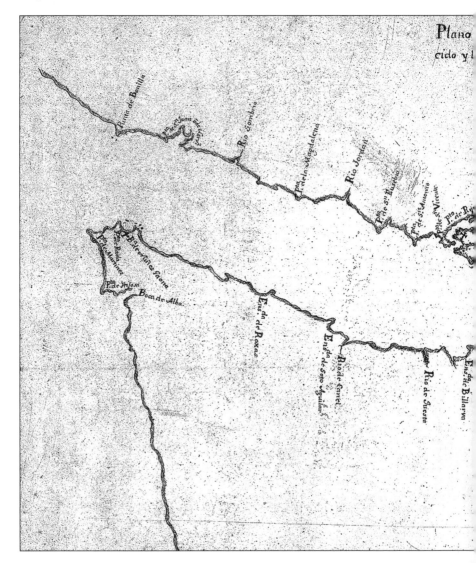

The local First Nations provided much information, on request. Quimper tells about questioning some of them: "After having made them some presents I asked them if there was a channel towards the east part of the strait. They answered with entirely understandable signs, that there was a very large and wide one which trended somewhat towards the northwest, and that at the end of the range of mountains on the south coast there was another like it. They made a sign that this trended towards

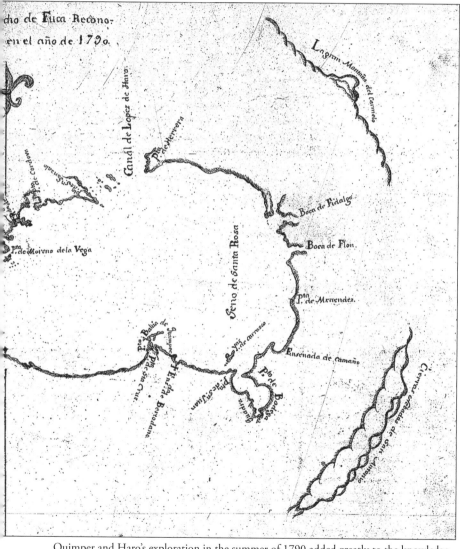

Quimper and Haro's exploration in the summer of 1790 added greatly to the knowledge of the Juan de Fuca Strait, but they mistakenly concluded that it was a dead end. FROM *BRITISH COLUMBIA: A NEW HISTORICAL ATLAS*, COURTESY OF DEREK HAYES

the southwest."[130] At 8:30 that evening Quimper returned on board the *Princesa Real.*

Fog cloaked the shores and sea, and lack of wind caused further delays, hindering his progress. But he took advantage of the opportunities when they presented themselves. And so his slow and methodical examination continued. In the circumstances, the heavy lifting of exploration was done by weary men at their oars. On 19 July Quimper sailed the *Princesa Real* into what he called Puerto de Córdoba, now Esquimalt Harbour and home to Canadian Forces Base Esquimalt. There he anchored. He named it after the 46th viceroy of Mexico. Esquimalt, or Is-whoy-malth (accent on the second syllable), means "place of gradually shoaling waters" or, by inverted definition, a place of deepness. The ambience was different from Sooke and delightful in its own way. "The harbour . . . ," wrote a Spaniard there two years later, "is beautiful and affords good shelter to ships but water is scarce in it . . . The land is very diversified, of no great elevation, and it appeared from the land round it that there is little depth of earth over the rock. It is certainly fertile, covered with trees and plants, which are almost the same in character to those of Nootka, wild roses being more plentiful. Birds were also rather more plentiful; there were special species of gulls, ducks, kingfishers and other birds."[131]

In this first written description of Esquimalt, the Spanish observer did not pronounce it heaven on earth, as well he might. When, in 1842, James Douglas visited Esquimalt's sister port, Victoria—or Camosun as it was known to those of the Hudson's Bay Company—he pronounced it "a perfect Eden." Douglas was on reconnaissance for the HBC, looking for a site where the company could build a fort and establish a marine depot for its coastal trade. He too pointed out that the availability of water for drinking and agricultural purposes would be a problem, as it is to this day. It is worth noting that Vancouver Island's first independent settler, Captain W. Colquhoun Grant, profusely praised Esquimalt. He pronounced it "a safe and commodious harbour for vessels of all sizes, with that of an open entrance, into which a line-of-battle ship might beat without difficulty."[132] He wrote this in 1857, and, true to his prediction, HMS *Ganges*, flagship of Rear Admiral Robert Lambert Baynes, made that entrance and dropped anchor in Constance Cove on 17 October 1858. Four years later, Esquimalt became the British naval base for the Pacific Squadron, the duties of which ranged far, from the Arctic westward to Hawaii and south to Chile.

Quimper had spied the possibilities. But now he hurried on with his burden of discovery. Steering east along the southeastern points of Vancouver Island he discovered Gonzales Point and Haro Strait, which he named in honour of his second-in-command, Gonzalo López de Haro. These place names survive from this first Spanish probing of the strait.

The next month Quimper crossed over the Strait of Juan de Fuca to the south side and New Dungeness. There he sent boats to have a cursory look at Admiralty Inlet, the entrance to which he named Ensenada de Caamaño. This widening of the Strait of Juan de Fuca farther east he called Seno de Santa Rosa. He entered a deep and commodious bay and named it Puerto de Bodega y Quadra, for the commandant at Nootka. (It is now Discovery Bay.)

Then he sailed west toward the strait's entrance, favouring the south shore. He came to Neah Bay, which he named Boca de Nuñez Gaona, after a Spanish admiral. Here he took formal possession of the country in the name of his king. His instructions called for him to be back in Nootka on 10 August, and he departed Neah Bay with full intentions of doing so. But this directive he could not fulfill because of heavy, foggy weather and westerly currents off Nootka. He was not the only mariner in the age of sail to miss his destination on the Northwest Coast. As Drake had put it, unerringly, "The wind commands." Accordingly, with food stocks dwindling, Quimper set course for San Blas via Monterey, which he reached 1 September. He was at San Blas 13 November 1790.

Quimper, like other mariners on the Northwest Coast, had found the sea-otter trade abundant and the Indians agreeable traders, and he carried 200 furs in his hold. Captain Walbran, who studied the history of Quimper when in command of the *Princesa Real*, makes this interesting observation: "On her way down the coast to Monterey the *Princess Royal* must have passed the released *Argonaut* in charge of her irate British commander, Colnett, with the order in his possession for the sloop to be delivered up to him at Nootka, and when he arrived there and found she was not in port, owing to the circumstances above related, he thought the Dons had again deceived him and did not intend to give her up, of which charge, however, the Spaniards were innocent."[133] Quimper remained in command of the *Princesa Real* only as far as Manila in June 1791, having faced a dramatic contretemps with Colnett in Hawaii that had been calmed by John Kendrick, Jr. Quimper returned from the Philippines to Mexico. The *Princess Royal*, as she was again, sailed with another crew to the British owners' agents at Macao in late 1791 or early 1792. In poor shape, she was further battered by a typhoon and sold for salvage.

How do we rate Quimper as an explorer? Highly. He did not know what was beyond his immediate position. All he could see was endless sea, sky, islands and mountains, and here, disbelief and enchantment met. His two months of sailing the Strait of Juan de Fuca and probing its wonders had brought great geographical results. This was thanks to his excellent capacities as a commanding officer and explorer, the sure qualities of his pilots Juan Carrasco and Gonzalo López de Haro, and his adroit diplomacy with the First Nations (he succeeded in keeping the peace where other Europeans had faced violence and sometimes death). As a good explorer should, he had asked advice from the locals, as he did at Esquimalt, and they had given generously of information.

His is, we can conclude admiringly, an unheralded achievement. He laid bare the essential geographical features of the Strait of Juan de Fuca. He had skirted the northern shore of the strait as far as the anchorage at Royal Roads, near present-day Victoria. He had discovered Esquimalt and disclosed the Canal de López de Haro. In the distance he had spied a pale blue hump that he named Lasqueti.[134] Time and circumstance closed his northern examination. Sailing south, he found a good harbour at the eastern end of the strait and named it Puerto de Bodega y Quadra. He concluded, incorrectly, that the Strait of Juan de Fuca really was a dead end, a cul-de-sac. Other Spaniards, Valdés and Alcalá Galiano, would change this record and press toward the first circumnavigation of Vancouver Island, effected before the British.

Thus closed the first phase of explorations directed by Bodega y Quadra. The year 1790 had terminated for the purposes of discovery; late August in any year in these waters is a turnaround time, foreshadowing change of season and approach of inclement weather. The tides and particularly currents are now known to be notoriously difficult, and Quimper was travelling with neither charts nor tide tables. This is not all. A mariner needed always to think of a return to port for refreshment and repair, to take on wood and water and, not least, to report proceedings to the officer commanding. So it was with Quimper, which is why in the next year, 1791, another navigator came on to expand the knowledge of the waters lying beyond where Quimper had made such remarkable discoveries.

Our story now shifts to the unheralded José María Narváez.[135] We have already met him in connection with Martínez's claim that he sent a pilot to find the Strait of Juan de Fuca in 1789. Narváez was born in Cádiz, that famous seaport, in 1768 and had entered the Real Colegio de Guardiamarinas, the Royal Naval Academy, which at that time had an intense course of practical instruction for trained pilots.

When we understand that it was the aristocrats who became the Spanish naval officers, it will be easier to see why this mariner, of no noble birth, became a warrant officer—in this case, a pilot. He had gone to sea early, fought against the British, and served on ships in the Caribbean. Promoted to *piloto habilitado* second class, he was sent to San Blas. By the time he sailed the waters of Juan de Fuca he had already been to Alaska, in 1788, with López de Haro in the *San Carlos*. He remained a senior pilot for many years, sailing to Macao, Manila and other places; married in Tepic, Mexico; settled in Guadalajara; and died there, age seventy-five. He was a man of considerable learning. His was a faithful life in imperial service, mainly afloat but also ashore, and we best see him as one of those essential persons with scientific qualifications in navigation and pilotage who kept up the communications of a world empire. In 1791, age twenty-three, he was about to embark on a mission that has made his name immortal.

The viceroy of New Spain had sent Eliza orders to make arrangements to complete the investigation begun by Quimper. In keeping with these instructions, the *San Carlos* under Eliza and the schooner *Santa Saturnina* (alias *Horcacitas*) under Narváez, provisioned for two months, sailed from Nootka with the puzzling and never properly explained intention of first going north to 60° N (it could have been a feint so as to keep the southerly course secret), then cutting south so as to examine Juan de Fuca Strait. Contrary winds lasting three days prevented the course northward, it is said, and soon Eliza had shaped one to the south, intending to enter the strait. A long and perhaps delightful summer lay before him, with ample time to do the work. It is odd that the winds deterred his Alaska plans, as most vaunted Spanish navigators were not similarly deterred. On the other hand, we do not know the secret file on this.

Be that as it may, the *San Carlos*, sailing south and east from Nootka, entered the strait on 26 May. Eliza, doubtless thinking his vessel too big for exploration, while the handy shallow-drafted *Santa Saturnina*, commanded by a junior officer, a pilot, could better do the work, decided to proceed directly to Puerto de Córdoba, with its sandy anchorage safe from stormy blasts, and use it as a rendezvous and base of discoveries. On the 29th the vessel came to anchor there. Subsequently, the *Santa Saturnina* arrived alongside and stayed there for four days beginning 11 June. There was now much paperwork to do: with all the sheets of paper unrolled and laid out before them, Quimper's charts were updated and completed to the satisfaction of the pilots, our first hydrographers.

The mariners must have thought they were in an interminable waterway. Even this far eastward in their progress, the strait stretched out farther before them, and who knew where the gaps in the distance might lead. In the early afternoons the sea and sky melded together on the limitless horizon, and from across the watery wastes mirages would have played their tricks on Spanish eyes, a squat island rising upward and becoming a strange apparition, a wall of rock, slate grey, the water in front a broad and waveless sheet. And always in the far and elusive distance, the snow-clad ramparts of the North American shore issued a more sombre message: forget trying to find a passage hereabouts.

Eliza remained in the eastern part of Juan de Fuca Strait from 1 to 22 July and sent boats to search out the geographical particulars. On the 31st he sent the armed longboat of the *San Carlos* eastward, under José Verdía, to explore the Canal de López de Haro and carry on Quimper's work. The longboat had thirteen oars and was a cramped craft for exploring duties, with practically no room for storing provisions for the crew.

Verdía returned at 10:30 that same evening to tell his superior that he had been forced to turn back. On entering the passage he had been surrounded by six canoes carrying many Natives, on whom he had been obliged to fire. He had escaped but was again surrounded, and Verdía was obliged to kill some of them so as to make a full escape.[136] Eliza, now alerted to the danger, deployed the *Santa Saturnina* and the longboat as a show of force. Well armed and well manned, the vessels were not to be intimidated. When the canoes made a repeat appearance, the schooner fired on them, then moved on in the imperial progress.

The two vessels passed between islands and then entered Active Pass.

At the far end the sailors saw Lasqueti Island in the distance. They continued east, anchoring at Patos, then passed Sucia and Matia islands. They spent several days investigating the troublesome and swift waters of the San Juan archipelago, mainly noting its extremities. Then they headed east for Lummi Island.

Eliza in the *San Carlos* and Narváez in the *Santa Saturnina* cruised eastward and northward into the Strait of Georgia. Eliza named that waterway grandiloquently the Gran Canal de Nuestra Señora del Rosario la Marinera. The name is not entirely lost, for it is now given to Rosario Strait, the passage between the San Juan Islands and the American mainland. Narváez named Saturna Island after his vessel, and Orcas Island, now on the American side of the line, after the alias, *Horcacitas*.

Having passed into the broader waters of the Gran Canal (Georgia Strait), the mariners had greater scope of the compass for their actions, and Narváez was about to make his most important discoveries. He cruised into Boca de Bodega (Boundary Bay), then sailed north from what is now Point Roberts, the mainland promontory jutting just south of the forty-ninth parallel, and for a distance passed through "a line of water that was more sweet than salty." The mariners assumed that there was a very copious river here, because they collected water from the sea surface some

Watercolour by Gordon Miller: San Carlos *and* Santa Saturnina *off Royal Roads.* Francisco de Eliza, the Spanish commander, played it safe and sent the shallow-draft *Santa Saturnina* into the straits to explore while waiting for news in the larger *San Carlos.*
COURTESY OF GORDON MILLER

distance from land and found that they could drink it. Below the river water flowed the tidal masses inward and out to the entrance to the Strait of Juan de Fuca. They must have wondered what kind of a world this was. Looking at the shoreline, they could find no trace of a river's entrance, for with the morning haze resting on the low mudflats and marshes, all seemed a vanishing flatness, sea and sky again melding into the limitless horizon. Bad weather checked discoveries there, too, and they did not investigate the source from whence this fresh water came. They therefore missed the great river, understandable in the circumstances.

Such evidence as Eliza and the pilot Juan Pantoja y Arriaga provide suggest that Narváez sensed the presence of the Fraser River, and that is as far as we dare go in saying that they made a specific claim to its discovery. A few personal remarks are due here. Having lived for some years in the municipality of Delta, both on the Boundary Bay side and on the South Arm of the Fraser River, with lots of time to explore these environs, I can say that this is a land of sloughs, marshes, muddy channels and brown water. It is a land of wildfowl, of low-lying landscape, and in that age of discovery there would hardly have been a tree to be seen. Tsawwassen Bluff would have looked like an island, as would, far to the north, Point Grey.

The Spanish vessels undoubtedly sailed near the western shores of what is now the City of Vancouver, but no documentary evidence survives as to their actual dates in the vicinity. The cartographic representation is suggestive but far from conclusive. On Narváez's sketch we note, curiously, Isla de Zepeda, which is Roberts Bank and the Tsawwassen bluffs. To the east, in the broad interior waters, we see Semiahmoo, White Rock and a mythical passage called Boca de Florída Blanca, after the Spanish prime minister—perhaps this is Burrard Inlet. Point Grey has greater definition and is Islas de Langara, high enough to seem an island. We are reminded that in the time of exploration, during and soon after the season of spring tides, snow-melt freshets and flooding rivers, the waters would be higher and the natural landscape of grasses and sloughs, as seen from longboats, seemingly lower in height than nowadays.

The travellers were met by a large number of the Musqueam nation in slim canoes. The Musqueams told the Spanish that the canal continued much farther, then carried on a considerable trade. Narváez's purser purchased an eleven-year-old Indian boy.[137]

Crossing to the Vancouver Island shore, Eliza went north to Cape

Lazo, on his way naming the Ballenas Islands (Islands of Whales), one of the few Spanish place names that still survives (along with Texada, Lasqueti and Cape Lazo).[138] Narváez, meanwhile, coasted north from Punta de la Bodega (doubtless Point Atkinson), looked in on the Bocas del Carmelo (Howe Sound), noted the Islas de Apodoccia (the islands stretching toward the Sunshine Coast, including Bowen Island), and continued north to Wilson Creek. He anchored at Thormanby Islands, probably in Buccaneer Bay, steered between Texada Island and the mainland, and reached as high as Hardy Island, in the latitude of Nootka Sound. He sailed toward Cape Lazo, looked into Comox Harbour, spotted an island to the north, then headed southwest across the Gran Canal, rounding Hornby Island. Denman Island appeared to be joined to Hornby. He looked in at Nanaimo harbour, which he called Winthuysen, after the head of the naval college in Madrid. He saw numerous large whales, which caused him to think they had entered by some other way than Juan de Fuca's strait. From Porlier Pass he crossed the Gran Canal into Rosario Strait, and on 22 July he was back in Puerto de Bodega y Quadra, his supplies exhausted. Eliza and the *San Carlos* lay there at anchor awaiting his return.

Any thought of examining the large entrance in the Ensenada de Caamaño (Admiralty Inlet) had to be set aside. Eliza had planned to explore it on his return, but the lack of fresh foods and an outbreak of scurvy among the crews necessitated a change of plans and curtailment of the expedition's activities. It was time to gather together the details of this grand voyage of discovery. Accordingly, he transferred Narváez to the *San Carlos* and gave command of the *Santa Saturnina* to Carrasco. Thus it was that Narváez found himself again in Nootka, this time to look after the paperwork. "If the commander hadn't given up his plan to accompany Narváez's exploration with the *San Carlos*," writes Jim McDowell, Narváez's biographer, with sympathetic insight, "he could have kept the smaller vessels supplied, and supported a longer expedition into Puget Sound to the south and through the Inside Passage to the north. The Spaniards missed a golden opportunity to make both discoveries one year before Captain George Vancouver sailed these waters. But Spain finally had its first picture of the size and shape of the inland sea that so many European navigations had sought."[139]

Eliza never lacked for self-assurance, and he was keen to press his case that the work had been accomplished as ordered. "Your Excellency may rest assured," he wrote unreservedly to the viceroy, "that the passage to the ocean, for which foreign nations have sought with so much zeal, lies, if it exists at all, nowhere save in this great channel."[140] His report was transmitted to the king, who was always keen to know about such developments. In consequence, instructions were sent by return that the examination should be further pressed on the basis of new disclosures. Thus was born the *Sutil* and *Mexicana* expedition, the subject of the next chapter.

It is impossible to tell what happened to each and every mariner who first explored the Strait of Juan de Fuca and the Salish Sea for the king of Spain during those distant days of 1790 and 1791. But of two of them some details are worth recounting.

Quimper continued for many years in the navy, and like Juan de Fuca he sailed to Manila and back. In later years he did some surveying ashore, married in Mexico and raised a large family. He is not lost to the pages of history after all, and is one of those secondary figures of the chronicles whose lives are so well worth the telling. Quimper Peninsula in Jefferson County, Washington State, that area between Port Discovery and Port Townsend, honours him.

And what about Narváez? He is the other great force in sailing these same waters, and he took the explorations farther. Among the first Europeans to see the Strait of Georgia, he explored well into it, determining the scope of the waters north of the San Juan Islands up beyond what is now called the Sunshine Coast on the mainland and Comox, well north of Parksville and Qualicum, on the Vancouver Island shore. Like Quimper he continued the life of a pilot at sea. He fought against Mexican insurgents, but after the Mexican Republic was proclaimed he joined the Mexican navy, became a provincial deputy for Guadalajara, served as commandant at San Blas (1822–27) and produced many a fine map of Mexican coastlines and boundaries. Narvaez Island, one of the Spanish Pilot Group southwest of Bligh Island in Nootka Sound, and Narvaez Bay, at the east end of Saturna Island, are named for him.

Chapter 7

ALCALÁ GALIANO AND VALDÉS: THE FINAL QUEST FOR THE ELUSIVE PASSAGE

*M*eares's bold if irresponsible contention regarding what he called "the probable existence" of a northwest passage set off alarm bells in the halls of power of the Spanish empire and echoed around the Iberian world. The king of Spain, his viceroys and their functionaries had long been nervous of Russian and British encroachments in the North Pacific. To the threat of these unwelcome and pestering fur-seekers had now been added a strategic worry. Such a pathway from the South Sea to the Atlantic would revolutionize the geopolitics of the western hemisphere if it existed and fell into enemy or rival hands. Meares, in a map accompanying the narrative of his voyage, had reported an inland sea, one whose western shore ran northwest from the Strait of Juan de Fuca and looped back to the Pacific just north of Haida Gwaii.

Given the tendencies of mapmakers to fabricate waterways where mountains stood, such a seaway as Meares projected made as much sense to the gullible mind as many another high-flying scheme. Charlatans inhabited the mapmaking world, taking the greatest of liberties with the known facts, or ignoring them altogether. Mapmakers seem to have been the last to take to the age of science and reason. It was far easier to dream than to quantify.

Alejandro Malaspina, with his co-commander José de Bustamante y Guerra, set off on an ambitious scientific and political expedition in 1789, planning to visit all of Spain's possessions. Among their accomplishments on the Northwest Coast, they thoroughly charted Nootka Sound and sent the *Sutil* and *Mexicana* to further explore the Juan de Fuca and Georgia straits. IMAGE A-01420 COURTESY OF ROYAL BC MUSEUM, BC ARCHIVES

Commodore Alejandro Malaspina, sailing for Spain in a grand reconnaissance of the globe in the name of scientific inquiry, got wind of the possibilities of such a strait long after he had sailed from Spain. News of it caught up with him at Acapulco.

Malaspina and his fellow captain in the Spanish navy, José de Bustamante y Guerra, had presented to the Minister of Marine in Madrid a plan for the most elaborate scientific expedition ever attempted in Spanish history. It was designed to rival the voyages of Cook and La Pérouse. "For the past twenty years two nations, the English and the French, in noble competition, have undertaken voyages of this sort in which navigation, geography and humanity have made very rapid progress," reads the introduction to the plan, which clearly reflects the Enlightenment ideals of its authors. "The history of human society has thus been founded on much wider research; natural history has been enriched with almost endless discoveries; and possibly the most exciting victory has been the preservation of health in the course of long sea voyages through different climates while facing the most challenging of labours and dangers. The proposed voyage would aim to accomplish these objectives."[141] In other words, the Malaspina expedition was fuelled by academic fervour, and it superimposed itself on the more workaday activities of the Naval Department of San Blas and its responsibilities for the Spanish shipping needs of the Northwest Coast.

Malaspina's and Bustamante's corvettes *Descubierta* (Discovery) and *Atrevida* (Daring), expressly constructed for this scientific and political expedition and containing laboratory and studio rooms, arrived at Acapulco. A surprise awaited Malaspina.

News of a voyage, said to have been made in 1588, that found a Pacific Ocean entrance at 59° 30' N had come to light in the private papers of a noble Castilian family. Was it a hoax? Malaspina was deployed to find out. He sailed there with great expectations. In fact, the bay in question dead-ended in a massive glacier. Malaspina dubbed it "Disenchanted Bay" and concluded that no passage existed.[142]

The Spanish warships came south to Prince William Sound, though strong winds prevented them from entering it, then bore away south to Nootka Sound, sighting Bering's Mount St. Elias on the way. When Malaspina anchored in Friendly Cove, the disposition of Nootka remained up in the air, undecided. South again they sailed and were at Monterey for two weeks in September before sailing to complete their other assignments in the Pacific Ocean. It was at this stage that Malaspina's higher rank as a Spanish naval officer coincided with the imperial duty of the viceroy of New Spain to find out what was happening on the Northwest Coast in regards to the new geographical fantasy floated by Meares. Malaspina did not have the right ships for close inshore navigation. In addition, he had other obligations and priorities. He therefore delegated the assignment to two junior officers.

Two *goletas*, or schooners, the *Sutil* and *Mexicana*, were ordered to sail from Acapulco in mid-May 1792 to undertake an examination—a reconnaissance, really, not an examination in depth, for they had neither the ships and men nor the resources for such as the British intended—of the Strait of Juan de Fuca. They were to determine its character and dimensions. Speed was of the essence. They were to do so "as quickly as circumstances would permit," as one of the party put it; accordingly, he explained, "we did not stop to examine the Coast which we sighted, but only took bases for determining some of them and rectifying the chart of the Coast drawn by the Officers and Pilots of the Department of San Blas, which we found in good detail."[143] They were sent to find out the northern and eastern limits of its inner reaches.

But what if, in fact, a strait existed such as Juan de Fuca had described? The viceroy, Revillagigedo, prepared new instructions.[144] In the eventuality that this inspection should discover any communication with the Atlantic by way of Hudson Bay or Baffin Strait, the commanders were to set their course by it to Europe as stealthily as possible. The passage had to be kept secret, and certainly out of the web of British intelligence-gathering. The

Spanish sought to find whether or not such a passage existed among the coastal islands. As late as this date they still did not have confirmation of a possible indentation somewhat south of Cape Flattery. Hezeta had referred to the mouth of the Boca de Hezeta (now the Columbia River) in 1775. That point needed clearing up, and Malaspina rather stretched the possibilities of what might be accomplished in one long summer. In any event, however, he gave directions.

To review: the designers of this expedition gave the commanders a long list of tasks, far too long to do any with much thoroughness. From Fuca's Strait south to San Francisco, the *goletas* were to examine the Boca de Hezeta, to determine the true position of the fabled Rió de Martín de Aguilar as reported by survivors of Aguilar's 1602 voyage, and, ultimately, to enter the port of San Francisco. It is clear that although this was a requirement of the survey, the priority was determining if there was a passage from the Pacific to the Atlantic originating in the Strait of Juan de Fuca.

Malaspina wanted to clear up one nagging point. He argued that it was necessary to demonstrate whether Meares's "River Oregon," which supposedly flowed into the southeast part of Juan de Fuca Strait, actually existed. "The principal and almost only objective of your commission," Malaspina advised with insight, "is that of exploring the internal channels of the strait of Fuca, giving priority to the maximum penetration of the sea or navigable rivers towards the east to decide once and for all the excessively confused and complicated questions of the communication or proximity of the Pacific Ocean and the Atlantic in this parallel [of latitude]. Afterwards, a secondary objective is to look into the veracity of the words of the English Captain Meares in relation to the discoveries of the *Lady Washington* and the *Princess Royal* and finally to ascertain for the true utility of Geography what are the true limits of the continent and how far to the east the archipelago extends, which so far has been explored between 48° and 56° of latitude."[145] It was a full agenda, cobbled together in haste, but as contemporary historians have pointed out, "It would have been a blunder if Malaspina had not ordered this final effort, only to have a foreign expedition uncover the fabled seaway."[146]

Francisco Antonio Mourelle, who had been with Hezeta and Bodega y Quadra in 1775, was the ranking available officer and had been chosen to head up the expedition. However, illness kept him ashore, and the viceroy of New Spain selected Dionisio Alcalá Galiano to go in his stead as commander of the *Sutil*. Cayetano Valdés was appointed first lieutenant of the *Descubierta*.

Alcalá Galiano, of aristocratic lineage and bearing, was born in the Andalusian town of Cabra, in 1762. He enrolled in the naval school in 1775 and began active service in 1779. He was involved with surveys of the Spanish coast and the eastern coast of South America, notably Brazil and Buenos Aires. Beginning in 1778 he studied under the famous cartographer Vicente Tofiño. He mastered the practice of lunar distances and determining longitude by use of the nautical almanac. Of a scientific bent, and fully trained in the principles and practices of surveying and of measuring longitude, he had been selected to accompany Malaspina on his circumnavigation in the capacity of astronomer and is listed as second lieutenant of the corvette *Atrevida*. In 1791 he spent a year in Mexico to update the maps and astronomical calculations he had collected since departing from Spain. Late that year he was given his first command, the *Sutil*.

Alcalá Galiano and Valdés had been left at Acapulco to await the arrival from San Blas of the two *goletas*. They must have been dumbfounded when they cast eyes on these vessels. Having sailed in the purpose-built corvettes of the Malaspina expedition, they were now to be confined to cramped quarters in vessels of 45 tons, each manned by thirteen sailors. The sailing distance to Nootka was formidable, the course a long one, stretching out toward Hawaii so as to get a westing, then the last track back to the Northwest Coast and their destination. The first thing the designated commanders did was have the vessels rebuilt: the deck was raised so as to increase stowage capacity and headroom; the gunwales were raised to increase freeboard; and tin was applied to interior spaces for the safeguarding

An accomplished navigator and surveyor, Dionisio Alcalá Galiano led the *Sutil* and *Mexicana* in their expedition to explore and map the Juan de Fuca and Georgia straits. MUSEO NAVAL

of foodstuffs. Mariners at Acapulco found it hard to believe that the vessels would stand up to the rigours of the voyage or that there would be sufficient water and provisions for the crew.

Be that as it may, the vessels left Acapulco, where they had been fitted out in the sweltering heat, on 8 March. They were driven south, then west. The *Mexicana*'s mainmast snapped, the carpenters made such repairs as were possible and the vessel, now unable to adhere to the prearranged course, was obliged to sail downwind much of the time, running fearfully toward the American coast, followed by the *Sutil* under shortened sail. The voyage was lengthened by weeks.

But all's well that ends well, and they raised the land at Nootka on 12 May, though the *Sutil* grounded at the entrance. They came to anchor in the lee of Nootka Island, joining there the dismantled frigate *Concepcion*, the frigate *Santa Gertrudis*, and the brigantine *Activo*. Bodega y Quadra, who had shifted north from San Blas and become commandant at Nootka as well as Spanish commissioner to carry out the Nootka Sound Convention, was waiting for the schooners. He could do less for them in the way of refitting and reprovisioning than they would have hoped or expected, for he had scanty provisions at his disposal and was preoccupied with many other duties.

The author of the account of the voyage, who may have been Espinosa y Tello, summarized the work done at Nootka to prepare for their exploration of the Strait of Juan de Fuca: "Our needs were limited to changing the principal ropes, which were constantly breaking owing to their bad quality; to providing for each schooner a supply of good tackle, five inches thick, to serve as a mooring rope; to making a mainmast and mizzen for the *Mexicana*; to lengthening her crossjack and topsail yards; to providing her with a launch, which was done by shortening a boat belonging to the corvette *Concepcion*; to lengthening the boom of the *Sutil*, to repairing her boat and for getting the two schooners supplies of tow, pitch and tar, and other necessities which were wanting; to increasing the complement [*sic*] of the *Sutil* adding two marines, a gunner, a caulker, and a sailor in place of one who was ill, and that of the *Mexicana* by adding a carpenter and three marines."[147] The clocks, or chronometers, were corrected. All was now in readiness for a voyage of what might be unexpected challenges. It may be observed that marines and a gunner were added to increase the defence capabilities of the vessels, memories of the previous two years of Spanish survey still fresh. Armed conflict with the Natives was to be avoided, but the Spanish were prepared for every encounter: in the Americas they seldom travelled light in gunpower or other weapons.

They made sail on the night of the 2 April but found such dirty weather, with strong winds from the south, that they returned to port to await more favourable conditions. On 5 April they tried again, this time successfully, and passed along the coast, reaching across the entrance of the Strait of Juan de Fuca to its southern sentinel and coming to the safe port of Nuñez Gaona, where they anchored. There they found riding at anchor the frigate *Princesa* under command of Salvador Fidalgo. The voyage account says: "He had set up a provisional establishment preserving good relations with the Indians. Besides the observations [made in the correction of longitude on the chart they had in their possession] . . . we made a plan of the port and tried out the eudiometer [a device for measuring gases, and commonly used for ascertaining the percentage of oxygen in the air]. This showed that the establishment enjoyed pure air."[148]

On 8 April they sailed for Puerto de Córdoba across the strait, taking with them Tetacú (described by Spanish sources as one of the principal chiefs of Neah Bay but he may have been from Esquimalt), who had voluntarily offered to go in the *Mexicana*. His wife, Maria, would not take

Keepers at the gateway: one of the principal chiefs and one of those most attached to the Spaniards, Tetacú, chief of the entrance of Juan de Fuca, and his wife, Maria. Drawing by José Cardero. The artist recorded that Tetacú was the principal chief of two villages at Neah Bay and Córdoba (Esquimalt). DAVID RUMSEY MAP COLLECTION

the passage. Of the chief, the diarist wrote in appreciation, "The conduct of this Indian during the crossing and the stay in Cordova, where we anchored on the 9th at 11 in the morning, caused us to draw very different inferences about these Indians from what up to the present time voyagers have said about them. What they call ferocious treachery only seemed to us to be bold manliness."[149]

From the southern tip of Vancouver Island they sailed east and slightly north, passed through Rosario Strait, and entered the Strait of Georgia. Before long they had coasted the continental shore, passed the salt marsh of the Fraser River, then crossed the strait on further reconnaissance. They were on the lookout for foreign ships and boats, and in due course they met up with the British, under Captain George Vancouver, as told in the next chapter. They had a busy month working these waters, and soon they came to Gabriola Island.

On 15 June the vessels dropped anchor in Cala del Descanso ("small bay of rest"), now Pilot Bay. During an exploratory expedition in a longboat the Spanish discovered, to their surprise and delight, a remarkable natural overhanging gallery about 300 feet in length, 10 to 15 feet wide, and 12 feet high, situated at the water's edge near Malaspina Point, on the western shore of Gabriola Island near the entrance to Descanso Bay.

Nature had created this ocean gallery; it has been hollowed out of soft sandstone strata by the erosion of the sea, and has a floor of a hard

Galiano Galleries near Malaspina Point on Gabriola Island was discovered by Dionisio Alcalá Galiano and then forgotten by Westerners for more than a century. MUSEUM OF HISTORY & INDUSTRY, PHOTO BY HOWARD R. GISKE, 2011.115.1

concrete-like substance, fretted and honeycombed with many diverse patterns. The lovely view of it, based on the now-lost original by artist Manuel José Cardero, was painted by Fernando Brambila. The scene was first disclosed to the wider world when it appeared in Malaspina's *Voyages*, edited by Pedro de Novo y Colson, of the Spanish navy, and published in Madrid in 1885. Then it gained much publicity in Europe. The gallery, sometimes called Malaspina Grotto, remained undiscovered until 1903. Alcalá Galiano named it Malaspina Gallery after his chief, but inasmuch as Malaspina never sailed these waters, the name has reverted to Galiano Galleries. Time has played tricks on this gift of nature. A writer in the *Vancouver Province* in 1925 described his visit there: "While admiring the unusual beauty of the grotto, one cannot but endeavor to resist the spell that arises to picture the small fleet of old-time sailing vessels rounding the head of the island in their search for a sheltered harbor—a search that was rewarded by their discovery of this unusual shelter. Then Nature had been the only artist to decorate the walls of the retreat. But rude carvings and inartistic monograms have since been drawn and painted on the inside wall by rash explorers of a later day."[150]

The *goletas* now worked their way northward, in company with the British vessels or away on more specific assignments. The Spanish officers seemed under compulsion to follow British directions, perhaps because the British had much more in the way of naval units—in addition to the two vessels, they had a number of boats and many more sailors. The Spanish were not bystanders, but in the circumstances, and given the difference in instructions—theirs of reconnaissance versus Captain Vancouver's of following up any and all leads on the continental shore—they had a more limited task. They did well with what they had, and in the time given. They worked up toward Seymour Narrows, and with the British awaited news of a seaway to the north.

On 23 August, on the basis of reports by Master James Johnstone, who Captain Vancouver had assigned to explore northward along the western shores of this inland sea, Galiano and Valdés came out into the broad and undulating swells of the Pacific Ocean by way of a passage they named Canal de la Salida de las Goletas, now Goletas Channel, and anchored in Nootka again on 1 September 1792.

They had circumnavigated (for the very first time) Vancouver Island, a remarkable achievement in two tiny 46-ton schooners. From Nootka they returned to Acapulco and then to San Blas on 23 November. Thus ended the last Spanish expedition of exploration on this coast in these latitudes.

The results of their discoveries were kept under the wraps of official-dom for years. When Vancouver's magnificent *Voyage of Discovery* was published in 1798, complete with a beautifully prepared *Atlas*, and French and

other editions followed in succession, the Spanish were finally spurred into action. The account of the expedition was published in 1802 as *Relación del Viaje hecho por las Goletas Sutil y Mexicana en al año de 1792 para reconocer el Estrecho de Juan de Fuca*, with a justly celebrated introduction by Martín Fernándes de Navarette. Not until an English translation appeared

The *Sutil* and *Mexicana* in the San Juan Islands with Mount Baker in the background, drawn by José Cardero. MUSEO NAVAL

in 1930 did the work attract much international attention, which is a pity, for it is one of the classics of voyage literature and a testament to the capabilities of Spanish mariners, who travelled the world's most difficult waters, with tide-rips and boiling channels, in vessels poorly designed and ill equipped for their tasks. As for Alcalá Galiano, he met a hero's death at Trafalgar when in command of the line-of-battle ship *Bahama*, seventy-four guns. He refused to strike his flag in the face of withering fire, but his ship was captured. He is memorialized in the Pantheon of Heroes, San Fernando, Spain.

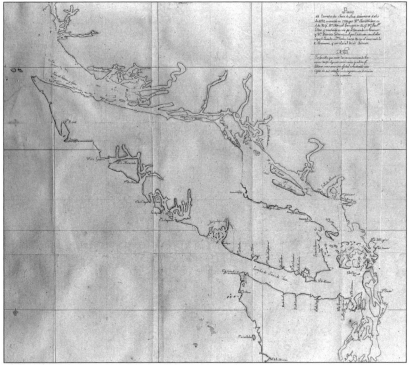

Produced by Bodega y Quadra in 1792 after the *Sutil* and *Mexicana* completed the first circumnavigation of Vancouver Island, this map shows contemporary knowledge of Vancouver Island and the surrounding waterways. OREGON HISTORICAL SOCIETY, BB009562

Chapter 8

CAPTAIN VANCOUVER
AND THE SALISH SEA

In the 1780s, Britain had unbounded ambitions to extend some sort of imperial control to the coast that James Cook had put on the map of the world, and where an abundant economy in the form of a trans-Pacific sea-otter trade to China had developed. These ambitions increased during the course of that decade. These years were crowded with a bewildering cluster of events on the coast; in Mexico, India and China; and in the capitals of Great Britain and Spain. Nootka Sound was vaulted onto the stage of the world. Its splendid isolation was no more, and the sounds of anchor chains being run out, officers barking orders, sailors chattering at their work, the blacksmith hammering on his anvil, and carpenters banging away with their tools as they repaired masts or built boats echoed across the water and into the forested hills beyond. By 1790, British merchant traders were regularly sailing in and out of the entrances to Nootka Sound, and John Meares and James Colnett had plans to set up a permanent factory, trade depot and shipyard at Nootka so as to increase their profits. The motivation was trade expansion, for such were the politics that ruled in London. The British ministry preferred trade to dominion. But, as in many other instances of the growth of the British Empire, on distant frontiers where rivals presented themselves, informal empire gave way to mechanisms of formal empire. Who would come to possess Vancouver Island in the land-hungry stakes of empire?

Even before the Spanish forced the issue at Nootka, the British government had considered various ideas for imperial aggrandizement on Vancouver Island. A novel scheme of convict settlement received attention, linking New South Wales with Vancouver Island. The frigate *Gorgon* was to be sent to Australia, where she would pick up about thirty convicts and officers, then sail for Nootka Sound, or perhaps to the shores of Queen Charlotte Strait. There would be built a stout settlement able to resist any attack from the Natives. It would lay the foundations of an establishment that could help British subjects pursuing the fur trade on the Northwest Coast. Eventually the plan for a convict settlement was dropped, but the government accepted as an official responsibility the need for a survey that would provide a more thorough knowledge of the coast from Nootka Sound north to Cook Inlet in Alaska. Here was the earliest hint of what eventually grew into the expedition of Captain George Vancouver.

At about the same time, the name of the vessel *Discovery*, which was to prove so important in the examination of the Strait of Juan de Fuca, the Strait of Georgia and waters beyond leading to the north end of Vancouver Island, first appeared in the Admiralty records. Originally destined to undertake a search, at the behest of Britain's whaling interests, to locate new harbours in the South Atlantic and the Southern Ocean that could be used for the rest, refit and repair of whaling vessels, she was deflected by the urgency of the crisis with Spain.[151] Her South Atlantic mission set aside, the *Discovery* was instead assigned to undertake the coastal survey.

However, in early January 1790, London received news, via diplomatic channels, of Spain's high-handed seizure of British ships and property at Nootka Sound and the incarceration of British captains and crew. The Spanish government considered itself the aggrieved party; the British had other ideas. The Spanish, under diplomatic pressure from London, confirmed the truth of the rumours. London replied with cautionary threats, seeking explanations. In April, Meares arrived fresh from China with all the details. He became useful to the British ministry as a first-hand witness to the unwarranted actions of Estéban Martínez, the Spanish commandant at Nootka. On 30 April the British began to increase the pressure, even threatening war, by raising a great fleet called "the Spanish armament." They called for the return of ships captured, the freeing of prisoners, and compensation for lost cargoes and other property. There is no doubt that Meares's arrival made clear the extent of Spanish conduct, which now appeared more hostile and injurious to the British Crown than the government had been given reason to imagine. To make known the details, Meares drew up, under editorial advice, his Memorial containing particulars respecting the capture of ships in Nootka Sound. It was dated 30th April and presented to the House of Commons on 13 May. An *Authentic Copy* of it became an instant bestseller and has since been reprinted at least twice.

Back and forth between London and Madrid passed the diplomatic pouches. The British dug in their heels; the Spanish resisted, then recoiled, then admitted their error. On 28 October the Nootka Sound Convention was signed at the royal palace, El Escorial, Spain (the same place where, so long before, Philip II had set aside Juan de Fuca's petition for compensation for his faithful services). Now, at last, a vessel, or vessels, could be sent from England to the Northwest Coast, but on a different sort of mission than previously contemplated. It was time for the Royal Navy to demonstrate the long arm of British power.

There was yet another pressing matter of concern. We have seen how the British sea-otter traders Meares, Charles William Barkley and Charles Duncan had recently provided startling details concerning the rediscovery of the Strait of Juan de Fuca. If, indeed, the western entrance to the northwest passage had been found at last, then confirmation was needed that the old riddle—the great geographical conundrum of its age—had been solved at last. British fixation on this subject dated to the age of Martin Frobisher, Michael Lok and other Elizabethans. Now the time had come to put the matter to rest, and none too soon, for the American traders were known to be challenging the British in the sea-otter business, and the Spanish, though apparently secretive in their discoveries, might rise to the challenge and assert their influence there.

In late November or December 1790, Meares had reinvigorated thoughts of the passage when he published his engaging book with the long-winded title *Voyages made in the Years 1788 and 1789, from China to the North West Coast of America, to which are Prefixed an Introductory Narrative of a Voyage Performed in 1786 from Bengal, in the Ship Nootka; Observations on the Probable Existence of a North West Passage; and some Account of the Trade between the North West Coast of America and China, and the latter Country and Great Britain*. In discussing the likelihood of a northwest passage, Meares, cheekily, disregarded the discoveries of Barkley and claimed them for himself. He was critical of James Cook and talked wildly and irresponsibly of a great northern archipelago, an inland sea, and a waterway in which the American vessel *Lady Washington* had sailed, making the land behind Nootka an island. He was interested, also, in settling the matter of the Río San Roque, the Bahía de la Asunción and the Entrada de Hezeta. In 1788, though he had not found the Columbia River, he had seen and named its prominent northern headland, Cape Disappointment, and found some sort of entrance that he called Deception Bay.

In his claims to discovery, he thought that Alexander Dalrymple, the hydrographer for the East India Company who was introduced in Chapter 4, might be an ally, but he got this wrong too. For Dalrymple came to distrust Meares, and he put far more faith in the news that Barkley and particularly Charles Duncan had brought or sent home from the Pacific. In time, a pamphlet war developed in London. Charges against Meares flew thick and fast and were equally returned. Gradually Meares found himself discredited. In the meantime, the British ministry accelerated its plans for a coastal survey, after some considerable delays because of all the complications arising from the Nootka crisis.

On 15 December 1790, George Vancouver hoisted the pendant of command aboard the *Discovery*, of 320 tons, then fitted out at Deptford on the Thames. The *Chatham*, built at Dover and purchased for the navy, and commanded by Lieutenant William Robert Broughton, was ordered to attend the *Discovery*. The *Discovery* had been fitted for the voyage to the South Atlantic before the dispute with Spain about Nootka. By the time Vancouver took command she was nearly fully rigged and had the greater part of the provisions on board. She was in all respects ready, but now a further delay ensued. Originally ordered to victual for twelve months, once it was found that she was capable of stowing a greater quantity, an order was issued to supply both vessels with such additional stores and provisions as could be arranged. Thus it was that surgeon's stores were increased, including the bark of cochineal used to produce quinine, an anti-malarial, and such other articles as were intended for a long voyage. The navy built on the experience of Captain Cook, but its planners also had advice from Sir Joseph Banks, who got his information from the naturalist and surgeon Archibald Menzies. (The latter had sailed with James Colnett in the *Prince of Wales* to Nootka and the North Pacific Ocean on a fur-hunting expedition for the King George's Sound Company.) The guns were taken on board at Longreach—"ten four pounders with proper ordnance stores for the voyage, besides four trap pieces of three pounds each to protect us on shore against the Indians," says Thomas Manby. The ships' companies came on board at Spithead. Vancouver received permission from the Admiralty to stop briefly at Guernsey in order to take in wine and other liquid necessities for himself and the officers. "A fair wind was the only thing wished for to carry us to Falmouth."[152]

On 1 April 1791 the *Discovery* and *Chatham* sailed from Falmouth. They made Simon's Bay, Cape of Good Hope, on 10 July 1791, leav-

Surveyor of the seas: After his mentor James Cook, Captain George Vancouver was the British explorer most responsible for exploring the Northwest Coast. A person of remarkable personal disposition and a tough commander, he carried his duties through to completion, though left by the home government to fend for himself—and face the consequences. IMAGE PDP 02252 COURTESY OF ROYAL BC MUSEUM, BC ARCHIVES

ing 17 August. They spent about a month surveying the western end of the southern coast of Australia before making for Dusky Sound in New Zealand, where they watered and refitted. After they departed, the *Chatham* got separated in a gale, and Broughton, proceeding independently, discovered Chatham Island. He arrived at the intended rendezvous, the beautiful tropical paradise of Matavi Bay in Tahiti, ahead of the *Discovery*. In fact, more often than not the *Chatham* arrived before the *Discovery*, the reason being that measures taken by the two commanders to properly ballast the brig resulted in much better sailing performance. They were about three weeks at Tahiti, then another five in the Hawaiian Islands, where they wintered preparatory to their intended spring arrival on the American coast.

On 16 March 1792 the vessels cleared the Hawaiian Islands for the Northwest Coast, now bound on their main duty. A month later, on 17 April, Vancouver made his landfall in 38° 27' N, slightly south of Cape

Mendocino. This was what the English, beginning with Drake, called Nova Albion.

The sight of the American continent brought this response from Vancouver, as given in his voyage account for 17 April 1792: "The land was now discovered at a distance of about two leagues, on which the surf broke with great violence. The rain and fog, with which the atmosphere was now loaded, precluded our seeing much. The shore appeared straight and unbroken, of a moderate height with land behind, covered with stately forest trees." Vancouver had an eye for the scenic and the majestic, but the apparent emptiness of the landscape always spoke to him of loneliness in the midst of loveliness, and to me this speaks of the isolation of a commander in, for himself, isolated circumstances.

A gentle breeze settled in the southern quarter and aided Vancouver's easy coastwise passage. The vessels worked their way north along the Oregon coast, where Vancouver named Cape Orford (now Cape Blanco). Vancouver had sailed a somewhat similar track with James Cook fourteen years before, and the landscape was familiar as to general character. On the 27th they reached a headland north of the Columbia River. Although not seeing the river itself, they recognized Cape Disappointment and Deception Bay from the description given by Meares in his *Voyages* (which had been published not long before their departure from England). Vancouver noticed signs of river water off Cape Disappointment. "The sea," Vancouver wrote, "had now changed from its natural, to river-coloured water; the probable consequence of some streams falling into the bay, or into the ocean to the north of it, through the low land. Not considering this opening worthy of more attention, I continued our pursuit to the N.W."[153] He therefore passed it by, and the mouth of the Columbia River, seen by Spaniard Bruno de Hezeta, though not entered by him, in 1775, remained as yet undiscovered by Europeans.

Vancouver continued coasting northward past 47° N, reporting several times that they were being affected by a strong and consistent northward current of near half a league per hour. His journal suggests impatience. "Notwithstanding the serenity and pleasantness of the weather, our voyage was rendered excessively irksome by the want of wind; our progress was slow, and our curiosity was much excited to explore the promised expansive Mediterranean ocean, which, by various accounts is said to have existence in these regions." Several large rivers and capacious inlets had by this time been identified as unnavigable brooks or bays, quite incapable of serving as an inland sea or even as harbours for refitting, and Alexander Dalrymple had suggested that only one entrance between the 40th and 48th degree of north latitude was still eligible for consideration. This was the one that, it was alleged, the Spanish had recently found "in the latitude of 47° 4' north, which in 27 days course brought them to the vicinity of Hudson's Bay; this latitude exactly corresponds to the ancient relation of Juan de Fuca, the Greek pilot, in 1592."[154]

George Vancouver followed his instructions to the letter. Dalrymple had recommended to the Admiralty that the expedition should look particularly for an entrance in 47.5° N, "supposed to be the Straits of Juan de Fuca, with directions to penetrate the same, or any other Inlet they might find, that should appear to have a water communication with the Lakes, Rivers or Inlets on the East side of the Continent, as far as the Shore is navigable."[155]

Remarkable encounters occur at sea—ships on different passages suddenly arrive at the same location, unmindful of the other's presence until the actual encounter and the chance to "speak" to the other. So it was with the rendezvous of the Americans and the British not too far from the entrance of the Strait of Juan de Fuca, where Vancouver encountered the *Columbia Rediviva* of Boston under Captain Robert Gray, with young John Boit, whom we met in Chapter 5, aboard. In their respective records, 28 April was Boit's date for the meeting and 29 April 1792 was George Vancouver's, an understandable discrepancy considering that Boit was using local time and Vancouver counted his days west of Greenwich.

Boit takes up the story: "This day spoke his Britannic Majesty's Ships *Discovery* and *Chatham*, commanded by Capt. George Vancouver and Lieutenant Wm. Broughton, from England, on a voyage of discovery." He reports that a boat boarded them from the *Discovery*, "and we gave them all the information in our power, especially as respected the Straits of Juan De Fuca, which place they was then in search of. They bore away for the Straits mouth, which was not far Distant. Stood in and drain'd the village we was at yesterday and then bore off after the English Ships." And the next day: "Pass'd Tatooche Isle, close on board, and left a large ledge of Rocks without us, and stood into the Straits of De Fuca. Many Indians came off, and brought plenty of furs. The English Ships came too [*sic*] towards evening on the South entrance of the straits. In the morning they got under way and stood up. We stood in and anchor'd to the Westward of Cape Flattery in 17 f[atho]m trade not very brisk got under weigh agin towards evening and stood to the S and E along shore."

For five more days the *Columbia* traded along the entrance of the strait close to Cape Flattery, beating to and fro when necessary in preference to anchoring, and working about two miles from shore, hoving to when required so as to allow the canoes to come up and stay alongside for trade. Soon it was noticed that the Indians brought no furs. It was time to sail away, this time for Grays Harbor. Unlike Vancouver, Captain Robert Gray in the *Columbia* decided to take a look at the river that entered the ocean near Cape Disappointment. The weather favoured his discoveries, and he and his men made their justly famous entry into the estuary of the Columbia River, which Gray named after his ship.

As for Vancouver's account of the meeting, when a ship's sail was first spotted, he noted it as "a very great novelty, not having seen any vessel but our consort, during the last eight months. She soon hoisted American colours."[156] He sent Lieutenant Peter Puget and surgeon-botanist Archibald Menzies to secure "information as might be serviceable in our future operations." The two were also to convey that the British expedition was scientific, not commercial. Puget and Menzies listened to Gray's account of his voyaging. "His relation, however, differed very materially from that published in England [by John Meares]. It is not possible to conceive any one to be more astonished than was Mr. Gray, on his being made acquainted, that this authority had been quoted, and the track pointed out that he had been said to have made in the sloop *Washington*."[157]

Scottish surgeon, naturalist and a fine diarist, Archibald Menzies sailed with George Vancouver. He proved to be a thorn in the commander's side. BY PERMISSION OF THE LINNEAN SOCIETY OF LONDON

Menzies puts it this way: "[We] entered the Straits of Juan de Fuca on the 29th [April 1792] . . . It may appear curious that on the day we made the Straits of Juan de Fuca we should fall in with the very same *Capt Gray* which in Meares's *Voyage*, it said, to perform that wonderful interior navigation in the Sloop *Washington*;—I accompanied one of the Officers on board his vessel, the *Columbia*, and he positively averred to us, that he was never above 50 miles up the Straits & came back the same way he entered.—& Mr. [Robert] Duffin who is in this port at present, waiting to carry our despatches to China, says that he himself was not above 14 Leagues [about 42 miles] up—on comparing this to Mr. Mears assertions you will see the difference."[158]

Gray assured Puget and Menzies that when he had penetrated the 50 or so miles into the strait, he judged the passage 5 leagues, or 15 miles, wide. He also declared that from the Natives he heard "that the opening extended a considerable distance to the northward"; that this was all the information he had acquired respecting this inland sea, and that he returned to the ocean not to the north but by the same way he had entered. The inlet he supposed to be "the same that De Fuca had discovered, which opinion seemed to be universally received by all the modern visitors."[159]

The British ships were now moving into an area of many hazards to navigation. Because of the shallower draft of the *Chatham*, Broughton was sent ahead to work through narrower approaches to the open strait beyond, the *Discovery* following. Vancouver puzzled over what he was observing on the shores below the cliffs of the promontory and Tatoosh island. "I anxiously looked out for the point which Captain Cook had distinguished by the name of Cape Flattery, of which I could not be completely satisfied, on account of the difference in latitude."[160]

On 29 April, the same day Gray was encountered, observers aboard the *Chatham* saw a pinnacle rock near Cape Flattery. We can imagine that Broughton had heard of Fuca's Pillar. Their view of it was from the north. James Johnstone, sailing master of the *Chatham,* wrote a day later, on the 30th, "What we took for pinnacle rock spoke of at the entrance [by Juan de Fuca and Charles Duncan] we saw after we got within the [Green] Island [near Cape Claaset]—and instead of laying in the entrance to the straits it is close on the Shore of Classat, by no means answering the idea which I had been led to form of its situation."[161]

Vancouver records afterward that he had been informed that, from the point of view of a ship passing by, this pinnacle rock was visible only for a few minutes. It was close to the shore of the mainland instead of lying in the entrance of the straits. He had been looking for it, of that there is no doubt, for he had in his possession the chart of 1790 published by Dalrymple and based on a sketch of the entrance of the Strait of Juan de Fuca compiled by Charles Duncan. (As noted in Chapter 4, the former Master in the Navy had sailed these same seas in August 1788 when in command of the trading sloop *Princess Royal* and had noted Fuca's Pillar.) The rock's precise location as indicated by Duncan did not square exactly with what Vancouver determined upon that day, and it's fair to say the always-skeptical captain was a bit suspicious of the whole matter.

> As we passed the outermost of these rocks the distance of a mile, we plainly distinguished the south point of entrance into De Fuca's straits . . . The opposite side of the straits, though indistinctly seen in consequence of the haze, plainly indicated an opening of considerable extent. About noon, we reached its south entrance [Cape Flattery], which I understand the natives distinguish by the name of Classet; it is a projecting and conspicuous promontory . . . Tatooche's island, united to the promontory by a ledge of rocks over which the sea violently breaks, bore from N. 17 E to N. 30 E.; and the rock lying off the island, as described by Mr. Duncan in his excellent sketch of the entrance into this inlet, N. 14 E. In the latitude, however, there appears to be an error of ten miles, which, from Mr. Duncan's accuracy in other respects, I was induced to attribute to the press. The south entrance is by him stated to be in 48° 37'; whereas, by our run, and making every allowance, we could not place it so far north as Mr. Gray. No great violence of tide was experienced; nor did we observe the Pinnacle rock, as represented by Mr. Meares and Mr. Dalrymple, in order to identify these as De Fuca's straits, or any other rock more conspicuous than thousands along the coast, varying in form and size; some conical, others with flat sides, flat tops, and almost every other shape that can be figured by the imagination. We followed the *Chatham* between Tatooche's island and the rock.[162]

Even so, this famous landmark—"this pinnacle rock," as Master James Johnstone called it—Captain Vancouver renamed Rock Duncan. It is now Duncan Rock. Johnstone also remarked that along this coast there were numerous rocks of various sizes and shapes. "I did not decidedly observe any prominence, so as to be able to be convinced which was the real Cape Flattery."[163]

The same chart that was Vancouver's pride showed the opening of the continent from the Pacific, and on it was Duncan's note that said the local Indians, the Makah, called the waterway a "great sea." Vancouver and Broughton continued along the south shore of what Vancouver was even then recording as "the supposed Strait of Juan de Fuca," working past Neah Bay, where, unknown to them, Manuel Quimper had previously made claims in July and August 1790. "As we proceeded we passed the village of Classet [Neah Bay] which is situated about two miles within the Cape and has the appearance of being extensive and populous."[164] The ships' companies were on the alert for any possible difficulties with any Indians encountered, for the ship commanders knew that in 1788 Meares's longboat under command of Robert Duffin had been attacked near Port Townsend. The Indians not only did not threaten but were noticeably polite.

The British warships, we are reminded, were entering waters used by the people of the coast for thousands of years. In a sense, the officers and men sailing these vessels were interlopers. Vancouver's book recounting the nature of his voyage is called *A Voyage of Discovery*, which reflects nicely the British discovery of a new world. But what about those who were looking out at these vessels with their masts, yards and sails, their longboats that were hoisted out or hauled back in as required, their noisy crews and the guns fired on ceremonial occasions? "Discovery" for the First Nations had a different connotation from that of the English language. Perhaps "encounter" is a better term from their point of view, and perhaps "involuntary encounter" is even better, for the First Nations had no ability to sail away as did the British, who were indeed transients. Robin Fisher, noted commentator on matters of contact and conflict, puts it this way: "In spite of the visits of Cook and others, much of the coast was still unknown to Europeans, so Vancouver was there to gather new knowledge. Over the next four years he would examine its entire length—from Baja California in the south to Cook Inlet in the north—in greater detail than anyone had ever done before . . . In one sense the word "discovery" was a misnomer, since the coast was not unknown to those who were already there. In another sense it was appropriate because this would be a voyage of mutual discovery, as the coast became a line for the meeting of cultures."[165]

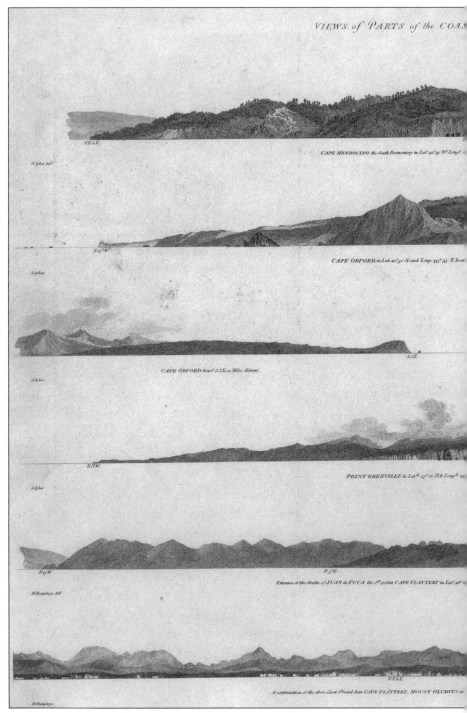

Engravings from George Vancouver's *Atlas* give the view of the coast from seaward. From Cape Mendocino north and into Juan de Fuca Strait: the stunning beauty and majesty of

RTH WEST AMERICA.

past S.E. dist.¼ Long.⁴ nearest Shore E.b.N. 10 Miles dist. Var.⁴⁵ 15.° East.°

_N. 64.° E._

ne nearest Shore N.° 64.° E. ¾ Miles ¾.⁴ dist. Var.°. 16.° East.°

N.N.E.

CAPE GREGORY in Lat.⁴ 45°45′ N.⁴ & Long.⁴ 235°50′ E. bear.⁴ N.N.E. ¼ Miles distant.

E.b.S.   S.E.b.E.

¼ Miles nearest Shore N.E.b.N. ¼ Mile dist.⁴ Var.⁴ 18.° East.°

bear.⁴ N. 5.° E.° dis.⁴ 6′¼ Long.⁴ The N.° point of entrance S. 33.° W. Var.⁴ 18.° Easterly.

East

36°51′ E.° bear.⁴ E.°dis.⁴ 13′¼ Long.⁴ nearest Shore N.E.b.E.⁴ Miles dis.⁴ Var.⁴⁵ 18.° Easterly.

the meeting of sea and land, with remarkable views of desolation and splendour, caught the awe-struck explorers by surprise. David Rumsey Map Collection

Views of the shores of the strait were often obscured or, at the least, indistinct due to haze and fog. "The evening of the 29th [of April] brought us to an anchor in very thick rainy weather, about eight miles within the entrance on the southern shore of the supposed straits of De Fuca," Vancouver writes. The next day brought transition.

> The following morning, Monday the 30th, a gentle breeze sprang up from the N.W. attended with clear and pleasant weather, which presented to our view this renowned inlet . . . We weighed anchor with a favorable wind, and steered to the east along the southern shore, at the distance of about two miles, having an uninterrupted horizon between east and N. 73 E. The shores on each side [of] the straits are of a moderate height; and the delightful serenity of the weather permitted our seeing this inlet to great advantage. The shores on the south side are composed of low sandy cliffs, falling perpendicularly on beaches of sand or stones. From the top of these eminences, the land appeared to take a further gentle moderate ascent and was entirely covered with trees chiefly of the pine tribe, until the forest reached a range of high craggy mountains, which seemed to rise from the wood-land country in a very abrupt manner, with a few scattered trees on their sterile sides, and their summits covered with snow. The northern shore did not appear quite so high: it rose more gradually from the sea-side to the tops of the mountains, which had the appearance of a compact range, infinitely more uniform, and much less covered with snow than those on the southern side.[166]

The dramatic vistas caught the Royal Navy explorers off guard, for only Meares's voyage account had given any sort of particulars, and those were unconfirmed and subject to reconfirmation. Manby, in the *Chatham*, provides a vivid commentary on the reaction of the officers and crew. "Never was contrast greater, in this days sailing than that we had long been accustomed too. It had more the aspect of enchantment than reality; with silent admiration each discerned the beauties of Nature, and nought was heard on board but expressions of delight murmured from every tongue. Imperceptibly our Bark skimmed over the glassy surface of the deep, about three Miles an hour, a gentle Breeze swelled the loft Canvass whilst all was calm below."[167]

The smoothness of the sea and clearness of the sky, Vancouver notes, "enabled us to take several sets of lunar distances . . . As the day advanced, the wind, which as well as the weather was delightfully pleasant, accelerated our progress along the shore. This seemed to indicate a speedy termination to the inlet; as high land now began to appear just rising from that horizon, which, a few hours before, we had considered to be unlimited. Every new appearance, as we proceeded, furnished new conjectures; the whole was not visibly connected; it might form a cluster of islands separated by large arms of the sea or be united by land not sufficiently high to be yet discernible."[168]

The people on shore on one occasion paid no attention to the British warships. The previous appearance of Spanish explorers and sea-otter traders had evidently satisfied the Salish curiosity about the newcomers. The ships were later visited by Natives who brought some fish and venison for sale, which was pronounced extremely good. There were no sea otter offered.

The enchantment experienced by the navigators grew as they entered farther into the strait. It was a wonderful world that had opened to them— of vast surroundings, spacious inland seas, numerous channels and islands of untold number. From the mast tops or from the decks of the ships, the sailors gazed on magnificent forests and great mountains, some to the north (now known as the Cascades) and some inland from where they were. At sea level they were thousands of feet below the great Olympic range, with its own sentinel, named by Meares Mount Olympus.[169] To the north, and in the immediate space that stretched out before them, lay the great slumbering strait connecting the Pacific and the Salish Sea. Native canoes there were, of that we are sure. No other sail was to be seen anywhere, no commercial traffic. It was an empty shipping lane. Across that body of water lay the continent, possibly (actually, as they were to learn after months of inquiry, it was a great island, later named Vancouver Island). What fantastic visions must have passed through the minds of the ships' companies. Thoughts of despair may also have crossed their minds: how were they to complete the exploration of this complex body of water and rock? What, indeed, were its secrets, and could these be unravelled? The challenges of command were daunting, and how was the whole to be arranged for this limitless exploration? Those who run George Vancouver down for his despotism fail to appreciate that this was no summer cruise among pleasant islands and lovely passages. He was answerable to the Admiralty and to King George III.

Vancouver desperately stood in need of a base of operations, an anchorage where his men could take on fresh water to drink and firewood for the stoves. Also of critical importance was the need to find a location to check the rates of the chronometers. This had to be done by setting up an astronomy station ashore where the long telescopes needed to observe lunar particulars, notably the satellites of Jupiter, could have a firm footing. At sea, with rocking decks, this was impossible. Sometimes the sky was overcast, also making astronomical observations impossible.

Progressing farther eastward, the *Discovery*, followed by the *Chatham*, passed Dungeness Spit. That evening, acting prudently, two boats from the *Discovery* and the cutter from the *Chatham* set out along the shoreline searching for a suitable harbour. The longboats returned to the waiting ships, having found a harbour six or seven leagues to the east.[170]

The vessels eased through a welcoming gap, and inside the justly named Protection Island a long deep-water harbour came into view. Vancouver described the surrounding landscape as being "almost as enchantingly beautiful as the most elegantly finished pleasure grounds in Europe."[171] When the English later learned that Quimper had been there two years previous and had named it Puerto de la Bodega y Quadra in honour of the senior Spanish naval officer on the coast at that time, they referred to it as Puerto Quadra. However, Vancouver did not know this at the time of his exploration; he called it Port Discovery, after his ship, and so it appears in the atlas accompanying Vancouver's famous published account of his voyage. It retains that name today, though many regret that it does not still bear the name of the great mariner Bodega y Quadra.

Here, in deep waters, *Discovery* and *Chatham* lay for sixteen days. The British took note, and even detailed examinations, of Salish and Klallam material culture. The collected items and companion notes made by Vancouver, Menzies, Peter Puget and others offer a rich body of evidence for the reconstruction of these people at a time when a great cultural crisis was approaching them. Already there were signs of deserted Native villages.[172] The mariners expressed surprise at how thinly populated was this apparently abundant land. Faces of some natives were much pitted by the smallpox, and there were other disfigurements. Vancouver, pondering this state of affairs, and noting the desolation of the human coastline, concluded that it would not be easy "to draw any just conclusions on the true cause from which this havoc of the human race proceeded: this must remain for the investigation of others who may have more lesure, and a better opportunity to direct such an inquiry."[173]

On 8 May, a three-boat armada—*Discovery's* yawl, *Discovery's* launch and *Chatham's* cutter, all properly armed and provisioned for five days— went to explore Admiralty Inlet, Puget Sound. They entered a labyrinth. The surveying parties examined the long and interlocking water corridors of the sound and found many a cul-de-sac. The details lie outside our focus here, though they are fascinating in and of themselves.

After much dreary fog, a rise in atmospheric pressure brought bright weather and, with it, a splendid view of that great sentinel Mount Rainier, to the southeast. Those in the boats had suffered terribly from exposure and hunger, but when they returned to the ships in Port Discovery, this chapter of the imperial progression came to a happy conclusion. It had been a boat voyage through waters of what seemed to resemble a new kind of paradise. To these hard-bitten sailors, the lands of the southern inlets had been most grateful to the eye. The snow-clad mountains overlooking the islands and channels provided a most agreeable prospect and even made it a land of enchantment, though far from home. It seemed as if this landscape had been prepared for the convenience of mankind, they thought. Even the trees were so situated as to display beautiful prairie lands on the rising grounds that led away from waterside. Little would be the labour required to cultivate this land, it was imagined, perhaps a little too easily. Captain Vancouver foresaw its value for settlement: "The serenity of the climate, the innumerable pleasing landscapes, and the abundant fertility that unassisted nature puts forth, require only to be enriched by the industry of men with villages, mansions, cottages and other buildings, to render it the most lovely country that can be imagined."[174]

At daylight on 18 May the ships weighed anchor at Port Discovery, and with light variable winds and the assistance of the boats they made their way out of that splendid harbour by the eastern channel of Protection Island. While this was happening, Vancouver went ashore on Protection Island to take some bearings, and Menzies took the opportunity to scramble ashore for some botanizing, happily discovering the prickly pear that grew plentifully, though in a dwarf state, on the eastern, sandy point of the island.

From a high point on Protection Island (the highest elevation is 200 feet), Vancouver scanned the horizon, taking in all the particulars that lay before him across this watery waste of seas, islands and mountains. His methods, in conformity with his instructions, called for him to follow the continental shore, taking no chance that a passage might be missed. Thoroughness, it is hardly necessary to say, was a Vancouver characteristic and is one of all good hydrographers. Therefore, Vancouver knew he would have to press along the continental shore southward, examining the maze of islands and passages of what we call Puget Sound, which Vancouver named after Peter Puget, one of the officers. Much of this work could be done in boats.

But in the northern quarter—in fact, almost due north from his place of observation—lay what appeared to be a cluster of islands and a possible canal or passage to the north. Was this the waterway that Meares said the *Lady Washington* had sailed? He did not have confirming evidence that the land on which Nootka lay was an island or just part of the continental shore. He knew that to the northeast lay Mount Baker, signifying another portion of the continental shore. But he did not know if there was a passage out to the distant Atlantic thereabouts, nor did he know that a strait, now known as the Strait of Georgia, or Georgia Strait, lay to the north of—that is, beyond—these many islands. It was all quite puzzling. Thus was born the requirement to examine these distant islands.

Menzies, an important observer to these proceedings, described the events of 18 May: "About noon the Vessels were advanced between the Island & the Main when in our return we called on board the *Chatham* where Captain Vancouver left orders for a short separation of the Vessels. At this time a fresh breeze sprung up at West with which we steerd for Admiralty Inlet whilst the *Chatham* hauld up to the North West ward being dispatched to look into a large opening that appeard in that direction on the other side of this large gulph, & after obtaining what information they could of the size & general direction of it & the other branches in that quarter they were directed to follow us into Admiralty Inlet pursuing the South East Arm that was left unexplored by the Boats & keeping the Starboard shore of it aboard till they fell in with us." This is an excellent resumé of the intentions of the discoverers at this important juncture: while

The arms of Admiralty Inlet proved to be a Byzantine maze, but at least on a clear day there was the majesty of Mount Rainier for consolation. FROM *BRITISH COLUMBIA: A PICTORIAL RECORD, 1778–1891*

Broughton in the *Chatham* would seek out the channels of the maze of islands to the north, Vancouver aboard the *Discovery* would press on south and eastward with the continental survey. In the end, it is fair to say the latter proved the more difficult task, so complicated and extensive were the interlinking passages of Puget Sound.

Even in our own time, and with all the mariner's aids available, navigating these straits and passages is tinged with anxiety and awe. The San Juan Islands lie like a tangle of rocks between the Strait of Juan de Fuca on the south and the Strait of Georgia on the north. We now know—Broughton did not—that three main channels lead from the east end of Juan de Fuca Strait to the southeast end of the Strait of Georgia. The first of these is Haro Strait, of which Boundary Pass is the continuation. This is the main channel and is now the international water boundary. Middle Channel and Rosario Strait are the other two channels, as well as the waters forming the east end of Juan de Fuca Strait. Haro Strait and Boundary Pass are deep and, for the most part, broad, as the *BC Coast Pilot* reminds us, but on account of the reefs which exist in some parts, the scarcity of anchorages and, above all, the rate and varying directions of the tidal streams, great caution and vigilance are necessary in their navigation.

Tidal streams set fairly through the middle of Haro Strait, and at Turn Point the flood or north-moving tidal stream divides, part flowing northwest through Prevost Passage and Swanson Channel, and part setting northeast toward Boundary Pass. A minor branch flows east through Spieden Channel. At Discovery Island, off Ten Mile Point or Oak Bay at what is now called Victoria, heavy tide-rips form. Through the whole length of the strait, the ebb or south-going tidal stream usually attains a much greater rate than the north-going tidal stream. Velocities of 3 to 6 knots can be expected. These are the conditions that mariners face today, whether under sail or power, and Broughton in the *Chatham* was obliged to venture into uncharted waters without the aid of sailing directions. There were no mid-channel indicators, no lights ashore, no radio communications—only a mass of rock and moving water.

Discovery Island lies in the approach to the south entrance of Haro Strait, with the Chatham Islands close to the north. Opposite it is Cattle Point, the southern extremity of San Juan Island, with Mount Dallas (elevation 1,036 feet) a conspicuous feature observable in fair weather. There is a local magnetic anomaly at that island's Bellevue Point, where 4-degree departures have been found in the compass reading, another peculiarity of navigation. Guarding the southern approach to San Juan Island are various islets and reefs, and we can only imagine that Broughton approached with the greatest degree of care.

From Protection Island to San Juan Island the Strait of Juan de Fuca is at its broadest extent of 20 miles. Broughton and the crew of the *Chatham* must have had a glorious sail across the strait that afternoon—truly a clear passage on a fine spring day, with fair winds from a favourable quarter. Perhaps it was just all in a day's work. The vistas would have been grand: it might have been possible in clear visibility to see Mount Rainier on the southern horizon and Mount Baker on the northeastern, white-coned volcanic sentinels of navigation even nowadays.

Broughton's reconnaissance of the San Juans was a necessary if time-consuming step in the British exploration of the inland waters leading from the Strait of Juan de Fuca. Like other aspects of the examination of these waters, notably Puget Sound and its annexes, thoroughness of task demanded time and energy, to say nothing of commitment to scientific excellence. The San Juan Islands are a sea of islands and a maze of passages. There are countless submerged rocks to imperil the navigator, and tides, currents and riptides of unknown quality. Broughton sent his boats out on daily missions, while he directed the survey from the cabin of the *Chatham*, recording the previous day's results and planning the work of the next day. He had to keep his eye on the calendar, for Captain Vancouver had called for an initial rendezvous on 7 June 1792. At dark they anchored in 26 fathoms, close over on the north shore within the sandy spits, says Master James Johnstone.

Broughton's explorations commenced on 18 May and concluded on 25 May, and his account is sparse and matter-of-fact. Of this archipelago, Johnstone was to write: "The Land is delightful, being in many places clear and the Soil so rich that the grass in several parts grew to man height. We were surprised in such fine Country to find scarecely any inhabitants, not a Smoke or a village was seen, and only two small Canoes with 3 people in each were met by the Boats in all their cruising."[175]

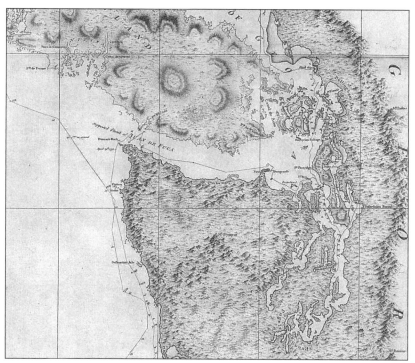

Detail from "A CHART shewing part of the COAST of N.W. AMERICA, with the tracks of His *MAJESTY's* Sloop *DISCOVERY and Armed Tender CHATHAM* . . . parts not shaded are taken from Spanish Authorities." Vancouver's 1798 map shows the route north in unbroken lines, and the route south in dotted lines—illustrating for the first time the navigational challenges of the San Juan Islands and the twisting dead ends of Admiralty Inlet. DAVID RUMSEY MAP COLLECTION

Broughton's principal discovery, and a discovery of immediate use to his superior officer, was that the archipelago, which Eliza called "Isla y Archipelago de San Juan," lay south of "an extensive arm of the sea which stretched as far as the eye could see in a variety of branches to the northwest and to the north-north east." Could this lead at last to the northwest passage or, failing that, northward behind Nootka Sound to the Pacific?

And what of the rest of the discoveries in these waters by the British navigators in 1792? Broughton was with Captain Vancouver on 4 June when the latter landed near Tulalip and took possession of the area. New Georgia is what the captain called it, named for the king of Great Britain. Vancouver writes, of that day: "Double allowance of grog to drink the King's health, it being the anniversary of His Majesty's birth, on which auspicious day I had long since designed to take formal possession of all the countries we had lately been employed in exploring, in the name of and for his Britannic Majesty." And again, "I went on shore and under the discharge of a royal salute from the vessels, took possession accordingly on the coast. The interior sea I have honored with the name of the Gulf of Georgia, and the continent binding the said gulf, and extending southward to the 45th degree, with that of New Georgia."

The two ships moved northward from Whidbey Island, working the long passage north toward Bellingham and Birch bays. The *Discovery* headed for Strawberry Bay; facing a strong tide, boats were put out and she was pulled in. She anchored at six in the evening. The *Chatham* was not so fortunate, for she was impelled by a strong flood tide into an opening a little more to the eastward. Archibald Menzies learned from those on board the brig that "neither helm nor canvas had any other power over her. All were alarmed for her safety & anxious to hear of her fate." At one stage in her exploration, the *Chatham* lost a precious anchor. The cable parted in the rush of tidal current.

At this stage Menzies went with Broughton to complete the survey of the San Juans to the latter's satisfaction. This, then, was the second of the two parts of exploration of this archipelago. Broughton, says Menzies in his journal, wanted "to finish his Survey of the Islands that were to the Westward of us, on the North side of the Gulph, & as the rugged appearance of these seemd to offer a new field for researches I accompanied him by a friendly invitation."[176]

184

Menzies came away from the San Juans with glowing things to say. He found them different from what he had recently seen, even though only two or three leagues separated them from other islands he had observed in the area. Here the land rose rugged and hilly to a moderate height and "was composed of massy solid Rocks coverd with a thin layer of blackish mould which afforded nourishment to a straddling forest of small stunted pines." Steep and rugged shores, chasms and many cliffs made it difficult to go ashore or land from the boats. But he was everywhere aware of its riches in natural history. He said that the expedition with

Unheralded explorer: William Robert Broughton commanded the armed tender *Chatham* in the first survey of the San Juan Islands and charted the lower Columbia River in 1792. He later made the first British exploration in Japanese seas.
COURTESY OF COLUMBIA RIVER MARITIME MUSEUM, ASTORIA, OREGON, 1977.98

Broughton to the San Juans "produced a pleasing variety in the objects of my pursuit & added considerably to my Catalogue of Plants."[177]

Meanwhile, from Strawberry Bay, as Joseph Baker reported, boat parties went out on daily survey and returned. They had found a large group of islands. Later still they sailed again and entered an extensive sound that appeared to lead to the north. This was Rosario Strait—not a sound at all, but a passage north of Orcas Island and leading to Georgia Strait. These discoveries indicated the way the ships should continue in their northern survey. The meaning was clear: the San Juans formed an island barrier between the Strait of Juan de Fuca and what lay to the north, the broad waters of the Strait of Georgia.

By late afternoon of 11 June, the *Discovery* and *Chatham* had tacked north through Rosario Strait, passed the dark shoulder of Lummi Island and entered the pleasing Gulf of Georgia, now Strait of Georgia or Georgia Strait. Menzies again: "On the 11th the vessels left Strawberry Bay and worked up the west side of Lummi Island. Rather than going through the channel leading to Bellingham and Samish bays, they entered an opening that was wide and spacious with "an unbounded horizon to the North

West." As they advanced they "could perceive that the South West shore was composed of a broken group of Islands intersecting by numerous islets branching in every direction while the opposite shore on our right appear'd streight [straight] ... stretching to the North West ward from Mount Baker."[178]

That evening the vessels cast anchor in a small bay on the continental mainland, now known as Birch Bay (for here the black birch tree grew abundantly), a few miles south of the present boundary between the United States and Canada. Birch Bay, said Vancouver, was "a very convenient situation for our several duties on shore." Here the ships lay until 24 June. Vancouver's experience in Puget Sound and Broughton's in the San Juans had shown the necessity of using boats to do the exploring, for experience had shown that this was the only way a survey of the maze of inlets and islands—"this broken country," Vancouver calls it—could be done with a sufficient degree of accuracy. This decision directed the work of three surveying seasons.[179] Subsequently, the vessels moved to another secure bay, within Point Roberts and near 49° N, which is now called Boundary Bay. From this place, Vancouver and his second lieutenant, Peter Puget, took the yawl and launch north. At the same time Joseph Whidbey, master of the *Discovery*, took the cutter and the *Chatham*'s launch south, where he found Bellingham Bay.

In the course of his inquiries, Broughton himself had set his eyes on the Strait of Georgia, a broad sheet of water fronting on shores and islands to the east, north and west. He did not speculate on what lay beyond it. Whidbey, however, had a different perspective. He wrote to a high-ranking member of the British administration, perhaps Henry Dundas, the guiding genius of trade policy, "We entered the Straights of Fuca in 48.23 and carried on inland Navigation to the above Latitude [52.10 N]—without the least possible signs of a N W Passage—nor do I think one exists—which no doubt will prove a great disappointment to our great Chamber Surveyors—I am sorry that the business of Nootka prevented our search farther North last season."[180]

In taking "formal possession of all the countries we had been lately employed in exploring," in the name of the king, his heirs and successors, Vancouver described the extent of these territories as "the coast, from that part of New Albion, in the latitude of 39° 20' north, and the longitude of 236° 26' east [approximately 124° W], to the entrance of this inlet of the sea, said to be the supposed Straits of Juan de Fuca; and likewise all the coast, islands &c. within the said Straits, as well on the northern as on the southern shores, together with those stationed in the interior sea we have discovered extending from the said Straits in various directions."[181]

The whole inland sea he proclaimed "the Gulph of Georgia" in honour of the king, George III; it was renamed Strait of Georgia by Captain George Henry Richards in 1865, but well into the twentieth century it was still called "the Gulf." John Walbran, famed historian of coast place names, in explaining this, made in 1909 this telling point: "The name of King George was a significant and potent one among the Indians of this coast in the days of the fur traders because, owing to his long reign, he was so frequently mentioned by British subjects and others that in the native mind his name became synonymous with power and authority, so much so, that all Britishers were called 'King George Men,' and their ships 'King George Ships,' in contradistinction to those of other nationalities with whom the natives came in contact. Other traders were styled 'Boston Men,' because nearly all of them belonged to American vessels which were fitted out and hailed from Boston, New England. In the Chinook trade jargon, which is

Watercolour by Steve Mayo: *June 9, 1792 — HMS* Discovery *&* Chatham *in Rosario Strait* (2012). The artist notes "I have followed, as closely as possible, a photograph of a wash painting of HMS *Discovery* done in 1790–91. The original was painted from life by a professional maritime artist, (possibly) Robert Cleveley, while the ship was moored in the Thames River just prior to her epic voyage." COURTESY OF STEVE MAYO

generally understood by the Indians on this coast, these meanings are still preserved."[182] Here the lingo of comparative empire had surfaced, with choices and preferences being made, and distinctions established. In due time all would be swept away in the lingo line, only the historical record speaking of these secrets of the past.

Leaving his ships at anchor in Birch Bay, Vancouver sailed north in two longboats—the *Discovery*'s cutter and the *Chatham*'s launch—and entered this Gulph of Georgia. The delightful excursion in this broad inner sea consumed eleven days, time spent away from the command ship. He was in Semiahmoo and Boundary bays on 12 June, and named Point Roberts.

Peter Puget worried that the rapid tide would prove dangerous for ships. Later that day, having left Point Roberts behind, the boats passed along the edge of a swampy bank, a low-lying landscape, which we now know was the Fraser River. Although Vancouver has been much rebuked for missing the mouth of this river, I think the criticism is unjust. Not having the advantage of an aerial view, he passed these features easily. Besides, Vancouver and his boat crews were looking for a passage through the mountain ramparts that they could see, and that muddy and scrubby foreshore apparently offered nothing in the way of a suggestion of a passageway. Indeed, Puget sensed a great river here but could detect no main, navigable channel. As he wrote in his entry for 12 June: "The land abreast to the Eastward is low & about three Leagues Distant. Two places in that Direction bear much the Appearance of Large Rivers [the Fraser and its North Arm], but the Shoals hitherto have prevented any Communication with them."[183] Light and shadow play tricks on an explorer's eyes.

To those on discovery, surprises always presented themselves, and there was an odd additional factor in the navigation that day—a powerful flow of water issuing from the mainland (the unseen river) swept the boats well out into the Strait of Georgia. Vancouver was obliged to pass across the strait to the vicinity of Gabriola Island. He hoped to find a place to anchor or moor for the night but in the end could find no place of safety. In consequence, the men had no option but to sleep in boats that night, a most inconvenient and unpleasant state of affairs, with no chance of good rest.

Wednesday 15 June was perhaps the most memorable day of the whole expedition. Approaching from the west, Vancouver saw Howe

Sound off to port—that is, on his left—and a point of land ahead and then to starboard, Point Grey. Could this broad entrance lead to a north-west passage? Hopes ran high. "From Point Grey we proceeded first up the eastern branch of the sound, where . . . within its entrance, we passed to the northward of an island [Stanley Park] . . . This island laying exactly across the canal, appeared to form a similar passage to the south of it [False Creek], with a smaller island lying before it."[184] Vancouver could see that the canal, about a half mile wide, continued eastward. He passed through the First Narrows into Burrard Inlet, on the shore of which the Canadian city bearing his name now stands, "the Constantinople of the Pacific," a promoter once called it. It was Cornelius Van Horne, superintendent of the Canadian Pacific Railway, who thought this railhead of his transcontinental railroad should bear the explorer's name.

To this point, Vancouver and his men had seen no Natives, and on 15 June Vancouver recorded that he had concluded that this part of the gulf was uninhabited. However, shortly after the boats passed through First Narrows, Vancouver notes, "We were visited by nearly forty of the natives, on whose approach from the very material alteration that had now taken place in the face of the country we expected to find some difference in their general character. This conjecture was, however, premature, as they varied in no respect whatever, but in possessing a more ardent desire for commercial transactions, into the spirit of which they entered with infinitely more avidity than any of our former acquaintances . . . Iron in all forms they judiciously preferred to any other article we had to offer." The anthropologist Charles Hill-Tout, writing in the early twentieth century, commented: "They have not altered much in these points of their character since Vancouver's visit . . . They are probably the most industrious and orderly band of Indians in the whole Province, and reflect great credit upon the Roman Mission established in their midst."[185]

Peter Puget wrote that the Natives came from a village on the "south side," but Vancouver noted that they came from "a small border of low marshy land on the northern shore." Vancouver is probably to be considered the best source here, for his comment is so specific. There were Squamish villages in both locations: Homulchesun on the north shore, just east of Capilano Creek, and Whoi-Whoi on the south shore, in what is now Stanley Park.[186] Puget also concluded that these people were not previously in contact with Europeans:

I . . . have no Doubt but we are the first Europeans who have penetrated thus far into the Streights, though it has been alleged that the Copper Ornaments in general Use with most of the Tribes we have met with must have been procured from Visitors; may not those Visitors be other Tribes on Commercial Pursuits who have collected such Articles from the Traders on the Coast and not Europeans. The only person we have had any account of is Mr. Grey [Captain Robert Gray, of the American trading ship *Columbia*] (vide Meares) [John Meares, who had alleged in his published *Voyages* that Gray had circumnavigated Vancouver Island] who denies his having performed that Circuit round Nootka & it now still remains a Doubt if such passage really exists. From these Circumstances, joined with their Surprize Admiration and fear of our weapons Boats Dress &c. I have no hesitation in venturing an opinion, that we are the Discoverers of this part of Fuca Streights.[187]

The expedition continued up Burrard Inlet to the vicinity of today's Port Moody. The shoreline was steep here, and tents could not be put up ashore, so the men slept in the boats. Some officers preferred to sleep on the beach but got wet when high tide came.

Having satisfied themselves that there was no northwest passage here, they began the return journey. On 14 June Puget wrote: "We set out early on our return down the Narrow Inlet keeping its North Side on board as the Continental Shore." They passed by a low, marshy portion of the north shore, Capilano, where they hoped that the Indians would come out to greet them. It was early; the canoes lay on the beach. The English passed unnoticed. As Puget noted, "We had no Visitors from the Tribe we passed yesterday & stopped [at or near Point Atkinson] to breakfast opposite Noon Breakfast Point [Point Grey] which bore due South about 3 miles."[188]

"The shores of this channel," Vancouver recorded, "which, after Sir Henry Burrard of the navy, I have distinguished by the name of Burrard's Channel, may be considered, on the south side, of a moderate height, and though rocky, well covered with trees of large growth, principally of the pine [fir] tribe. On the northern side, the rugged snowy barrier, whose base we had now nearly approached, rose very abruptly, and was only protected from the wash of the sea by a very narrow border of low land. By seven o'clock we had reached the N.W. point of the channel, which forms also the south point of the main branch of the sound; this also, after another particular friend, I called Point Atkinson, situated North from Point Grey."[189]

There were more surprising events to come on 22 June. "As we were rowing on Friday morning for Point Grey," Vancouver wrote, "we discovered two vessels at anchor under the land . . . These vessels proved to be a detachment from the Commission of Señor Malespina [*sic*]." Vancouver learned that Malaspina had visited the Northwest Coast the previous year, and that he had arranged for the two *goletas* to sail "in order to prosecute discoveries on this coast." From Alcalá Galiano, who spoke a little English, he learned that they had arrived at Nootka on 11 April. From there they had sailed on the 5 June in order "to complete the examination of this inlet, which had in the preceding year been partly surveyed by some Spanish officers, whose chart they produced."[190] (Alcalá Galiano was, presumably, squeezing their two years of explorations—1790 and 1791, respectively—into one). The chart Vancouver refers to still exists. It constitutes the state of Spanish knowledge of these straits to the end of the year 1791 and is formidable in its geographical comprehension. It was the first cartographic record of these waters produced by the Spanish and is remarkable for its

The surfing canoe: An engraving by Frederic Remington, published in *Harper's New Monthly Magazine* in 1892, depicts Natives on their way to a potlatch. COURTESY OF FREDERIC REMINGTON ART MUSEUM, OGDENSBURG, NEW YORK (PUBLIC LIBRARY COLLECTION)

thoroughness as well as its beauty. It showed the main features, including the chief islands and passages, although, of course, it lacked the detail of later charts compiled on the basis of information gathered from British, Canadian and American surveys.

Menzies, the surgeon, recorded that Alcalá Galiano told Vancouver that the Spanish had been "sent from Mexico by an order of the Court of Spain on the same service as us."[191] This was alarming news, and a surprise to Vancouver, who had been told nothing of these developments. He later admitted: "I cannot avoid acknowledging that, on this occasion, I experienced no small degree of mortification in finding the external shores of the gulph had been visited, and already examined a few miles beyond where my researches during the excursion had extended."[192]

If Vancouver was mortified by meeting the Spanish and finding they were well advanced on their explorations, the Spanish could well have had the same feeling on learning that the British were now examining waters they had long neglected as part of their claimed hemispheric preserve. It was a meeting of destinies, a strange encounter of empires.

The Spanish had caught a distant view of some survey boats (those under Joseph Whidbey, master of the *Discovery*) working in Lummi Bay, and thus the appearance of the British warships was not unexpected. The Spanish narrator says: "We did not doubt that they belonged to the two English ships which according to the information from our friend Tetacus [the Indian chief they had met at Neah Bay] were in the strait." That evening, after dark, the Spanish vessels sailed past Birch Bay "and saw lights within it, which told us that the ships to which the smaller vessels belonged were lying at that anchorage."[193]

The Spanish commanders pressed Vancouver to tell of his discoveries and his search in the wake of Juan de Fuca. Vancouver, however, says that the Spanish were far better acquainted with the discoveries of Juan de Fuca than he was. Valdés, says Vancouver, had been on the coast the previous year. That is true: he had been with Malaspina at Nootka. From Natives there he had learned that Georgia Strait communicated with the ocean to the northward, "where they had seen ships." But Valdés did not trust this Native evidence: he was not prepared to say how far remote such an ocean might be.[194] In short, the Spanish were as much in the dark as the British concerning waterways lying north of Georgia Strait.

From a position well within Georgia Strait on a clear day, the view in all directions provides a great theatre of nature, of boundless beauty—the Olympics lying to the south, Mount Baker off to the east, the mountain flank of Vancouver Island to the west and, above all in magnitude, the immense Cascades and Pacific Coast Range that form a portion of the Pacific Cordillera, of which the Rocky Mountains are but a part. Imagine trying to find a northwest passage in all of this, more particularly overwhelming because numerous islands and passages present themselves toward the north and east, suggesting only vague and unknown prospects of some sort of breach in the coastal landscape—ridge upon ridge and mountain upon mountain stretching beyond. Coming down to this landscape from Peace River, the North West Company trader and explorer Alexander Mackenzie called it "a sea of mountains." Vancouver was looking at it from sea level from other directions.

Peter Puget, who we get to like the more with the telling, had no doubts about the daunting challenges ahead: "The land to the WNW [in Howe Sound] had now the appearance of a cluster of Islands. We could not help regretting that our pursuit of these Narrow Branches from the Main NW Channel, greatly impeded our progress to the Northward & as the Season was fast advancing it might take a considerable time to determine the real extent of Juan de Fuca's Streight especially as they are so broken into these narrow intricate inlets."[195] Master Joseph Whidbey refers to this welter of islands and channels spanning northern Georgia Strait, seemingly the terminus of the broad passageway, as "the Head of Fuca Streights."[196]

For a time the Spanish and British worked agreeably in concert. Accepting the division of labour suggested by Vancouver, the Spanish tended to survey, chart and name the east coast of Vancouver Island (though they sailed across to the mainland on occasion). As for the British, they had the uncompromising obligation placed on them by the Lords of the Admiralty and the British Ministry: they had to disprove the existence of a northwest passage in these latitudes. Thus it was that they examined all the great fjords, or inlets, on the mainland side—Princess Louisa, Desolation Sound, Toba Inlet and many such as were similar. No Spanish charts were of help in these latitudes; they did not meet the British imperial mandate of definitive survey. The waters in some of the inlets were literally unfathomable, and the shores were steep and unforgiving. The grandeur of the place knew no bounds, but the labour was tedious and unremitting. Each day boats would go from the mother ships to some distant spot, where the surveying would be recommenced. Long hours at the oars were the nature of the business; no pleasure cruise this, only the tedious business of running surveying lines, putting up triangulation points, using lead and line, writing down statistical data, and continuing with the imperial progression of measuring space.

In Desolation Sound, contrasts came by way of surprise. The Spanish vessels, fresh from their own exertions, joined the British at anchor in Teakerne Arm, Redonda Island, a delightful spot with high rocky shores, warm water and a waterfall. Every day, says Menzies, they rowed over to the falls and used it as a resort. Vancouver, moody now with the drawn-out expectation of bringing the season's survey to a conclusion at last, seems to have been overcome by the gloomy and dismal aspect of the environment—"an awful silence pervaded the gloomy forest." The fishing was poor and shellfish hard to find. Master Johnstone, out on survey, found a well-engineered but deserted Native village that was home to ferocious fleas, obliging his men to beat an immediate retreat, up to their necks in water.[197] But of greatest importance was Vancouver's observation, made on the basis of advice reaching him from the boat parties, that the waters were flooding in from the north as well as the south. In other words, there must be sea to the northwest.

Acting on this promising news, he sent James Johnstone in the *Chatham's* cutter and the young master's mate Spelman Swaine in the launch to investigate. The date was 5 July, still early summer admittedly, but the problem was how to work their way out of the watery maze. Johnstone led the two boats north into what became known as Johnstone Straits (now Johnstone Strait), 40 miles in length, and ventured beyond it some distance until at last he got a clear though distant view of the expansive Pacific Ocean.[198] This was a tortuous passage in tight waters with rapids and many rocks at the top end, but beyond lay a narrow strait, Broughton, just where Alert Bay and Port McNeill are now, leading to the broader waters of Queen Charlotte Strait and far beyond. Thus was the last clue found. This, as it proved, was the triumph of the Vancouver expedition's voyage, for it proved the insularity of Vancouver Island.[199] If Juan de Fuca had made this passage, this would have been his course.

Until Johnstone's return on 12 July, after more than a week away from the mother ships, there were long hours of worry for the ship companies of the *Discovery* and *Chatham*, and, truth to tell, for the Spanish as well. Depending on the results of his reconnaissance, a decision would have to be made to take a navigable passage to the northwest or be obliged to return to the Pacific by the way they had come, "by De Fuca's entrance," as Menzies called it.

With the assurance of Johnstone's report, it was time for Vancouver to say goodbye to Alcalá Galiano and Valdés and make his own passage to the Pacific.[200] The date was Friday, 13 July. Vancouver was highly satisfied with this advancement of his expectations and reconsidered the summer's remaining obligations accordingly. "Senr Galiano and Valdés I made acquainted with our discoveries; and with my intention of departing, in consequence of the information we had gained, the first favourable moment."[201] Carrying a copy of Alcalá Galiano's notes and survey of this inlet of the sea, plus a letter of introduction to Bodega y Quadra waiting at Nootka, Vancouver left the two *goletas* at anchor.

The captains of the *Sutil* and *Mexicana* intended "to pursue their researches to the westward through the channel Mr. Johnstone had discovered."[202] Still taking mainly to the solid flank of Vancouver Island, they extended the cartography of the Strait of Georgia in that direction and added many details to the chart. Quimper, Eliza and Narváez had lit their path through and into the Strait of Georgia, but here, much farther north, it was the report of open ocean from James Johnstone that offered light. Now Alcalá Galiano and Valdés could trace the waters north through Johnstone Strait into widening Queen Charlotte Strait. Passing through the appropriately named Goletas Channel, they worked their way round Vancouver Island's northernmost edge, then rode the wide swells and glassy seas characteristic of this entrance to seaward, reaching the limitless Pacific at last before cutting south and southeast into welcoming Nootka. We might think the Spanish had the less arduous task as geography dictated, for to starboard all along Johnstone Strait many more channels and inlets had come into view, all rather unwelcome at this time. But the labour continued, and one after another the details of the water maze were laid down on paper. The loneliness of these water reaches, these canyons of dark, forested walls and fathomless seabeds, made thoughts of home even more fetching.

Vancouver was the more pleased with the coastal topography the farther north he travelled from Desolation Sound, pleased that the shores were not "wholly composed of rugged rocks." The British ships made their way silently through sporting whale pods: "Numberless whales enjoying the season were playing about the ship in every direction, as were also several seals."[203]

Vancouver might well have considered himself to be in a never-ending channel in which the farther he proceeded, the more it lay out before him. The meeting of channels added great velocity to the tides, and a river of turbulence could appear in the middle of a passage, as in the case of the Yuculta Rapids, named for the local First Nations. Arran Rapids and Seymour Narrows had to be negotiated with care.

On the evening of the 14th, now happily through that "confined passage" (Seymour Narrows), where the tidal stream attained velocities of up to 15 knots and the ebb likewise in the opposite direction, they were able to find a channel that gradually widened and communicated with Johnstone Strait. Boat parties, returning, had met twenty canoes, and the occupants showed every civility and friendship, wrote Vancouver. "These," he added, "were observed to be more variously painted than any of the natives our gentlemen had seen before. The faces of some were made intirely white, some red, black, or lead cover; whilst others were adorned with several colours; and the generality had their hair decorated with the down of young sea-fowl. In these respects they evidently approached nearer to the character of the people of Nootka, than any other we had yet seen, either in the entrance of the straits of De Fuca, or in the gulf of Georgia."[204]

There were other nations encountered, including those of the village of Cheeslakees, numbering about five hundred. Menzies made a shore visit here, and Vancouver likewise recorded his valued observations gathered from others. This social intercourse proved an ethnographic bonanza for the itinerant observers. Ceremonies and displays were mounted for the visitors, and a petty trade in peltry occurred. "Mr. Menzies informed me, that these [sea-otter skins] had been procured at least an hundred per cent. dearer than when he visited the coast on a former occasion, which manifestly proved, that either a surplus quality of European commodities had been since imported into this country, or more probably, that the avidity shewn by the rival adventurers in this commerce, and the eagerness of an unrestrained throng of purchasers from different nations, had brought European commodities into low estimation. Iron was become a mere drug; and when we refused them fire arms and ammunition, which humanity, prudence, and policy directed to be with-held, nothing but large sheets of copper, and blue woolen cloth engaged their attention in a commercial way; beads and other trinkets they accepted as presents, but they returned nothing in exchange."[205]

Farther north and yet again the survey continued, with Broughton in the *Chatham* sent on ahead in special assignment to probe Havannah Channel, which led to Call Inlet and then into Knight Inlet. "The shores of it, like most of those lately surveyed, are formed by high stupendous mountains rising almost perpendicularly from the water's edge. The dissolving snow on their summits produced many cataracts . . . the fresh water that thus descended gave a pale white hue to the channel, rendering its contents intirely fresh at the head, and drinkable for twenty miles below it."[206] Otherwise it was a dreary landscape. The ships were in many a tight scrape, and they found safety and comfort in Port Safety, Calvert Island.

Now Vancouver sailed waters known to the British fur-trading captains since the late 1780s. He had among his charts some plans drawn by Samuel Wedgborough, which Dalrymple had collected. Wedgborough had been there in the *Experiment*, under Captain Guise, in August 1786. Charles Duncan, already introduced as having made that precious chart of Cape Flattery area, had made another plan in this northern location and, like other mariners, had named islands and ports for patrons and friends. Vancouver knew that James Hanna had traded there that same year of 1786 and had named Fitzhugh Sound. "These being the names given, as far as I could learn, by the first discoverers of this part of the coast, will be continued by me, and adopted in my charts and journal."[207]

On 17 July the brig *Venus*, out of Bengal and commanded by Henry Shepherd, suddenly appeared off the entrance in the cove where the *Discovery* rode at anchor. Shepherd was hoping for a better trade here than in the outer waters, where the price of skins was exorbitant. Vancouver received the good news that the *Daedalus*, storeship for his expedition and sent from England, had arrived at Nootka with provisions and stores for their use. The bad news was that a letter from the master of the *Daedalus*, Thomas New, informed Vancouver that Lieutenant Richard Hergest, commanding the *Daedalus*; the astronomer William Gooch; and one of the seamen belonging to that vessel had been murdered in Oahu while on shore procuring water. (Vancouver would later deal with this matter when he reached Hawaii, and he let the Hawaiians exact the justice.) The loss of Hergest, his "particular friend"—they had been messmates under Cook—was a terrible personal blow. The loss of the promising young Gooch, a barber's son who had been educated at Gonville and Caius, Cambridge, was a disastrous blow to the scientific aspects of the interlocking businesses of astronomical observation, navigation and chart-making.

Hergest's death meant that there was no commissioned British officer at Nootka to liaise with the Spanish until Vancouver could arrive there, and this among other reasons led Vancouver to conclude that it was time to wind up the survey for the 1792 season. He knew he had perhaps another month that he could have used to continue the work, but all officers and men under him must have been relieved when news was passed that they were heading for Nootka. They sailed out of Port Safety in serene and cheerful weather, under a pleasant breeze from the southeast. They were soon out beyond the Scott Islands and Cape Scott, with its hills of moderate height, and before long they saw Woody Point, where Vancouver had been with Captain Cook fourteen years previous. They dodged rocks and shoals and faced fogs and squalls, and in the end, inshore sailing being out of the question as dangerous, Vancouver had

An occupational hazard for explorers: the *Discovery* in peril on the rocks in Queen Charlotte Sound, near the north end of Vancouver Island. No harm was done, and the ship floated free with the returning tide. The brig *Chatham* is shown in the distance.
ENGRAVING FROM A SKETCH BY ZACHARY MUDGE. FROM *BRITISH COLUMBIA: A PICTORIAL RECORD, 1778–1891*

to give up the prospect of charting the shores of Vancouver Island south to Nootka Sound. On the British chart, at least, they were still *terra incognita*.

From the time they had entered the Strait of Juan de Fuca at Cape Flattery to their safe arrival at Nootka, the work of discovery had been arduous, the speed of progress often that of the inchworm. Coastal geography had played many a potential trick on these mariners. With warm appreciation, Menzies commented on the survey work in his journal entry for 18 August 1792: "And if we look back on the different winding channels & armlets which the vessels & boats traversed over in following the Continental Shore ever since they entered De Fuca's Streights, it will readily be allowed that such an intricate & laborious examination could not have been accomplished in so short a time without the cooperative exertions of both Men & Officers whose greatest pleasure seemed to be in performing their duty with alacrity & encountering the dangers and difficulties incidental to such service with a persevering intrepidity & manly

Vancouver's Legacy: removing doubts of a Northwest Passage in the latitudes shown on his great chart of 1798. This section of the chart "Coast of N.W. America" shows curiosities, among them "Quadra and Vancouver's Island" (so named by him to honour his friendship with Bodega y Quadra), the "Gulph of Georgia" (as he called it) and long passages leading north to the Pacific by Johnstone Strait and Queen Charlotte Strait. Unshaded parts are from Spanish sources. Northernmost anchorage of Alcalá Galiano and Valdés is noted. DAVID RUMSEY MAP COLLECTION

steadiness that afforded a most pleasing omen to the happy issue of our future endeavours in this arduous undertaking."[208]

As a charmed observer, Menzies had many a fine phrase for what he had seen in these inland waters. "It remains for me still to give you a short account of New Georgia with the Seas which intersect it in various directions; and which is now called in general the Gulf of New Georgia."[209] So did he write to his patron, Sir Joseph Banks, the presiding genius of science and exploration of his age. Menzies put an imperial stamp on his prose, and with a naturalist's touch he was advancing a botany of desire. He continued:

> From the Lat. of 47° N., which was our Southernmost extent, to 48 1/2° N. is a delightful level country chiefly covered with Pine [sic] forests and abounding here and there with clear spots of considerable extent, forming excellent pastures favourable for new settlements, if it was not for the scarcity of fresh water, which was a general complaint in all our excursions through it. The Climate appeared to us exceedingly favorable in so high a latitude and the Soil, tho' in general light, would, I am confident, yield good and early crops of most of the European Grains: its being so intersected with branches of the Sea afford easy and commodious communications, and its short distance from the free access to the Ocean of De Fuca's Straits may likewise in time be much in its favour, for its Eastern boundary is not above fifty Leagues inland from the entrance of the Straits, and is formed by a ridge of high rugged Mountains in many places covered with perpetual Snow, running nearly in a North and South direction . . . But an Inland situation is by no means favourable for what I conceive to be the chief object of establishing settlements on this distant coast, which is the Fur Trade; as we saw but few Sea Otters, in our interior navigation, and indeed very few furs of any kind, so that the first settlements should be placed along the outer edge of the Coast, where furs and inhabitants are more abundant.[210]

To his way of thinking, the best place for a settlement would be the north end of Haida Gwaii, for those islands and the shores adjacent had supplied more furs for the China market than all other parts of the coast combined.

The sooner settlements were formed and this trade brought under regulation, Menzies thought, the better it would be for the advantages to be expected of it: "for you will hardly believe it when I tell you that with us and the Spaniards there has been in all no less than thirty Vessels on the N.W. Coasts this last summer—English twelve, Spanish six—American 7, Portuguese four—French one."[211]

That letter reached Banks by way of messages sent home to England via the *Daedalus* from Monterey. And all the while, Vancouver awaited further instructions. They never arrived.

If ever he had reason to doubt it, he now confirmed he was very much on his own and facing a challenge of a rather different but no less difficult order. The Spanish flag flew at Nootka, which Vancouver saluted with thirteen guns. The salute was returned, and on going ashore accompanied by some officers, Vancouver had the honour of being received with the greatest cordiality and attention from the commandant. However, rocky diplomatic shoals lay ahead.

Chapter 9

NOOTKA SOUND 1792

Waiting patiently at Nootka to give George Vancouver an official welcome was the Spanish commissioner and commandant at Nootka, Juan Francisco de la Bodega y Quadra, age forty-eight. By all accounts he was a paragon of virtue. All histories and biographies present him with high praise, and rightly so, for he exhibited qualities not always found among the rougher lieutenants and pilots who were junior to him in rank and station. Adjectives to describe these qualities include intelligent and hospitable, cordial and determined, ethical and honest—and, of course, devoted to the king's service. Much has been made of the fact that he was not born in Spain but in one of its colonial territories, a disadvantage to advancement. Bodega y Quadra overcame every obstacle in his rise to prominence. There was a bit of the grandee to this fellow, as was his right by seniority and station.

He was of a kindly and benevolent disposition, and those who came into contact with him were disarmed by his apparent disinterestedness.[212] But his genial exterior belied an icy disposition in treating with the English on matters of international substance, which from his viewpoint naturally meant Spanish imperial rights dating back to the Treaty of Tordesillas if not before. Doubtless he was personally disposed to resist English entreaties. He had equally to go by the letter of his instructions. Like his opposite, as we shall see, he went by the book. He was, in all but name, a viceregal figure. But sadly, from his viewpoint, his empire was fast crumbling beneath him, and he was caught in a swirl of international politics in which he was cast to the winds of fate. His exit plan was to depart the scene with dignity and with his king's power and influence in no way impaired.

Bodega y Quadra was born in Lima, Peru, and trained in Cadiz at the Real Colegio de Guardiamarinas under Juan y Santacilla and Vicente Tofiño.[213] When Spain became defensive about the Falklands and strengthened its base at the port of Lima, Bodega y Quadra was reassigned from the Mediterranean to El Callao and to Mexico. From there in 1775, the year after his arrival, he sailed north in the expedition of Bruno de Hezeta. The

Servant of the King of Spain: Juan Francisco de la Bodega y Quadra, a man of large vision, served a long and illustrious career as an explorer and administrator on the west coast of America, including a stint as commander of the Nootka settlement where in August 1792 he exchanged views with his equally determined opposite, the British commissioner George Vancouver.
MUSEO NAVAL

command ship was the *Santiago*. Bodega y Quadra was commander of the 36-foot schooner *Sonora* and a sailor without equal. Hezeta only got as far north as Vancouver Island before returning to Mexico, but Bodega y Quadra, in one of the great ocean voyages that tested every capacity of a skipper, reached the high latitudes of Glacier Bay, Alaska, the farthest north that any Spaniard had sailed to that time.[214] In 1779 he was again in Alaskan waters, this time in command of the frigate *Favorita*, and reached Cook Inlet. After subsequent assignments in Cuba and Spain he was sent to San Blas, there to take charge of the naval base and arsenal.

In 1792 Bodega y Quadra sailed to Nootka as Spanish commandant and commissioner. This voyage is often referred to as the Expedition of the Limits to the North of California. His assignment was to implement the Nootka Convention of 28 October 1790 and to do so in agreement with his British opposite, Vancouver.[215] Upon arrival at Nootka, Bodega y Quadra learned from the Yankee trader Joseph Ingraham, of the brigantine

Hope, that there had been next to nothing of a British house or establishment there.[216] The British would conclude that information such as this coloured the Spanish response and cast a pall over the negotiations. The Yankees chose to forget that the British were there long before Martínez had carried out his desperate measures. The Americans and Spanish had much in common, but what attracted them most in this truly distant corner of the world was their shared dislike of British sea-otter traders who subverted their power and their profits.

Bodega y Quadra entertained in lavish style, as had been common in Lima for men of his class. Opulence ruled the empire. Porcelain and glass were extravagant imports, but high-quality silver ore was abundant within the viceroyalty of Peru.[217] All plate and flatware used at table in his house ashore in Nootka were of solid silver—a sharp contrast to the Royal Navy's tin, pewter and brass. He thought nothing of having two dozen persons sitting down to a meal, and he always gave pride of place to Maquinna, whom he favoured over all chiefs at Nootka. A five-course dinner, served with great elegance, was the standard. To ships in harbour he sent newly baked bread, goats' milk and fresh vegetables. This was kindness with a purpose, an imperial intent. His expense allowance, agreed upon with the viceroy, had as its underlying intent the showing of the Spanish court's influence in this most remote of locations.

So odd was this largesse at Nootka that it has been imagined that Captain Vancouver was shamed because of his relative impoverishment.[218] The record shows much visiting back and forth between ship and shore, and on many occasions the Spanish provided the eatables and the British the drinkables. There is no doubt that Bodega y Quadra exceeded his allowance and increased his debts to a ruinous extent. And there is some indication that playing the munificent host was becoming ruinous to his health. But being a guest could be hazardous too. "Cap. Van. has got quite fat," reported Thomas Manby, Vancouver's first lieutenant, in a gossipy letter to a friend.[219] But Vancouver was facing ill health by this time. Not only was he overweight. He was showing symptoms of something more serious—puffiness, hair loss, irritability and short temper, and he would die at age forty, not long after his return to England. Bodega y Quadra would die even sooner, in 1794, at age forty-nine, of causes related to increasingly severe headaches.[220]

For the moment, however, there was much to discuss.

Vancouver bore a commission from the British government to settle, with his opposite, Bodega y Quadra, the differences of opinion about the seizure of British ships and cargoes at Nootka Sound in 1789. Also, and of a more tricky nature, he had to negotiate the return to Britain of a small beach at Nootka Sound where Meares had a factory—part storehouse, part marine establishment—where the first coastal trading vessel, the *North West America,* had been built and commissioned.

Bodega y Quadra decided not to return all the houses, gardens and occupied premises as they stood. When the Spaniard showed Vancouver the paltry acreage he could receive, Vancouver wisely declined and wrote home for new instructions. Had he accepted Bodega y Quadra's more narrow interpretation, he would have been, as he put it, either a consummate fool or a traitor. Vancouver was exasperated, and rightly so.[221]

These are the brief details of the story. The correspondence between the two commissioners tells much more, however, and throws light on the motivations and the tactics of these two men. Bodega y Quadra took the initiative, and he had had a good deal of time to think through what he would say to Vancouver when he arrived at Nootka. He had the Spanish empire to defend against the interloper at this distant spot.

In these circumstances, Bodega y Quadra brazenly wrote to Vancouver on 29 August and claimed that all was settled at Nootka Sound. It was his first letter to his opposite and seems to have adopted the tactic that the best defence is attack. He gave Vancouver a history lesson on recent developments, but, in addition, provided a long retrospective about the rights and claims of Spain in comparison to those of Great Britain. "By solemn treaties; by discoveries; and by a possession immemorial, well confirmed; it has been known to all nations the propriety which ours has in the Coast to the North of California. Founded in this right we have gone without violence, gaining the love of the natives, with the cost of innumerable sums, in different expeditions by sea and land, and in sustaining the department of Sn. Blas, without any other view than as an auxiliary to other establishments, and to extend them." Continuing in the same expansive tone, Bodega y Quadra breezily reported that all had been fixed at Nootka:

> Things thus established to their primitive state, it is clear that Spain has nothing to deliver, nor the smallest damage to make good. But comprehending the spirit of the King my Master, is

to establish a solid peace, and permanent with all nations, and consulting to remove obstacles which influence discords, far from thinking to continue in this port, I am ready, without prejudice to our legitimate right, nor that of the Courts better instructed resolves, generously to cede to England the Houses, Offices, and gardens which has with so much labour been cultivated; and retire to Fuca; and for never to be disturbed or molested, the one or the other party.[222]

"Fuca" was to be the northernmost Spanish establishment, exclusive to the Spanish.

On receiving this missive, George Vancouver must have drawn a breath and fought back anger. We can imagine his astonishment, for had he sailed all this way to be told that the game was up? He was not one to back away or stand down. Bodega y Quadra had met his match. When treating with Bodega y Quadra at Nootka Sound on various matters of restitution and on the rival rights of the two governments, Vancouver brought up the matter of the most recent Spanish attempt at "pegging out empire." This was the expedient construction in May 1792 of a Spanish base at Neah Bay, just inside the entrance to the Strait of Juan de Fuca, a short distance east of Cape Flattery and Fuca's Pillar. It was a poor port, the Spanish knew, and although safe from difficult winds outside and the sweeping tides and currents that ran along this shoreline, it was laced with boulders and rafts of kelp and thus made for a hazardous anchorage. It nonetheless had imperial importance and strategic merit in the game of statecraft then being played out. The Spanish had put up the place within days of Vancouver sailing past in early May, and Vancouver had learned of it from Alcalá Galiano. The weather had been horrid when the *Discovery* and *Chatham* had passed this way, and Vancouver had not seen the port, a point of insignificance in any event.

Bodega y Quadra waxed eloquent: he saw "Fuca"—that is, Neah Bay— to be "our last establishment"—by which he meant "our most northerly es- tablishment." In a strange foreshadowing of the 1846 boundary agreement between Great Britain and the United States, he said that Neah Bay would "fix the dividing point; and from thence to the Northward to be common the free entrance, use, and commerce, comfortable to the 5th Article of the Convention and that no others may be able to form themselves without the permission of the respective Courts: neither for the English to pass to the South of Fuca."[223]

By "others" the Spanish captain had in mind the Russians, rumoured to be coming south out of the fog banks of the Aleutians and Alaska with their destination the mouth of the Columbia River and Alta California. And he may have had in mind, too, the voracious Americans, principally Bostonians, already ranging these coasts in search of sea-otter pelts for the China market. Gray, Kendrick and Ingraham, among others, came in steady succession from Boston in their fast schooners and brigs. These intruders were making the Spanish claims of exclusivity ever more difficult to enforce. Neah Bay was the last line of defence, for if the Spanish could not retain their new base at Nootka Sound, they would have to fall back on "Fuca." To Bodega y Quadra this made eminent good sense.

George Vancouver would have none of it. The points Bodega y Quadra made counted for little with the British captain, who was more concerned with the here and the now and what Spain intended to do to keep its part of the Convention signed at El Escorial two years previous, on 28 October 1790.

In his reply to Bodega y Quadra, dated 1 September 1792, Vancouver gave his opposite a lesson in international law, reciting the exact words of the fifth article of the Convention. "Fuca," he pointed out, had been made a post after the Convention had been agreed. The telling point, Vancouver said, was that the article did not give Spain exclusive control at Fuca or elsewhere. Rather, the article specified that settlements made by subjects of either power since April 1789 would be open to "free access and carry on their trade without disturbance or molestation." In other words, Fuca would be a free port. He had Bodega y Quadra literally "dead to rights."

There is a bit of wry cynicism in Vancouver's concluding paragraph to his opposite on this matter: "This being the exact words of the said article, I should suppose the Establishment His Catholic Majesty has made in the mouth of Fuca, to come under the denomination of, a port of free access, as well as such as may have been, or may hereafter be made from thence South to Port St. Francisco, conceiving that port to be the Northernmost part of the said coast when occupied by Spain; and I believe the Establishment at the mouth of Fuca to have been made no longer than last May, when I was myself, employed in surveying the said coast."[224] And this was reason enough for Vancouver to conclude that he could go no further in his arrangements with Bodega y Quadra.

A second exchange of letters followed but to no effect.[225] It was time to close the wearying matter. Vancouver had been authorized to deal only with the issues that concerned Nootka Sound and Meares's establishment. His instructions did not include discretion to deal with post-April 1789 Spanish actions. His opposite might do as he wished and carve out a new imperial stronghold or watchtower, but Vancouver wisely left that to others in London to negotiate. In the circumstances, all he could do was send home for further instructions. Thus it was that his next junior to him, William Robert Broughton, an officer of conspicuous abilities and much

Tide of Empire: Friendly Cove, Nootka Sound, 22 September 1792. A drawing by Hewitt Jackson depicts one of the most important moments in the history of western North America, when warships and trading vessels gathered at the celebrated harbour of trade and international intrigue: (left to right) *Columbia Rediviva* and *Adventure*,

observation, according to Whidbey, was sent home by way of Mexico with dispatches and explanations. As it turned out, Broughton was escorted to San Blas by his friend Bodega y Quadra, then across Mexico, and thence to Spain. His arrival was eagerly anticipated in London, and he brought with him the details of Spanish discoveries on the Northwest Coast, their search for the Strait of Juan de Fuca, and their establishing of their new imperial toehold at "Fuca," Neah Bay.

In short, the British and Spanish rode at anchor in the salubrious surroundings of Nootka Sound, going about the heady business of comparing notes and dealing with the complications of implementing the Nootka Convention, which, it turned out, was a task impossible to complete

American traders; *Aránzazu*, Spanish frigate; *Margaret*, American trader; H.M. sloop-of-war *Discovery*; *Fenis & St. Joseph*, trader; *Jackall*, English trader; H.M. armed tender *Chatham*; H.M. storeship *Daedalus*; *Activo*, Spanish armed brig. OREGON HISTORICAL SOCIETY, BB009556

because of differing interpretations. Accordingly, the business passed back to the respective national capitals.[226] For some months there was much to-ing and fro-ing between the British and Spanish governments. The diplomatic pouches bulged with explanations and demands. Differing positions on international law were taken. Ancient rights were proclaimed, new ones pronounced. The British never wavered. They increased their pressure, and they refused to back down on their interpretation of the original Convention.

At the same time, the French revolution was reaching new intensity. By order of the National Convention, Louis XVI was executed. Four days later, a shudder of war passed over Europe, and Britain immediately decided to mend fences with the Spanish as a counter to French aggrandizements. An alliance was concluded in May and ratified in London, effective July 1793. The old antagonists who had quarrelled about ships and shipyards at Nootka were now allied against a greater menace.

Having patched up their differences, the metropolitan governments could now solve the Nootka riddle. On 11 January 1794 they signed the Convention for the Mutual Abandonment of Nootka. And thus the final act of the drama, an anticlimactic one, naturally, was brought on stage. Spanish prime minister Manuel Godoy instructed the viceroy to send a new commissioner to Nootka. Brigadier-General José Manuel de Alava was selected. The British arranged for theirs, too, a young marine first lieutenant named Thomas Pearce, who had recently been with Captain William Bligh on his successful *Providence* voyage. Pearce sailed north from San Blas with his Spanish counterpart. At Nootka, the Convention specified, the Spanish officer would convey "the Buildings and Districts of Land" to the British officer. Subsequently, the British officer would raise the Union Jack, or Flag, as a token sign of possession. To conclude, the officers of the two Crowns would withdraw their subjects from Nootka Sound.

On 16 March 1795 the *Activo*, bearing the commissioners, arrived at Nootka. Pearce, aided by the American trader John Kendrick, who served as an interpreter, inquired of Maquinna and the Nootka people the precise extent of Meares's factory, the details of which were now of no importance to the proceedings. Pearce confided in Maquinna and told him that the British offered protection and friendship. "With this account they all seemed much pleased," Pearce reported to his superiors in London, "observing that the English had ever been their good friends—but were very anxious to know if the Spanish should return, whether they were to be friends with them; from which I inferred that they had not been treated very kindly by them." The Spanish dismantled their establishment and took away their guns. They delivered over to Pearce the site of Meares's factory. Pearce went to the flagstaff, hoisted and then lowered the Union Jack. He gave the flag to Maquinna for safekeeping, instructing him to hoist it whenever a ship appeared.[227]

The British retained their right of using that port and having a shore establishment should they wish. But in the spirit of the times they were content to let the paper world of claims and rights of access serve as sufficient claim to the world that John Meares had commenced. The spirit of the British mercantile classes was unbounded at this time, as the British ministry knew, and it had to be satisfied. Commerce ruled, and the British had global ambitions.

Vancouver spent two more summers on the Northwest Coast, 1793 and 1794, making laborious surveys of the coastline. He pushed his inquiries up the mid-coast of British Columbia, then up to Alaska, making detailed surveys of the complicated coastline with all its islands, and searching for the passage he had been sent to discover. He closed his survey at the end of the 1794 season and headed for home via Cape Horn, completing a mammoth assignment that resulted in outstanding charts and navigational details about one of the most complex coasts of the world. It was the climax of a world quest going back to the age of the Portuguese mariners and the Spanish circumnavigators.

Vancouver was back in London on 17 October 1795 with 65,000 sea miles under his keel. Now in declining health, he left the preparation of his journals for publication to his brother John, who saw the volumes and an atlas of charts through the press. From this great work the world derived most of its knowledge respecting the Northwest Coast and Alaska. In it, George Vancouver confirmed in print what he had advised the Admiralty on 20 October 1795—that his "very extensive and accurate examinations removed every doubt and set aside every opinion of a Northwest Passage within the limits of our researches." That was, undoubtedly, a magnificent achievement.

And so, one by one in curious procession by sea, they had all made their approaches to or even passages into the strait. Barkley and his young wife, the seasoned ship master Duncan and the young mate Duffin reached the entrance and probed within. None of them discounted Juan de Fuca's claim of first passage into the waterway. Meares, who sent Duffin, was content to apply the name to the strait in honour of Juan de Fuca, the Greek mariner who had sailed in the service of the king of Spain. Robert Gray and those who sailed from Boston with or in competition with him did not object to its name and also sailed its waters. Captain George Vancouver acted similarly, perhaps with the knowledge that his fellow countrymen and others were content to let the appellation stand. The Spanish mariners—Eliza, Quimper, Narváez, Alcalá Galiano and Valdés—also kept the name, which appears as Entrada de Juan de Fuca on the Cardero map of 1792.

What are we to make of all this? James A. Gibbs, the well-known historian of shipwrecks, has wisely observed that whereas the mariners of the eighteenth century accepted the old pilot's claim that he had entered the strait, recent historians have taken greater exception to it.[228] In short, the early explorers are the ones who laid down the confirming basis of this story, and we have to give them credit for appreciating the difficulties of those who went before them. None of them, we can further note, quarrelled with the Juan de Fuca story as told to Michael Lok, and none of them took up alternate positions. And note what happened to John Meares when he began to fudge the record and make claims that it was he who made the discoveries and he who applied the names: Charles Duncan, who drew the first chart of the entrance that survived, called Meares to account in a famous pamphlet war. George Dixon, the famous maritime fur trader, did likewise.[229]

The most jaded opponent of Juan de Fuca is never likely to be convinced to the contrary, and is welcome to hold that view. But it does not deny the importance of the work of the mariners on discovery, those looking for the golden prospect of navigating a famous passage written into legend and lore. Empirical science and historical examination can never expunge the claims of those who seek farther horizons.

We may be content in reading what that distinguished mariner Captain Vancouver had to say on the topic. He had thought about it a good deal. He had quizzed Colnett, who knew the coast and those who had sailed it as well as any sea trader.[230] Vancouver also followed the pamphlet war involving the British discoverers and the untrustworthy Meares ("the lying Meares," the Natives of Nootka called him). Now in his last days, as he readied the massive text of his book *Voyage of Discovery* for the press, George Vancouver took pains to reexamine the Juan de Fuca claim in the concluding chapter.

What he says about a discovery of a strait in 1592 is well worth our consideration. For in 1798, two centuries after the rumoured event, no one was more aware of Juan de Fuca's claim than Vancouver. Further, no person was more aware of all the mariners of the late 1780s through 1790s— his very contemporaries, whether British, Spanish or American—who had probed the strait, gone through or by the San Juan Islands, explored Haro and Rosario Straits, transited Georgia Strait and its islands and annexes, then probed carefully through the dangers to Johnstone Strait and to the Pacific again.

In addition, and in regards to the complex geography of the Northwest Coast, Vancouver knew the dead ends, the interlocking waterways, the points of no return. In three long summers of surveying, the ships and men under his command had mastered the geography of an intricate water world all the way from the entrance of the strait to the Gulf of Alaska. He had worked in concert with the Spanish. He had studied their findings and examined their charts. Now it was time to put ghosts to rest and end the speculation. But he had to choose his words carefully.

Not long before, in 1795, Alexander Dalrymple, London's reigning literary booster of the Juan de Fuca claim, had been appointed the first hydrographer to the Admiralty. He was the reigning authority on discoveries of the age and knew more about charts and atlases than probably any person living. Taking him on in a public discussion about Juan de Fuca was a task to be done with care. But Vancouver, not one to shy away from the challenge, wrote: "With respect to the ancient discoveries of De Fuca, they appear to be upheld by tradition alone, and ought therefore to be received with great latitude and to be credited with still more caution." Referring to Dalrymple as "a celebrated writer on geography" who had advanced Juan de Fuca's claim in his *Plan for Promoting the Fur-Trade* (1789), a work which Vancouver identifies, Vancouver wrote that Dalrymple appeared to have been completely convinced that Juan de Fuca's oral testimony—and oral testimony was the only evidence—was correct, although he acknowledged that the story as given to Lok, and the promise to make further discoveries in that region, had been given on condition of payment for the great losses Juan de Fuca had suffered at the hands of Thomas Cavendish.

Dalrymple had candidly stated that "John de Fuca, the Greek pilot, in 1592, sailed into a broad inlet between the 47th and 48th degrees, which led him into a far broader sea, wherein he sailed above twenty days, there being at the entrance on the north-west coast, a great head-land or island, with an exceeding high pinnacle or spired rock, like a pillar, thereupon."[231]

Now it was time for Vancouver to tell his own tale, for he was conversant with all the views of the interested mariners of the age who had been on the Northwest Coast:

> This is the whole that can be collected from the information of this supposed navigator; which Mr. Dalrymple says exactly corresponds with the discoveries of the Spaniards, who "have recently found an entrance in the latitude of 47° 45' north, which in twenty-seven days' course brought them to the vicinity of Hudson's bay." On making inquiries of the Spanish officers attached to the commission of Sen[io]r Malespina [Malaspina], as also of Sen[io]r [Bodega y] Quadra, and several of the officers under his orders [Alcalá Galiano and Cayetano Valdés, among others], who, for some time past, had been employed in such researches respecting so important a circumstance, I was given to understand by them all, that my communication was the first intelligence they had ever received of such discoveries having been made; and as the navigators De Fuca, De Fonte, and others, these gentlemen expected to have derived intelligence from us, supposing, from the English publications, that we were better acquainted with their achievements than any part of the Spanish nation. A commander of one of the trading vessels met with such a pinnacle rock in the latitude of 47° 47', but unluckily there was no opening near it, to identify it being the same which the Greek pilot had seen; but this circumstance can easily be dispensed with, for the sake of supporting an hypothesis, only by supposing the opening to be further to the northward. That such a rock might have been seen in that latitude is not to be questioned, because we saw numbers of them, and it is well known, that not only on the coast of North-West America, but on various other coasts of the earth, such pinnacle rocks are found to exist.

Vancouver states that on these grounds alone stands "the ancient authority for the discoveries" of Juan de Fuca. And however erroneous they might be, they had been acknowledged by most of the recent mariners who had visited that coast. But at this point he made his departure from this prevailing wisdom. Vancouver was aware that if he continued to use the name of Juan de Fuca in his reports and maps, this would be seen as a tacit acknowledgement of his discoveries.

> [This] I must positively deny, because there has not been seen one leading feature to substantiate his tradition; on the contrary, the sea coast under the parallels between which this opening is said to have existed, is compact and impenetrable; the shores of the continent have not any opening whatever, that bears the least similitude to the description of De Fuca's entrance; and the opening which I have called the supposed straits of Juan de Fuca, instead of being between the 47th and 48th degrees, is between the 48th and 49th degrees of north latitude, and leads not into a far broader or Mediterranean ocean.[232]

He also pointed out that Drake had not made such an error in longitude, although those who subscribed to the Juan de Fuca observations excused his inaccuracy by arguing the ignorance of those days, or the incorrectness in making such observations during that era.

Vancouver had disproved the existence of a northwest passage in these latitudes. This was his achievement. He had put to rest John Meares's preposterous claim of the probability of a passage in those latitudes. Then there were the wide-eyed dreamers to deal with, those possessing the unscientific maps that lacked the statistical data of accurate latitude and longitude, those with the whales in the corners and the mermaids in the margins.

And what about these geographical speculators? Again we turn to Vancouver. He despised the "closet philosophers" who, instead of advancing the worthy causes of the mariners who actually made the explorations and disproved the speculative, made it their pernicious business to advance the causes and misconceptions of ancient mariners. Vancouver, for his times, was a modernist. Indeed, he had written the great volume of his stupendous navigations to prove as conclusively as possible that a hyperborean or northern ocean between the Pacific and the Atlantic did not exist. The whole was a fable, an illusion.

Canadian fur traders had also proved this. The Hudson's Bay Company made several attempts to find the passage. Samuel Hearne pressed overland from Hudson Bay to the Coppermine River on the Arctic shore. Peter Pond, a trader attached to the North West Company, reached Lake Athabasca, and this formed the base of explorations north and west for the next generation or so. In both his expeditions—the first to the Arctic in 1789 and the second to the Pacific four years later—Alexander Mackenzie disproved the existence of a sea passage in those latitudes. Mackenzie shared Vancouver's distrust of Meares, and in his *Voyages from Montreal* pointed out categorically how wrong Meares was.[233] Together Mackenzie and Vancouver laid to rest the idea of a northwest passage between 47° N and 60° N.

The quest for the passage had been abandoned in the early 1700s, when some regarded it as futile a pursuit as the search for the philosopher's stone, the mastering of perpetual motion, or the determination of longitude. The quest was resurrected in the late 1700s after the merchant sea traders found the entrance to the Strait of Juan de Fuca, but it was again abandoned when Vancouver disproved its existence. Mackenzie's overland journey in the same latitudes was the last nail in the coffin. In the nineteenth century the Admiralty again took up the idea of a sea lane, though this time in much higher latitudes, an icy passion that engulfed British naval officers including Ross, Franklin and Parry. By then Arctic exploration was being pushed on by some new requirements, not least the fear of Russian pre-emption, the need to provide employment for half-pay or unemployed Royal Navy officers, and the alluring news that there was a breakup in Arctic sea ice, as reported by whalers in the Greenland fishery.

Each age, it seems, has had a polar passion of some sort. Hakluyt and Purchas published accounts of adventure and daring in these high waters and ice-blocked lands and passages. The poet Coleridge, writing "The Rime of the Ancient Mariner" in 1797–98, borrowed North-west Fox's narrative about his voyage to the High Arctic in 1631–35, which contained Lok's testimony about his meeting with Juan de Fuca. When at last the Northwest Passage was transited by a Norwegian ship skippered by Roald Amundsen (1903 to 1906), it was in the latitudes north of 70°. It was not until the industrial age, when land surveyors found the passes and railway engineers laid down the grades, that Juan de Fuca's dream of a passage from Atlantic to Pacific in southern latitudes was realized.

Juan de Fuca's tale had a long lease on life, and his influence lingers still. Like the Ancient Mariner, he tugs at our sleeve, while all the time the more exciting bridal arrangements develop, luring us away to exotic flights of fancy.

In his last and sorrowful years, Juan de Fuca was an aggrieved party. Of that there can be no doubt. He had hoped for better at the hands of that great Christian prince, the Spanish king, whom he had served for so long with such faithfulness and professional zeal. Similarly, he had hoped for compensation from the English Crown for his grievous losses to the pirate Cavendish. Heaven knows the wealth that the flamboyant young Cavendish had splashed around London made robbery at sea seem such easy pickings. All Juan de Fuca wanted was his rightful share in compensation. He even promised to find the strait if a royal ship could be lent.

Juan de Fuca may have known how Elizabethan seadogs acted in violent and high-handed fashion on the high seas, pilfering on a grand scale their main line of work, but the world of London's politics and commerce was quite beyond his knowing. In that hard-driving English world of commerce, strategy and naval power, where aristocratic, mercantile and even municipal jurisdictions and interests were competing for the same sort of favouritism—whether charters of grant, monopolies on certain trades, or whatever else—an illiterate Greek mariner had no chance. That Juan de Fuca had served the king of Spain was enough to label him a threat to the British realm. This was especially so when he was backed by Michael Lok, whose status at court and in the city made him a dubious patron. Everything Lok had done—the Frobisher expedition especially—made him a discredited force. These two, Juan de Fuca and Michael Lok, though attractive to us now, perhaps, were an unsupportable combination. They had no power, only tales to tell that were suggestive of great riches and adventures—and of dreams unfulfilled. And we leave them now with not a little regret, for the world's history is full of dreams unfulfilled, of promises broken, of missed opportunities, of aggrieved hearts.

Before closing, we need to remind ourselves that not all history needs to have final results. In tangled tales there are, invariably, loose ends to tie up. Sometimes there are yawning gaps in the record, missing files in the annals—in this case lack of supporting or collaborative evidence—but it does not make the account any less significant. Nor does it necessarily disprove the event. Perhaps the surviving Spanish evidence is slim because the files were weeded out. At least two Spanish explorations to northern latitudes after Juan de Fuca left only fragmentary documentation. The particulars of discovery, these cabinets of curiosities, the Spanish kept entirely to themselves, for they were state secrets—and of potential danger in the hands of others. Indeed, the Mexican archives may offer more leads than the Spanish files.

Warren Cook, the eminent historian of Spain and the Pacific Northwest, thought Juan de Fuca's evidence commendably possible, as did the famous historian of cartography Henry Raup Wagner. The distinguished historian of early California voyages Michael Mathes remains convinced, on the basis of what he has seen, that there is little to support Juan de Fuca's claim, though he, too, wisely, does not discredit the possibility of such a voyage.[234] Noted marine artist Steve Mayo recently took me to the site of Fairhaven, Bellingham, Washington, where the Spanish are reported to have careened and watered their vessels from this early time. He told me that the Lummi had an encounter with early Europeans and their ship, or ships, on the bay near Fairhaven. Could these have been Juan de Fuca's vessels? Farther north, the Musqueam people said to Narváez as he stopped to visit with them in 1791, "Well, we have seen these sorts of vessels before," or words to that effect. It is all rather fantastic and the naysayers will pronounce strongly against it, but it is not outside the realm of possibility and would happily accord with Native contention that strength and accuracy lies in their oral tradition.

"Historians may have decided that his whole story is a myth," wrote that historical man-about-town John Crosse, "but local mariners know better." As Crosse correctly pointed out, Earnle Bradford demonstrated in *Ulysses Found* (1963) that the odyssey described by Homer was not a myth. He also reminded us that every time we honour Captain Vancouver we should also honour Apóstolos Valerianos, "that old Greek, who was here in the service of Spain 400 years ago."[235]

Muriel Wylie Blanchet describes delightfully in *The Curve of Time* (1961) how she often thought of Juan de Fuca as she sailed these waters with her children. Blanchet, intimately familiar with the upper Strait of Georgia and points northwest from summer voyaging, concluded that

Juan de Fuca followed the tides north of the broad inlet of the sea, beyond the San Juan Islands "and other divers islands." She concluded that somewhere close to Nanaimo the pilot emerged "into a much broader sea than that at the said [Cape Flattery] entrance." The expanse of the Gulf of Georgia would have stretched out before him. North again, in twenty days of rowing and sailing, he would have come to the great hump of Texada Island, and beyond that again Johnstone Strait. "Natives clad in skins of beastes," he says, "that being entered thus far into the said Straits and being come to the North Sea already, and finding the sea wide enough everywhere, to be thirty or forty leagues wide—he thought he had well discharged his office and done the thing he had been sent to do." As Blanchet wrote, he thought he had found the Strait of Anian and the passage into the North Sea.[236]

And though not proof but maritime oral history printed later, as Crosse put it magically, the statistical probability of Juan de Fuca correctly describing the location of his rock, the San Juan Islands and the open water beyond, if he had not been here, is no more improbable than winning the triple exactor at Hastings Racecourse in Vancouver.

Norman Hacking, venerable marine editor of the *Vancouver Province* and a noted historian himself, wrote, "Historians have been arguing for centuries as to whether Juan de Fuca ever existed. The Mexican and Spanish archives, which are very full of the early explorations, make no mention of his existence. If his voyage was invented, as many were in those early days, somebody did some remarkably good guesswork in placing the strait at almost its exact location." Hacking has a point, and he concludes this way: "Whether or not the old Greek ever existed, he has the credit for discovering the entrance to our inland sea as long ago as 1592, and nobody will begrudge him the honor."[237]

From the far distant margins of continent and country, as also from interior recesses, even places of exile and loneliness, come details of the past that enrich the larger narrative of our histories. This is why Juan de Fuca's tale takes its rightful place, and this, too, is why those quests by mariners in days now long ago deserve our attention. They deepen our humanity in the telling and the reading. They call out to us still.

Epilogue

TO THE TOTEM SHORE AND BEYOND:
A HISTORIAN'S ODYSSEY

*I*n 2005, on the occasion of the bicentenary of the Battle of Trafalgar—fought by the fleet of Britain's Royal Navy, under the command of Horatio Nelson, against the Combined Fleet of France and Spain—a cluster of scholars and learned commentators gathered in the town of Cabra, Córdoba, Spain, under the auspices of the local cultural association and its partners to celebrate the life of Dionisio Alcalá Galiano.

That famous navigator and explorer, a master of the advanced astronomy of his times and the senior officer who conducted the Spanish explorations of the Strait of Juan de Fuca and inland waters leading to the north end of Vancouver Island in 1792, had fallen at Trafalgar when in command of the 74-gun ship of the line *Bahama*. His had been a notable life, and a cultural association of his hometown had been established that same year, 2005, to pay homage to its most famous son. A suitably worded plaque was unveiled at the door of the family townhouse where he was born. A Mass was said in his honour. An artillery band paraded the national colours. A great display of ship models was provided by the Spanish navy and the naval leagues. Photographic and cartographic treasures were on display, including a great map of the Estreco de Juan de Fuca. Drawings of First Nations of the Northwest Coast were prominently shown, as was the handsome portrait of the great sailor. Books and articles were on exhibit too, emblematic of those times and how Spanish voyages have been portrayed down the years. It was a time of celebration and a rare chance to pay tribute to the past.

When I told friends at home in Canada that I had accepted an invitation to speak at a conference to the memory of Alcalá Galiano, who died at Trafalgar, more than one reply shot my way was "Why would the Spanish want to remember Trafalgar? They lost!" My explanation to the uninitiated in the nuances of history was simply, "They were participants in one of the greatest battles of history. They want to acknowledge it."

I had been brought in from half a world away to tell the Spanish about their native son's contributions as a surveyor and explorer in 1792—more particularly, how he had cooperated with his British naval opposite, Captain George Vancouver, and how he had been the first to circumnavigate Vancouver Island (though not the first to complete the inland navigation, Vancouver's triumph).

The whole comprised the sort of story a historian loves to tell. But how to gauge my audience? That was the trick. Those who read early history in my native part of the world, British Columbia, or in the nearby United States may know some of the details of voyaging those little-known waters in those distant days in surprisingly small vessels. But my audience, as I assumed correctly, had no such knowledge of these events on what was to them a faraway shore. What they knew about was the heroic death of the person most famous in their town's past. I therefore had to be the storyteller of a voyage of discovery that had passed into the fog banks of memory, if ever known there. Here was a chance to pay tribute to the close connections of Canada and Spain, allies in NATO, and I took pains to steer clear of the bitter episode of 1995, when the Spanish fishing trawler *Estai*, working within the margins of our 200-mile inshore limit on the Grand Banks, poaching fish, was seized by Canadian authorities—much to the indignation of the government of Spain. I was relieved when no one in the audience asked me about it.

I took my listeners on a crash course in Northwest Coast history, featuring the Spanish voyagers and ships from Juan Pérez, who arrived off the entrance of Nootka Sound in 1774, all the way through to Malaspina's notable scientific expedition of 1791. All this, however, was a mere warm-up for the story of the local hero, Alcalá Galiano, and the expedition that he led in those unimaginably small schooners *Sutil* and *Mexicana*. I praised his skills as an astronomer, navigator and surveyor. I lauded his discoveries.

I explained the circumstances of his meeting with Captain Vancouver and his cooperation with him. With his voyage in 1792, the Spanish effectively ended their voyages of inquiry and science on the Northwest Coast, though other ships came to Nootka when the Spanish dismantled their establishment there, recognized the right of the British to be there and left the location to the First Nations. Thus closed the chapter of Spanish expansion on the Northwest Coast, when imperial overstretch caught up with the Iberian kingdom and, at the same time, the Spanish Crown showed declining interest in these northern latitudes and lands.

I could not in all conscience avoid discussion of the Spanish relations with the First Nations of Vancouver Island's west coast (principally Moachat and Muchalat and, to the south of Nootka, the Clayoquot). Generally, harmony had reigned in cross-cultural relations. But there had been reprehensible and violent incidents, even deaths.[238] The "contact," I explained to my Spanish audience, was neither benign nor indifferent; in fact, it was marred by the killing of the chief Callicum. But, as I took pains to explain, Francisco de Eliza, the senior officer and commandant, was past master at good relations, and his colleague Don Pedro Alberni, the captain of the Catalonian Volunteers, composed lyrics, set to the popular Andalusian folk song "El Marabú," that contained these flattering and soothing words, which attracted the otherwise hostile and revengeful Maquinna: "Macuina, Macuina, Macuina/ Asco Tais hua-cás;/ España, España, España/ Hua-cás Macuina Nutka." This translates, in effect, "Maquinna is a great prince and friend of ours; Spain, Spain, Spain is the friend of Maquinna and Nootka." Alberni taught his troops to sing it.

It was a charming, effective stratagem. Taking in the scene was José Moziño, the botanist-naturalist. In his treasured account—would that we had many more like his (but, sadly, do not)—he professed to the Natives' singular affection for Alberni. The same went for the Spanish generally. Moziño puts it this way in his *Noticias de Nutka*: "The memory of Senores Malaspina and Bustmante, [Alcalá] Galiano and Valdés, will be eternal in that nation for the friendly and generous manner in which they behaved during the short time they remained among its inhabitants." Maquinna had been assured by Commandante Eliza that "the land would revert to the First Nations as soon as the Spanish left and so that he could establish his village there, as had all of his ancestors and he himself had done during the first years of his government."[239] And indeed that is what happened:

three years after Alcalá Galiano sailed away on other assignments, the Spanish legacy was but a memory.

There were other details to explain to my Spanish audience: the reasons why the Spanish had gone to Nootka in the first place—so as to keep the Russians out—and how they had unexpectedly found the British. There was need to speak of the cluster of buildings they had thrown up at Nootka, which boasted 200 residents in 1791; the British response to Spanish seizure of ships and shore establishment, and the arrival of Alcalá Galiano on this scene in that intense summer of 1792. I had to wrap my story in the politics of the time. I recounted the background of Malaspina's incarceration in a jail in Coruña,[240] and explained how the voyage account of Alcalá Galiano and Valdés had been released in 1802. Had that account never been published—and a most truncated and massaged account it was—Alcalá Galiano's northwestern explorations would hardly be known.

Then my story took on a more urgent tone as it passed to the stirring events of Trafalgar. On 8 October a council of war, comprising seven French and six Spanish officers, was held on board the French flagship *Bucentaure*. Admiral Pierre Villeneuve, with two flag officers, one of whom was Magon, and a bevy of French captains faced Admiral Frederico

Captain Vancouver's ships seeking the limits of upper Juan de Fuca Strait in 1792, near Desolation Sound. Here, against the magnificent panorama of the Northwest Coast's inner waters, the *Chatham* leads the *Discovery* into largely unknown waters. OIL PAINTING BY THE AUTHOR'S FATHER JOHN GOUGH, 1978. PRIVATE COLLECTION.

Gravina and his flag officers, plus the two senior Spanish commodores. One of them was Churruca, the other Alcalá Galiano.

The French admiral opened proceedings. He stated that in his view the Combined Fleet should set to sea as soon as convenient. The Spanish objected; in their opinion, delay favoured the Combined Fleet. They argued that Nelson's fleet could not maintain station for much longer for want of supplies. Besides, the Spanish levies for the strengthening of the fleet needed further training. These were sensible viewpoints. But the insensitive Admiral Magon used a phrase damaging to Spanish susceptibilities, one which seemed to convey a slight to the honour of the Spanish officers. "The suggestion instantly provoked a scene. One of the Spaniards, Commodore Galiano, leapt angrily to his feet. He laid his hand on his sword-hilt, and with flashing eyes turned on the French rear admiral as though about to offer him personal violence. Only with great difficulty, it is said, was Galiano kept back from challenging Magon to a duel on the spot."[241] The Spanish had many reasons to despise the French at this time, not least because Napoleon had made Spain almost a vassal state, and French coffers, museums and galleries were being enriched at Iberian expense.

Of the battle and its results the Spanish chose their words carefully. The official dispatch on the events of the naval battle, written from Cadiz by Rear Admiral Antonio de Elcano, Admiral of the Ocean Fleet, and published in *Gaceta de Madrid* on 5 November 1805, reported in mournful explanation that "All our endeavour and heroic unconcern for our own lives did not prove sufficient to prevent our sustaining losses which would have been overwhelming had we not been convinced to a man that there was nothing more we could do and so come off with honour unscathed." The Admiral's heart was full of sadness. The Spanish vessels had known the evening before of the enemy ships, eighteen in all, ranged in line of battle; accordingly, the Spanish had suggested to Villeneuve, the senior commander, that they likewise form a line of battle. This had been agreed to. But then the enemy had fallen off to leeward and drawn into two separate lines, and Villeneuve had ordered an immediate wheel, leaving Captain Gravina's observation squadron, in which Alcalá Galiano's *Bahama* was, to follow as best it could. Once again Villeneuve ordered the resumption of course.

At eight minutes to twelve in the morning, the British three-decker

Victory, Nelson's flagship, with pennant flying at the topmast, cut the Combined Fleet's line at the centre, with the support of various ships following at her stern. The lead vessel of each enemy column did likewise and passed round the stern of a French or Spanish ship.

The results were as cataclysmic as they were unexpected. The sad Spanish report continued: "From that moment on, the action was restricted to particular encounters, ship to ship, of a very bloody nature, and the greater part of them carried on by an exchange of pistol-fire. This between the whole of the enemy fleet and but half of our own, with the inevitable consequent boarding of some ships."

In fact, Nelson used a hitherto untried tactic, though it was well known to "the band of brothers" who were his captains. The effect was lethal, for many of the French vessels were literally out of the action, ahead of the line, while the British doubled up, as it were, on those in the rear. The individual ship losses could not be described in detail, nor could the doubling back of the ships in the van aid those under attack. All was too little, too late. "What I certainly can assure Your Excellency," the report concluded, "is that every single vessel that it could see, be it French or Spanish, carried out its duty to the full in battle, and that this ship, after engaging three or four of the enemy in horrifying combat, was relieved just in time, all her rigging in shreds, her stays cut adrift, and in a sorry plight, her masts and her mainmast riddled by shot and quite unable to sail . . . Commander Cayetano Valdés lies gravely wounded from three balls he caught during the battle, as does Captain Ignacio María de Alava. The English have also suffered important losses in the battle, during the course of which Lord Nelson and other officers of distinction perished, according to a report from Gibraltar." So ended the sad commentary.

The warm and languid evening was drawing on, challenging enough for a lecturer, but from the podium I could sense a stir in my Cabra audience, the locals wanting to hear what I had to say of their natal hero. After all, the death of Alcalá Galiano had been a headline story in *El Pais*, in the edition of 21 October 1905. What about his status in 2005? Had it faded, become tarnished with the passing of the years? They had only a brief time to wait, and I did not intend to disappoint.

I took my cue from the classic account. "Galiano," wrote the great narrator Benito Pérez Galdós in 1905, "reviewed the crew at noon, went round the gun-decks, and made the officers an address: 'Gentlemen,' he said, 'you all know that our flag is nailed to the mast. I charge you to defend it.' Turning to the marine infantry captain, Don Alsonso Butron, he said: 'No Galiano ever surrenders, and no Butron should either.'"

A rousing Spanish cheer went up in the Cabra Theatre at that point. Perhaps I should have expected it, but I didn't and was not playing to the crowd in its anticipation. In thousands of lectures I had given, never, to that point in time, had a cheer been issued—and with such passion. Some deep but hitherto well-restrained Spanish passions had been boiling in anticipation of my words. I did not disappoint, and it spoke to me of Spanish patriotism and pride.

In the event, the *Bahama* had first encountered the enemy's *Bellerophon* and then the *Colossus*, both of equal power in guns. The British proved formidable foes in gunnery and in close combat. It is said that the Spanish sailors, following the word and example of their leader, put up a stubborn defence, overcoming some deficiencies of training. The circumstances facing *Bahama* were chaotic and unrelenting. The enemy riddled the ship with broadside to port and to starboard. Officers and men displayed highest courage in the face of overwhelming odds.

About three in the afternoon, standing on the quarterdeck, telescope in hand, Alcalá Galiano was observing the chaos of a deteriorating situation. A strong wind passed by, and then the strong breath of a cannon ball, staggering him, causing him to lose his telescope, which flew to the deck. He fell, with a bruise to one foot and a splinter to the head, and with it a deep gash. He fought on, declining to see a surgeon. A coxswain came to his rescue but turned out to be the object of a cannon ball, which cut him in two, covering Alcalá Galiano in blood. A second ball struck the Commodore, knocking him down and taking part of his head away. "Un Galiano sabi morir, pero no rendirse" were his last words—"A Galiano knows how to die but not surrender."[242] His body was covered with a flag so as to show the crew that the commodore was dead, and the officers and men soon faced the inevitable surrender. The nailed flag was stripped down and a British Jack put in its place. The *Bahama's* fight ended, and soon a lieutenant from the *Colossus* came on board to take formal possession. Of the 690 officers and men, 75 were killed and 67 wounded, and it is recorded that the moment when Alcalá Galiano fell was the turning point in available resistance.

His name stands high in the naval annals of Spain, his fame as a fighter far ahead of his renown as a scientific navigator. "El inclito Galiano," the fallen, heroic one, is how he is remembered in the present Armada of Spain. Perhaps he could imagine the outcome of this battle, fought against fearful odds. But would it be false to imagine that he could foresee his own death? He was trained for combat, and national honour dictated all, besides his own fealty to the idea of an immortal memory. The heroic age of which he was a part holds no equal nowadays, and the true glory stood before him in undeniable clarity.

"His only mistake," says Donald Cutter, in sympathy for Alcalá Galiano, "was to be a martyr on the losing side." This is so. For had he been in Nelson's position, a martyr on the winning side, he would have been vaulted into international fame. "But midshipmen in the naval academies of Spain know of Dionisio Alcalá Galiano as one of the great figures of the Spanish navy, commanding one of the ships of the line in the most famous battle of modern history—the last great battle of the age of sail. At Trafalgar Alcalá Galiano got his head shot off; not much fun, but it makes you a rather impressive martyr."[243]

As for Cayetano Valdés, who had sailed the Northwest Coast on discoveries with Alcalá Galiano in 1792—"El intrepido Valdés"—he fought to the end at Trafalgar, the last Spaniard to surrender. Neither able to fight nor fly away, he ordered the flag struck aboard his ship *Neptuno*. Valdés was to become a very important man: when there was an attempt to replace Fernando VII, Valdés was one of three men who controlled the government. He paid twenty years in exile for that, in England, and that on top of ten years in prison in Alicante. It is said that Valdés would have been released had he begged the royal pardon, but that the great sailor would not do, and rather than face death, England was the last resort.[244]

Cayetano Valdés commanded the *Mexicana* on the circumnavigation of Vancouver Island. He later led a tumultuous naval career due to the political upheavals of Spain. MUSEO NAVAL

Thus ended my Cabra excursion, an interesting inversion of the Alcalá Galiano story from the point of view of Northwest Coast historians, for whereas in North America we know about his work as a navigator and surveyor of Northwest Coast waters, we know little or nothing of his death as a fighting sailor at Trafalgar—exactly the reverse of what the Spanish know of our coast history, or, for that matter, of Alcalá Galiano as a surveying explorer! Why this great gap of understanding?

A series of conferences on the Spanish theme has enriched our appreciation of the work of Malaspina, Alcalá Galiano, Quimper and many others. Spain's Pacific horizons of cultural diplomacy have similarly broadened. The Spanish government and its associated ministries, notably of Culture and Defense, and the Spanish Association for Canadian Studies have been strong proponents of advancing the cause. Expo '86, held in Vancouver, was the initial in-Canada enterprise, the first flowering of great expositions devoted to the theme. The exhibition was titled *To the Totem Shore*, and a brilliant catalogue, with learned commentary included, was published, in which some of the great artistic drawings of the age of discovery on the Northwest Coast appeared for the first time. To my understanding, this was also the first time Spanish artistic treasures of the Northwest Coast from the voyage of 1792 had been placed on display for a global audience. The Australian bicentenary was another Spanish opportunity, this time for South Pacific disclosures. Then along came the Quintocentenario, the five-hundred-year anniversary of Columbus's first voyage, and thus was born, for the Northwest Coast, *Nutka 1792*, a beautiful catalogue published in Spanish and English editions. Conferences on Pacific voyaging yielded similarly resplendent catalogues—showcases, as it were, of history, anthropology, botany and much else.

While the Spanish were carefully telling their story from the point of view of official disclosure, other forces were gathering public attention in an example of what we can call "the politics of history." In the lead-up to 1992, there was much spilt ink about the Columbus discovery of America; some writers irresponsibly talked about "stolen continents" and much else, all in the space of a single volume! Others talked of five hundred years of genocide in the Americas. These simplistic themes and appreciations are well known and they play to the uninformed and the gullible. The Spanish made no apologies and struck the Spain '92 Foundation to aid informed scholarship and counteract the volatile. New journals sprang up, including

IDEAS '92, from the Iberian Studies Institute in Florida, to which I contributed, for the Spring 1991 issue, its sole Canadian content, "The Chains of History: Canada, 1992 and Christopher Columbus."[245] It was my call for Canada to learn more Spanish history in the Canadian context and to use the discovery theme not as a rant against Spain, Columbus or Europe generally, but to explore the interface of cultures and so take from the encounter a greater appreciation of the complexities of White-First Nations interaction in Canada, beginning with the French.

By this time I had a good deal of anthropology and ethnology under my belt, having had to prepare myself in these fields for the writing of my book *Gunboat Frontier: British Maritime Authority and Northwest Coast Indians, 1846–1890* (UBC Press, 1984), arguably the most complicated work I have crafted and one of my favourites. Moreover, I was at this time teaching Canadian First Nations history, among the first lecturers to do so in Canada, with a goodly quotient of Inuit and Métis material in a decidedly Indian-dominated curriculum. With colleagues in Ontario I had founded the Laurier Conference on Ethnohistory, and with help from the Museum of Civilization, Ottawa, and the university, multi-authored publications appeared. I could not, in all conscience, let the attention-seeking critics of Columbus go unaccounted for, because you cannot reverse the course of history. It has its own dynamics even if it does not have its own logic. By blaming Columbus you actually take the story away from the indigenes, whose histories deserve more than rants and postulations.

At a conference in Spain that same year of 1992—held like a travelling circus in Madrid, Cadiz and Seville (site of that year's World's Fair), with side trips to Valladolid, Salamanca and other high points of the age of Ferdinand and Isabella, and a glance at El Escorial, Philip II's monastery-like centre of imperial administration, north of Madrid—I got a chance to see the insides of academies and institutes where formality of an earlier age still rules and where continuity from the eighteenth century to our own times persists. In one academy the fellows wore flowing robes of yesteryear's design, and membership was of the highest honour. Among the members was our hostess, Mercedes Blanco Palau, who for this conference and for many others since has been the prime mover in promoting Spain's cultural expansion overseas. Her work has been parallelled by directors and staff of the Museo Naval. In my spare time I visited Colon Square, Madrid, the memorial to Christopher Columbus, and was as surprised as

I was delighted to find carved in stone the name of every known sailor who had sailed in the *Nina*, *Pinta* and *Santa Maria*. Each had taken a place in history. Their names are not forgotten. Then as now, I wondered if Cartier's or Cabot's sailors have been memorialized somewhere. I think not, and their names are sadly lost to history.

Back in Vancouver that same year, at Simon Fraser University's urban campus, we took pains to discuss George Vancouver's 1792–1795 voyage. There were new twists given to the story: details of chronometers used and error factors of same, discussion of surveying practices, viewpoints about the Nootka First Nations, and side glances at Alexander Mackenzie, plus some comparative perspectives on the Spanish on the coast at the same time. As much as the planners might have wished this to be more of a Spanish theme, it could not, for the George Vancouver story will always be central to the history of the Northwest Coast, and in Washington and Oregon and Alaska the Americans were making plans to salute him that same year. The Vancouver Maritime Museum put on an exposition, and a very fine one it was, except for the fact that the local press, always wanting to put a political twist on a historical subject, railed against Vancouver as a misguided imperialist and the brunt of jokes back home in Georgian England.[246] Later I learned a golden rule: never rely on newspapers for history.

Just as the backstory of Alcalá Galiano is his gallant death at Trafalgar, so that of George Vancouver lies back in the streets of London and his last days in Petersham, Surrey. It seems useful to recount some of the details here, because they help to explain how difficult it is for the historian to complete the account without reference to the side-stories, which sometimes seem arcane but which, willy nilly, form part of the whole.

George Vancouver would dearly have loved to fight in the naval battles leading up to, and perhaps past, Trafalgar. But his last years consisted of one problem after another. Declining health prohibited any seagoing appointment, even though he had been posted to the rank of Captain before his return to England. Vancouver was a marked man politically. He had had a quarrel with Archibald Menzies concerning the Admiralty's requirement that all journals kept on board the voyage of discovery be handed over. Menzies argued that he was answerable to Sir Joseph Banks of the Royal Society, his patron. Vancouver won on this point, but not before senior political figures in London learned about the squabble. Then there was the dispute with Lord Camelford, young Thomas Pitt, whom Vancouver had sent home for conduct unbecoming. Camelford was kin to the powerful Whigs of the day, the Pitts and the Grenvilles. The irascible Camelford took his cane to George Vancouver in Conduit Street, Mayfair, and the satirist James Gillray made great work of it. Vancouver inescapably bore the brunt of the joke. He also made a claim for a ship captured from the enemy near St. Helena and got no prize money for that on grounds of a disputed rival claim. He had to fight tooth and nail to get money to pay for the engraving of his charts and even had to put up the money for the publication of his *Voyage of Discovery*.

No wonder he was a beaten man, old before his time, riddled with illnesses, tired of lonely command and distant voyaging. The First Lord of the Admiralty, the indolent Lord Chatham, a relation of the prime minister, would not respond to his written entreaties. And thus it was that Vancouver died, age forty, forgotten and neglected, even the anti-hero according to some who sailed with him.

But his lasting testament was his *Voyage of Discovery*, published in three volumes plus an atlas, in 1798. The record of discoveries prompted the French and the Spanish to produce something that might rival Vancouver's book, but to no avail. The account of the Alcalá Galiano and Cayetano Valdés voyage to the Strait of Juan de Fuca and beyond was written by a third party and was a feeble response, in my opinion, to Vancouver's great account. It would take two centuries for the Spanish side of the story to be told by the likes of Warren Cook, Donald Cutter, Jim McDowell, Jack Kendrick, Iris Higbie Wilson Engstrand, Freeman Tovell, Christon Archer and Robin Inglis. We are in their debt, and so are the Spanish. The early modern history of the Northwest Coast could not be properly written without the accounts, journals and letters of those engaged in the expedition of George Vancouver.

As for myself, the voyage in the discovery of history continues, seeking always to make sense of the past and, more, to explain it to the reader as best I can. The pleasant work is fuelled by memory as much as it is done to satisfy curiosity. In and out of my local waters had flowed the tides of empires on ceaseless change. The Strait of Juan de Fuca has held the destiny of nations in its ebb and flow. From its portal the waters extend and open out to the ends of the earth.

Visions of the great ships of yesterday pass by my window. One by one they pass through Juan de Fuca's strait. Here she comes now, Vancouver's elegant *Discovery* on exploration, accompanied by Broughton's strangely tubby *Chatham*. They are followed by Alcalá Galiano's remarkably small *Sutil* and Cayetano Valdés' *Mexicana*.

But wait a minute: only forty years or so after, a smoke-belching steamer comes into view, rounding Cape Flattery rather effortlessly, heading purposefully against tides and currents for Puget Sound and Fort Nisqually. This is the Hudson's Bay Company's *Beaver*. Out of the fog bank comes the barque *Harpooner* with supplies and mine workers and men for business and for the land. In 1850 the British paddlewheel sloop *Driver* is seen bringing a young lawyer, Richard Blanshard, to take up the governorship of the young Vancouver Island colony. The *Tynemouth* and other bride-ships will leave from London, and a hundred marriageable women will step onto the settlement's docks. During the Fraser River gold rush and the occupation of the San Juan Islands by the United States Army, the three-decker *Ganges*, a British ship of the line, built in Bombay of teak, enters Esquimalt under sail. This place Rear Admiral Robert Lambert Baynes, echoing its Spanish discoverers, finds glorious and suitable for a naval base,

A second phase of hydrographic survey: HMS *Plumper* and Captain G.H. Richards, in Port Harvey, Johnstone Strait, with survey boats. Working the inlets and passages and taking numberless measurements was long, hard work; the resulting charts are arguably the greatest legacy of the British tide of empire. FROM *BRITISH COLUMBIA: A PICTORIAL RECORD, 1778–1891*

which it becomes, not long afterward—a British anchor of empire in the North Pacific. Captain George Henry Richards, heading a diligent team of six surveyors, has charted the turbulent waters from Cape Flattery right through to the Strait of Georgia on both the Vancouver Island and continental shores, and has even marked the Fraser River for safe navigation up to New Westminster, the newly sited capital of the Colony of British Columbia.

Now the vessels come in increasing number and in greater tonnage. The United States and Royal Navy send some of their largest battleships. The Canadian Pacific Railway develops a trans-Pacific service, and the romance of steam is now in full view as the sleek *Empress of Japan* speeds for Yokohama with mail and passengers and a mixed cargo from the new railhead port of Vancouver. Inbound cargoes of tea and porcelain from the exotic East arrive, and, in the steerage class, Chinese and Japanese on indenture or other permit.

Back and forth, despite the triumph of steam navigation, the sailing ships still pass on their peaceful occasions. There goes the *Ardnamurchan*, a typical steel carrier, working out through the interminably long strait with a cargo of lumber recently loaded at Port Blakely, Washington. And lo and behold, from her Victoria home port, there's the old *Thermopylae*, fastest of the clippers and famous for beating her rival, the *Cutty Sark*, in a race home to London from Shanghai, with tea. There sails HMS *Herald* to western Arctic waters to search for Sir John Franklin. There goes the old whaler *Karluk*, to serve Stefannson in the Canadian Arctic Expedition, and here, inbound, comes the *St. Roch*, fresh from a return transit of the Northwest Passage.

In May 1901 the Indian canoe *Tilikum* is seen working down the strait toward open ocean under sail but driven to the lee shore of Vancouver Island's hard coast. Now out of view, we imagine her finally escaping the clutches of the storms, tides and currents off Cape Flattery with destination London, then home again by curious circumstances on the deck of an ocean tramp. Others are not so lucky: the American steamer *Pacific*, past her prime and loaded with Victoria passengers, sinks with catastrophic losses, and later the British naval corvette *Condor* disappears with all hands.

Now the big ones steam into view. The mighty British battle cruiser *Hood* arrives as an exhibit of British naval might in 1923; in 1940 she will be sunk in the famous action with the *Bismarck* and *Prinz Eugen*. In 1942 the massive liner *Queen Elizabeth* ghosts into Esquimalt Graving Dock for upgrades as a troopship—her existence kept secret, a gang of Victoria High School lads pressed into work parties—then departs urgently on a wartime mission, the fates of democracy hanging in the balance. The British super dreadnought *Warspite*, veteran of Jutland, refitted recently in a Puget Sound yard, heads out to become flagship of the British Eastern Fleet near war's end. There she passes, under tow, the battleship USS *Missouri*, destination Pearl Harbor as the United States Naval Memorial; the signing of the Japanese surrender in 1945 took place on her decks.

The grey, armed ships continue their transits, en route to Korea or Vietnam, taking the military power of the American continent to the Far East, returning battle-hardened. The smart, brightly coloured P & O liners like the *Orsova* and *Oronsay*, links of Empire shipping, come and go and then suddenly disappear from our waters. All the while, and for three generations, Canadian Pacific steamers toil on passage to and from Seattle and Vancouver, sometimes crossing to Port Angeles, and are, sadly, no more. Meantime, the Black Ball Line's MV *Coho* outlives them all and still bridges the strait, linking communities on both side of the watery divide, a reminder of what we have in common and hold dear.

Acting by stealth and never seen by us, the Trident nuclear-powered submarines of the United States Navy steal out and back from Puget Sound on silent patrol. They are the new bearers of Neptune's trident in an uncertain world. More than half a century ago, in 1958, USS *Nautilus* departs Seattle and exits the strait with a secret destination of the North Pole, under the icecap, then completes a history-making polar transit. Even to Jules Verne this would be heady stuff.

Now, and almost one an hour by my reckoning, the stupendous container ships parade past in designated sea lanes. They have carried the goods of Asia inbound. Now, in exchange, they freight the resources of North America outbound. It's the new reciprocity. In the endless succession of ships, Canada pours out its mineral wealth, its fossil fuels, its oil and natural gas, its wheat and its potash. The sea-otter trade of yesteryear has burgeoned into something quite beyond anyone's imaginings. And, if looked at from another angle, the northwest passage has been achieved at last—by rail across North America and from the portals that lead to and out of the Strait of Juan de Fuca.

Who knows what technological changes will come to the marine world or how the world's political and military shifts will unfold. But mark my words, the Strait of Juan de Fuca, growing in importance every day, will become a choke point of history. Their security will require every care by the nations who share its waters.

No longer on the margins of empires or the subject of inquisitive discoverers, the Strait of Juan de Fuca, like the English Channel, Suez Canal, the Straits of Gibraltar or Malacca Straits, takes its position as a great portal of the world, Canada's Pacific Gateway, and that of the United States as well.

The magic of the waterway is unsurpassed, and when we gaze on it the enchantment of the scene is unforgettable. Daily the view changes, with different shades of blue, green and grey, white and pink mixing in new profusion. Juan de Fuca would shake his head in disbelief if he could see it now. Perhaps, if he thought others would credit his story, the stalwart old pilot would give us a chance to tell what we know from our own times to him in his times, more than four long centuries ago. He reported the existence of one of the world's great waterways. It is worth a glass of ouzo to contemplate, especially with the snow-clad Mount Olympus in view or, to those who do business in great waters, the light at Cape Flattery flashing out its welcome though urgent warning.

ACKNOWLEDGEMENTS

*M*y inquisitiveness about the history of the waters that are the subject of this book dates from when I was a lad. Whether cruising with my father, John Gough, in his Monk-design *Klahanie* out of Canoe Cove, Sidney, or under canvas in the old Lightning out of the Royal Victoria Yacht Club, I learned much about tide-rips off Cadboro Bay, gushing waters powering through the sloughs of Guemes Channel, and the all-too-shallow waters of the eastern approaches to Puget Sound. The visual memory of my father sitting disconsolately on *Klahanie*'s foredeck while the mud flats surrounded the vessel, high and dry, for half a mile or more, at low tide, is not soon to be forgotten. For myself, I had to take greater care in reading the charts! The charts, Canadian and American, fascinated me, as did tide tables and weather forecasts. From Sooke to Quadra Island was my beat, with summertime explorations of Discovery and the Chatham Islands of particular memory, plus excursions in the San Juan Islands under steam or canvas. The way to university and home again was likewise by sea, and I first saw Vancouver city from a porthole. When asked why I got into maritime history, I have only this delightful answer: I sailed the waters and learned some of their secrets—and how to survive the perils. To my father I owe the greatest of gifts, and once again I pay tribute to his editorial skills, exhibited in my early books, notably *The Royal Navy and the Northwest Coast* (1971). It was my baptism in the literary world, the launch at the Vancouver Maritime Museum a most suitable venue. It was UBC Press's first book.

This present book has had many contributors for whose help, advice and criticism I express my gratitude and thanks. Over the decades the list of persons who have aided in my research and often answered my queries, from distant locations, has lengthened considerably. Because maritime research is global, I have had to press my inquiries in those places uniquely connected to the history of the Northwest Coast of North America. These are, in turn, the United Kingdom, Spain, the United States, Australia, New Zealand and Canada, particularly British Columbia. A long list of thanks would perhaps bore the reader, but I am particularly obligated to thank the staff of the National Archives, Kew, England, and of the National Maritime Museum, Greenwich. I also thank the Natural History Museum, Kensington, which houses a collection of Banks letters, and Cambridge University Library, which has the Board of Longitude papers. Once again it is a pleasure to thank the master and fellows of Churchill College Cambridge, the director and staff of the Scott Polar Research Institute, and the keepers of the British Library Manuscripts Division and Map Library for unfailing help during a time when methods of cataloguing have undertaken seismic shifts as we move toward the digital age. Those who keep the hydrographic records at Ministry of Defence (Navy) at Taunton, Somerset, as well as the staff at the London Library, and the library of the Athenaeum also deserve thanks. These are the chief places for the sources, English and Spanish, which are used in this book.

In Spain I have benefited from much advice from a generation of scholars and archivists who, partly in keeping with the push to make the Columbus Quintocentenario the beginning for an extension of historical inquiry that would embrace 1792, a key year in Nootka Sound and Northwest Coast history, have made Spanish naval history global. In particular, I thank the Museo Naval and the Ministerio de Asuntos Exteriores and particularly its Relaciones Culturales y Cientifícas department. A participant in a number of conferences and symposia in regards to 1492/1992, I travelled to such places as the Cadiz naval academy, the archives in Valladolid, and Coruña, where Malaspina was jailed for revolutionary ideas. Of unique connection was Alcalá Galiano, especially a chance to speak at the congress dedicated to his memory, and held in his home town of Cabra on the occasion of the bicentenary of his death at the battle of Trafalgar. For this, I thank the Asociación Cultural Dionisio Alcalá-Galiano.

In the United States, the Washington State Museum and Archives in Tacoma and the Oregon Historical Society library and archives in Portland have, as always, been of utility. The Bancroft Library, University of California Berkeley, and the Beinecke Rare Books Library, Yale University, have assisted my work.

In New Zealand, the Alexander Turnbull Library, Wellington, and in Australia, the National Archives, Canberra, and the Dixon Library, Sydney, New South Wales, house pertinent materials. In Canada, the National Archives in Ottawa keep excellent illustrations and maps.

But it is in my native British Columbia that I have been most blessed. Willard Ireland and W. Kaye Lamb backed my pursuits from the beginning, and Margaret Ormsby and Brian R.D. Smith gave me the opportunity in those distant days when I was a student at Point Grey. The British Columbia Archives in Victoria have been the polar star of my research voyaging for forty years and more: outward and progressive acquisitions have brought the world into its stacks and vaults. Hard-pressed librarians and archivists, weary under the importunate requests for genealogical data or ministerial requests, still found time to locate a recondite file or the rarest book. Likewise, the Maritime Museum of British Columbia, also in Victoria, and the Vancouver Maritime Museum—both have unheralded collections—have helped, as has Rare Books and Special Collections, the University of British Columbia, Vancouver.

My indebtedness to the many who have helped with this book would make a very long list indeed. But I wish to thank in the United Kingdom Michael Barritt, Andrew Cook, Andrew David, Eric Groves, the late David Quinn, who sparked my interest in the Lok and Juan de Fuca partnership, and Glyn Williams; in Spain, Leoncio Carretero Collado, Dolores Higueras, Luísa Martín-Merás, Mercedes Palau and Francisco Salamanca Moreno; in the United States, Donald Cutter, E.W. Geisecke and especially Greg Langdon; in Australia, Robert King; in Canada, Christon Archer, Norman Collingwood, Nicholas Doe, Derek Hayes, Robin Inglis, Grant Keddie, Michael Layland, Gary Little, Gary Mitchell, the late John E. (Ted) Roberts and the late Freeman Tovell, also Simon Robinson and Carrie Schmidt of the Vancouver Maritime Museum. For the loan of materials or for answers on specific and editorial points I wish to thank the late John Crosse, Kim Davies, Heather Harbord, Michael Harrison, Christopher Hyde, John Whittaker, Jean Wilson and Bill Wolferstan. My thanks and appreciation for his foreword are due to that master mariner Martyn Clark, who knows these seas as well as anyone and shares the zeal for maritime affairs.

The art of Steve Mayo, Gordon Miller and the late Hewitt Jackson graces these pages; permission to include their works here is acknowledged with gratitude.

In the development of this work the assistance of Camilla Turner is greatly appreciated. The skill and care taken by Audrey McClellan as editor deserves my enduring gratitude. In this new printing, matters in need of rectification have been attended to. Once again it is a pleasure to thank the team at Harbour Publishing for its care and dedication to the making of this book.

GLOSSARY

Spanish items are in italics.

adventure: A speculation in goods to be sold or bartered for profit; officers, pilots, and sailors were customarily allowed to carry on board small amounts of goods on their own account and to trade for native curiosities and other items of value

***boca*:** Inlet, mouth, entrance

brig: A two-masted, fully square-rigged vessel, with a fore-and-aft sail on the lower mainmast

brigantine: A two-masted, square-rigged vessel, differing from a brig in that it does not carry a square mainsail and has a square sail on the main topmast; fast vessels used for communications in the Spanish empire

cable: (a) Strong, thick rope to which the anchor is fastened; (b) Hawser used to hold a ship temporarily in a river or other haven, or in emergency; (c) Unit of measure that differs from country to country (in the Royal Navy it is equal to 100 fathoms or one tenth of a sea mile—approximately 200 yards or 185 metres) *canal*: Channel

capitán de fragata: Frigate captain

capitán de navío: Ship's captain

caravel/caravela: A generic term used for a one- to three-masted lateen-rigged craft—small, light and fast—used principally in coasting trades; in time they evolved into one of two types: (a) the two- and three-masted lateen-rigged caravel (*caravela latina*), with close-wind possibilities and able to ease into the wind; and (b) *caravela rotunda*, with a square rig on the fore and main (for running downwind) and a lateen mizzen, chiefly Portuguese and Spanish of the fifteenth and sixteenth centuries

carriage gun: A cannon set on a wheeled support

chronometer: A mechanical watch, used for determining time from one location to another, and thus longitude

commandante: Chief officer of a Spanish naval ship, regardless of rank

cutter: (a) A fore-and-aft-rigged, sharp-built vessel with a jib, forestaysail, mainsail, and single mast; (b) A medium-sized ship's boat

East Indiaman: A large, armed ship of about 400 tons or more, privately built, engaged in trade to the East Indies

ensenada: Inlet

entrada: Entrance, usually of a river

estreco: Strait or straits

fathom: A measure of six feet, used to describe the depth of water by taking soundings (a Spanish fathom was five and a half feet)

frigate: A fast cruising, ship-rigged, three-masted warship, with more than one sail per mast, carrying between twenty and forty-four guns on more than one deck

galley: A long vessel of war or trade using both sails and oars

gig: A light clinker-built boat carried by a warship and favoured by captains for their own use

goleta: Schooner

hawser: A large rope or small cable

heave down: To place a vessel on its side for caulking or repairing; also called "careen"

heave to: To bring a vessel's head to the wind and adjust the sails so it will remain stationary, or nearly so

ketch: A small vessel rigged with two masts set nearly where the two after masts would be set in a three-masted vessel, leaving a clear deck forward of the mainmast; the mizzen mast is set forward of the rudder

larboard: A word for port, the left side of a vessel facing forward, and preferred for helm orders (abandoned 1844)

latitude: Angular distance on a meridian (in degrees, minutes etc.), and measured north or south of the equator

league: A measure of distance of three nautical miles (five kilometres) or 3,041 fathoms (one fathom equals six feet)

lee: The direction away from the wind, or downwind, hence **lee shore** (the shore on which the wind is blowing and thus hazardous, notably in the face of strong or gale-force winds)

lieutenant: Most junior commissioned rank in the Royal Navy of the era

longitude: Angular distance east or west from a standard meridian, as that of Greenwich, to the meridian of any place, and now reckoned to 180° east or west

lugger: A small fishing or coasting vessel carrying one or more lugsails, four-sided sails attached to a yard that hangs obliquely on a mast and is hoisted and lowered with the sail

mast: An upright spar rising from the keel or deck of a ship and supporting the yards, booms and rigging

master: An officer in the Royal Navy by warrant (as opposed to royal commission), and responsible for piloting and sailing the vessel under the officer commanding; sometimes also ship's purser

midshipman: A candidate for commissioned rank in the Royal Navy; messed in the gunroom

nautical mile (or sea mile): Equivalent to 6,076 feet, or one minute of latitude; approximately 1.15 statute miles

pendant: Pennant, any of various nautical flags tapering to a point or swallowtail and used for identification or signalling

piloto: A rank in the Spanish navy, of three classes: *piloto piloto*=master, *pilotín*=master's mate, *práctico*=coastal pilot. They were institute-trained and not strictly considered members of the *marina de guerra*

pinnace: A warship's boat, usually with eight oars and carried on a man-of-war; also, a small ship or ship's boat, especially one used as a tender

port: To the left of the ship, when looking forward; thus, port side

privateer: An armed, privately owned vessel commissioned to cruise against the merchant shipping or warships of the enemy

pirate: A lawless person or vessel, sailing under a pirate flag; before changes to international law, acts of piracy were deemed acts against humanity and thus punished summarily by death

prize money: A part of the proceeds of a captured ship ("the prize") divided among the officers and men making the capture

puerto: Port or, sometimes, sound

quarter, to give: The clemency of not killing a defeated enemy

quarters: (a) The stern of a ship's sides; (b) Assigned stations or posts

rada: Roadstead, road or roads, an open anchorage

rigging: A general name for all ropes employed to support and work masts, yards, sails, and so forth

salida: Channel or strait

schooner: A fore-and-aft rigged vessel having two or more masts with a smaller sail on the foremast and with the mainmast stepped nearly amidships

ship rig, or ship: Technically speaking, a ship is a three-masted vessel, and **ship rig** is the arrangement of a vessel carrying eleven or twelve square sails on the masts, extending by yards, and also a number of fore-and-aft sails

sloop: A fore-and-aft rigged vessel with one mast and a single headsail

sloop of war: A vessel of war next in size to a frigate; also smaller than a corvette

snow: The largest two-masted vessel of the period; usually served as a merchant vessel

spar: A stout rounded piece of wood, used as a mast, boom, gaff, or yard, to support rigging

swivel gun: Small cannon fixed on a pivot

tack: (a) The direction of a ship with respect to the trim of the sails (a vessel is on the starboard tack when the wind strikes the starboard side, and on the port tack when the wind strikes the port side); (b) To change the direction of a vessel from one tack to another when close-hauled by bringing the head into the wind and causing it to fall off with the wind, by using the helm and sails

tender: A vessel sent to accompany, or attend, often as an insurance policy against disaster, a larger one while on trade or discoveries, and selected for shallow draft and economy of operation

teniente de navío: Lieutenant

viceroy: An executive position of administration in the Spanish empire, carrying viceregal authority in that jurisdiction, or viceroyalty

wear (as in "to wear ship"): To bring a ship on the other tack by bringing the wind around the stern; done unintentionally is "to gibe."

weigh: To raise the anchor

yawl: A ship's jolly boat with four or six oars, two-masted and rigged to carry fore-and-aft sails, the mizzen-mast stepped abaft the rudder post

SOURCES

The following is structured in such a way that the reader may consult works by types: Place Names, Atlases and Reference; Voyage Accounts, Pamphlets and Editions; Studies including Biographies.

Place Names, Atlases and Reference

Burney, James. *A Chronological History of North-Eastern Voyages of Discovery*. London: John Murray, 1819.

David, Andrew, ed. *The Charts and Coastal Views of Captain Cook's Voyages: The Voyage of the* Resolution *and* Discovery, *1776–1780*. Vol. 3, Hakluyt Society Extra Series. London: Hakluyt Society, 1997.

Griffes, Peter L. *Pacific Boating Almanac 2004. Vol. 1, Pacific Northwest*. Culver City, CA: Pacific Boating Almanac, 2004.

Harris, Cole, ed. *Historical Atlas of Canada. Vol. 1, From the Beginning to 1800*. Toronto: University of Toronto Press, 1987.

Hayes, Derek. *America Discovered: A Historical Atlas of North American Exploration*. Vancouver: Douglas & McIntyre, 2004.

———. *British Columbia: A New Historical Atlas*. Vancouver: Douglas & McIntyre, 2012.

———. *Historical Atlas of the North Pacific Ocean: Maps of Discovery and Scientific Exploration, 1500–2000*. Vancouver: Douglas & McIntyre, 2001.

Howay, F.W. *A List of Trading Vessels in the Maritime Fur Trade, 1785–1825*. Kingston, ON: Limestone, 1973.

Inglis, Robin. *Historical Dictionary of the Discovery and Exploration of the Northwest Coast of North America.* Lanham, MD: Scarecrow Press, 2008.

Litalien, Raymonde et al. *Mapping a Continent: Historical Atlas of North America, 1492–1814.* Montreal: McGill-Queen's University Press, 2007.

Little, C.H. *18th Century Maritime Influences on the History and Place Names of British Columbia.* Madrid: Editorial Naval/Museo Naval, 1991.

New, Donald. *Voyage of Discovery: Gulf Island Names and Their Origins.* Sidney, BC: Peninsula Printing, 1966.

Phillips, James W. *Washington State Place Names.* Seattle: University of Washington Press, 1971.

Quinn, David, ed. *The Hakluyt Handbook.* 2 vols. London: Hakluyt Society, 1974.

Scott, Andrew. *The Encyclopedia of Raincoast Place Names: A Complete Reference to Coastal British Columbia.* Madeira Park, BC: Harbour Publishing, 2009.

Scott, James W., and Roland L. De Lorme, *Historical Atlas of Washington.* Norman: University of Oklahoma Press, 1988.

Speake, Jennifer, ed. *Literature of Travel and Exploration: An Encyclopedia.* 3 vols. New York and London: Fitzroy Dearborn, 2003.

Strathern, Gloria. *Navigations, Traffiques & Discoveries 1774–1848: A Guide to Publications Relating to the Area now British Columbia.* Victoria: Social Sciences Research Centre, University of Victoria, 1970.

Suttles, Wayne, ed. *Handbook of North American Indians.* Vol. 7, *Northwest Coast.* Washington: Smithsonian Institution, 1990. Contains many unique studies, also comprehensive bibliography to date of publication.

Walbran, John T. *British Columbia Coast Names, 1592–1906, to Which are Added a few Names in Adjacent United States Territory: Their Origin and History.* 1909. Reprint, Vancouver: J.J. Douglas, 1971.

Voyage Accounts, Pamphlets and Editions

Anderson, Bern, ed. "The Vancouver Expedition: Peter Puget's Journal of the Exploration of Puget Sound, May 7–June 11, 1792." *Pacific Northwest Quarterly* 30 (April 1939): 195–205.

[Anon.] "Recollections of Six Months in Puget Sound." *Nautical Magazine* 21 (May–June 1852).

Baker, Simon. *The Ship: Retracing Cook's* Endeavour *Voyage.* London: BBC, 2002.

Barwick, G.F., English trans. *Viaje de las Goletas Sutil y Mexicana en el Año 1792 al Estrecho de Juan de Fuca.* Madrid, 1802. Typescript in the library of the Maritime Museum of BC, Victoria, British Columbia.

Beaglehole, John C., ed. *The Journals of Captain James Cook: The Voyage of the* Resolution *and* Discovery, *1776–1780.* 3 vols., volume 3 in 2 parts. Cambridge: Hakluyt Society, 1967.

Beals, Herbert, ed. *For Honor and Country: The Diary of Bruno De Hezeta.* Portland: Western Imprints/Oregon Historical Society, 1985.

Blanchet, M. Wylie. *The Curve of Time.* 1961. Reprint, North Vancouver: Whitecap Books, 1987.

Blumenthal, Richard W., ed. *The Early Exploration of Inland Washington Waters: Journals and Logs from Six Expeditions, 1786–1792.* Jefferson, NC: McFarland, 2004.

———, ed. *With Vancouver in Inland Washington Waters: Journals of 12 Crewmen, April–June 1792.* Jefferson, NC: McFarland, 2007.

Busch, Briton C., and Barry M. Gough, eds., *Fur Traders from New England: The Boston Men in the North Pacific. The Narratives of William Dane Phelps, William Sturgis & James Gilchrist Swan.* Spokane: Arthur H. Clark, 1997.

Craig, Hardin, Jr., ed. "A Letter from the Vancouver Expedition." *Pacific Northwest Quarterly* 41, 4 (October 1950).

Dalrymple, Alexander. *Plan for Promoting the Fur-Trade, and securing it to this Country, by uniting the Operations of the East India and Hudson's Bay Companies.* London, 1789.

Dampier, William. *A New Voyage Round the World.* Printed 1686.

David, Andrew et al., eds. *The Malaspina Expedition 1789–1794: The Journal of the Voyage by Alejandro Malaspina.* 3 vols. London: Hakluyt Society in association with Museo Naval Madrid, 2001–2005. The first English edition.

Donno, Elizabeth Story, ed. *An Elizabethan in 1582: The Diary of Richard Madox, Fellow of All Souls.* London: Hakluyt Society, 1976.

[Espinosa y Tello, José?] *Relación del Viaje hecho por las Goletas Sutil y Mexicana en el Año de 1792 para reconocer al Estrecho de Juan de Fuca.* Madrid, 1802. The first publication of this important account was wrongly attributed by some bibliographers to Alcalá Galiano, commander of the expedition. Fernández Navarette, who prepared the work for publication in 1802, states that Espinosa wrote the *Relación* and that he himself wrote the introduction. The former detail of attribution has been doubted. Beware further that the 1930 English edition, noted below as Cecil Jane, ed., *A Spanish Voyage to Vancouver and the North-West Coast . . .* , contains a truncated version of the Navarette introduction. The full version in English appears in the typescript version based on the translation from the Spanish by G.F. Barwick, former Keeper of Printed Works, British Library. A copy of this survives in the library of the Maritime Museum of BC, Victoria, British Columbia.

Flannery, Tim, ed. *The Life and Adventures of John Nicol, Mariner.* New York: Atlantic Monthly Press, 1997.

Forsyth, John, ed. "Documents Connected with the Final Settlement of the Nootka Dispute." *British Columbia Historical Federation Second Annual Report* (1924): 33–35.

Fuster Ruiz, Francisco. *El final del descubrimiento de América: California, Canadá y Alaska (1765–1822): aportación documental del Archivo General de la Marina.* Murcia: Servicio de Publicaciones, Universidad, 1998.

Galois, Robert, ed. *A Voyage to the North West Side of America: The Journals of James Colnett, 1786–89.* Vancouver: UBC Press, 2004.

Grant, W. Colquhoun. "Description of Vancouver Island, by its First Colonist." *Journal of the Royal Geographical Society* 27 (1857): 268–320.

Hakluyt, Richard. *Voyages and Discoveries.* Edited and abridged by Jack Beeching. Harmondsworth, Middlesex: Penguin Books, 1972.

Hill-Tout, Charles. *The Far West: The Home of the Salish and Dene.* London: Archibald Constable, 1907.

———. *The Salish People. Vol. 2, The Squamish and Lillooet.* Introduction by Ralph Maud. Vancouver: Talonbooks, 1978.

Howay, F.W., ed. *The Dixon-Meares Controversy.* Toronto: Ryerson, 1929.

———, ed. *The Journal of Captain James Colnett aboard the* Argonaut *from April 26, 1789 to Nov. 3, 1791.* Toronto: Champlain Society, 1940.

———, ed. *Voyages of the* Columbia *to the Northwest Coast 1787–1790 & 1790–1793.* 1941. Reprint, Portland: Oregon Historical Society Press, 1990.

James, Thomas. *The Dangerous Voyage of Capt. Thomas James, in his intended discovery of a North West Passage into the South Sea.* 2nd ed. London, 1740. This work was first published in 1633.

Jane, Cecil, ed. *A Spanish Voyage to Vancouver and the North-West Coast of America, being the Narrative of the Voyage made in the Year 1792 by the Schooners* Sutil *and* Mexicana *to Explore the Strait of Fuca.* London: Argonaut, 1930. See my note on page 249 in connection with Espinosa y Tello, José. *Relación del Viaje . . .*

Kaplanoff, Mark, ed. *Joseph Ingraham's Journal of the Brigantine "Hope" on a Voyage to the Northwest Coast of North America, 1790–92.* Barre, MA.: Imprint Society, 1971.

Kendrick, John, ed. *The Voyage of* Sutil *and* Mexicana *1792: The Last Spanish Exploration of the Northwest Coast of America.* Spokane: Arthur H. Clark, 1991.

Lamb, W. Kaye, ed. *George Vancouver: A Voyage of Discovery to the North Pacific Ocean and Round the World, 1791–1795.* 4 vols. London: Hakluyt Society, 1984.

———, ed. *The Journals and Letters of Sir Alexander Mackenzie.* Cambridge: Hakluyt Society, 1970.

———, ed. *Vancouver Discovers Vancouver: An Excerpt from the Rough Logs of Second Lieutenant Peter John Puget.* Burnaby: Vancouver Conference on Exploration and Discovery, Department of History, Simon Fraser University, 1989. From the original in the British Library.

Manby, Thomas. *Journal of the Voyages of the H.M.S.* Discovery *and* Chatham. Fairfield, WA: Ye Galleon Press, 1988.

McDermott, James, ed. *The Third Voyage of Martin Frobisher to Baffin Island 1578.* London: Hakluyt Society, 2001.

Meany, Edmond S., ed. *Vancouver's Discovery of Puget Sound: Portraits and Biographies of the Men Honored in the Naming of Geographic Features of Northwestern America.* New York: Macmillan, 1907.

Meares, John. *Voyages made in the Years 1788 and 1789 from China to the North West Coast of America.* London, 1790.

Mourelle, Francisco Antonio. *Voyage of the* Sonora *from the 1775 Journal.* 1920. Reprint, Fairfield, WA: Ye Galleon Press, 1987. Originally published by Daines Barrington, 1781.

Moziño, José Mariano. *Noticias de Nutka: An Account of Nootka Sound in 1792.* Translated and edited by Iris H. Wilson Engstrand, foreword by Richard Inglis. Seattle: University of Washington Press, 1991. The 1970 edition contains a foreword by Philip Drucker.

Newcombe, C.F., ed. *The First Circumnavigation of Vancouver Island.* Memoir 1. Victoria: Archives of British Columbia, 1914.

———, ed. *Menzies' Journal of Vancouver's Voyage April to October 1792.* Memoir 5. Victoria: Archives of British Columbia, 1923.

Nuttall, Zelia, ed. *New Light on Drake: A Collection of Documents Relating to His Voyage of Circumnavigation, 1577–1580.* London: Hakluyt Society, 1914.

Olson, Wallace M., ed. *Through Spanish Eyes: Spanish Voyages to Alaska, 1774–1792.* Auke Bay, AK: Heritage Research, 2002.

Purchas, Samuel. *Hakluytus Posthumus: or, Purchas His Pilgrimes.* 4 vols. London, 1625.

Quinn, David, ed. *Last Voyage of Thomas Cavendish, 1591–1592: The Autograph Manuscript of His Own Account of the Voyage, Written Shortly before His Death.* Chicago: University of Chicago Press, 1975.

Rundall, Thomas, ed. *Narratives of Voyages towards the North-West, in Search of a Passage to Cathay and India 1496 to 1632.* London: Hakluyt Society, 1849.

Smith, Derek G., ed. *The Adventures and Sufferings of John R. Jewitt, Captive Among the Nootka, 1803–1805.* Edinburgh, 1824. Reprint, Toronto: McClelland & Stewart, 1974.

Tovell, Freeman M., Robin Inglis, and Iris H. Wilson Engstrand, eds. *Voyage to the Northwest Coast of America, 1792: Juan Francisco de la Bodega y Quadra and the Nootka Sound Controversy.* Norman: University of Oklahoma Press, 2012.

Vancouver, George. *A Voyage of Discovery to the North Pacific Ocean and Round the World.* 3 vols. and atlas. London: C.J. and J. Robinson; J. Edwards, 1798.

Vaux, William S.W. *The World Encompassed by Sir Francis Drake, being his Next Voyage to that to Nombre de Dios: Francis Drake, Francis Fletcher.* London: Hakluyt Society, 1854. This text dates from 1628, three years after Purchas's publication of the Juan de Fuca account.

Wagner, Henry Raup, ed. *Spanish Explorations in the Strait of Juan de Fuca.* Santa Ana, CA: Fine Arts, 1933.

Wells, Richard E. *Calamity Harbour: The Voyages of the* Prince of Wales *and the* Princess Royal *on the British Columbia Coast, 1787–1788.* Sooke, BC: the author, 2002.

Wood, James. "Vancouver Island—British Columbia." *Nautical Magazine* 28 (December 1858).

Studies including Biographies

Archer, Christon I. "Retreat from the North: Spain's Withdrawal from Nootka Sound." *BC Studies* 18, 3 (1973): 19–36.

Arima, Eugene, and Alan Hoover. *The Whaling People of the West Coast of Vancouver Island and Cape Flattery.* Victoria: Royal BC Museum, 2011.

Bancroft, Hubert H. *History of the Northwest Coast.* 2 vols; San Francisco: History Press, 1886.

Bartroli, Tomas. "Discovery of the Site of Vancouver City: A Tentative Account." Unpublished text from 1986, with additions to 1988. Vancouver Maritime Museum. Important as a correction to some historical claims by Major J.S. Matthews.

———. *Genesis of Vancouver City: Explorations of its Site 1791, 1792 and 1808.* Rev. ed. Vancouver: Tomas Bartroli, 1997.

Bawlf, Samuel. *The Secret Voyage of Sir Francis Drake, 1577–1580.* New York: Walker & Co., 2003.

Bowen, Catherine Drinker. *The Lion and the Throne: The Life and Times of Sir Edward Coke (1552–1634).* Boston: Little, Brown, 1956.

Boyd, Robert T. *The Coming of the Spirit of Pestilence: Introduced Infectious Diseases and Population Decline among Northwest Coast Indians, 1774–1874.* Vancouver: UBC Press, 1999.

Clark, Robert. *River of the West: Stories from the Columbia.* New York: Picador USA, 1997.

Colson, Elizabeth. *The Makah Indians.* Manchester: Manchester University Press, 1953.

Cook, Warren L. *Flood Tide of Empire: Spain and the Pacific Northwest, 1543–1819.* New Haven, CT: Yale University Press, 1973.

Cooke, Alan. "Martin Frobisher." *Dictionary of Canadian Biography,* Vol. 1. Toronto: University of Toronto Press, 1966.

Crosse, John. "Honour Juan de Fuca Too." *Vancouver Sun,* 13 June 1972.

Cutter, Donald. "The Malaspina Expedition and Its Place in the History of the Pacific Northwest." In Inglis, *Spain and the North Pacific Coast.*

———. "Malaspina's Grand Expedition." *El Palacio: Quarterly Journal of the Museum of New Mexico* 82, 4 (Winter 1976): 28–41.

David, Andrew. "A Fresh Look at the Meeting of Dionisio Alcalá Galiano and George Vancouver and their Joint Survey." MS., 2006, Andrew David Archive.

Davies, K.G. *The North Atlantic World in the Seventeenth Century.* Minneapolis: University of Minnesota Press, 1974.

Deane, Philip. *The Land and Isles of Greece.* New York: Doubleday, 1966.

Dewhirst, John. "Nootka Sound, a 4,000 Year Perspective." In *"nu-tka: The History and Survival of Nootkan Culture,"* ed. Barbara S. Efrat and W.J. Langois, *Sound Heritage* 7, 2 (1978).

Doig, Ivan. *Winter Brothers.* New York: Harcourt Brace Jovanovich, 1980.

Downie, Mary Alice and Mary Hamilton. *"And Some Brought Flowers": Plants in the New World.* Markham, ON: Fitzhenry & Whiteside, 2002.

Drucker, Philip. "Northern and Central Nootkan Tribes." *Bureau of American Ethnology, Bulletin 144,* House Documents, vol. 49. Washington, DC: GPO, 1951.

Drury, Devon. "'That Immense and Dangerous Sea': Spanish Imperial Policy and Power During the Exploration of the Salish Sea, 1790–1791." Masters thesis, University of Victoria, 2010. Online at https://dspace.library.uvic.ca:8443//handle/1828/3007.

Dulles, Foster Rhea. *Eastward Ho! The First English Adventurers to the Orient—Richard Chancellor—Anthony Jenkinson—James Lancaster—William Adams—Sir Thomas Roe.* 1931. Reprint, Freeport, NY: Books for Libraries Press, 1969.

Durell, Lawrence. *The Greek Islands*. New York: Viking Press, 1978.

Fireman, Janet R. "The Seduction of George Vancouver: a Nootka Affair." *Pacific Historical Review* 56, 3 (August 1987): 427–43.

Fisher, Robin. *Vancouver's Voyage: Charting the Northwest Coast, 1791–1795*. Vancouver: Douglas & McIntyre, 1992.

Franks, Michael. *The Court, the Atlantic and the City: Sir Walter Ralegh v William Sanderson*. Mapledurwell, Hampshire, UK: South and West Books, 2009.

Fraser, Edward. *The Enemy at Trafalgar: Eye-Witness Narratives, Dispatches and Letters from the French and Spanish Fleets*. London: Chatham, 2004.

Fry, Howard T. *Alexander Dalrymple (1737–1808) and the Expansion of British Trade*. Toronto: University of Toronto Press, 1970.

Galdós, Benito Pérez. *Trafalgar*. 1905. Reprint, Madrid: Arlanza, 2005.

Gerhard, Peter. *Pirates on the West Coast of New Spain 1575–1742*. Glendale, CA: Arthur H. Clark, 1960.

Gibbs, James A. *Shipwrecks off Juan de Fuca*. Portland, OR: Binfords and Mort, 1968.

Glover, Richard. "Hudson Bay to the Orient." *The Beaver* 281 (December 1950): 47–51.

Gough, Barry. "The Chains of History: Canada, 1992 and Christopher Columbus." *IDEAS '92: A Journal to Honor 500 Years of Relations among Spain, Latin America and the United States* 8 (Spring 1991): 45–55.

———. *First across the Continent: Sir Alexander Mackenzie*. Norman: University of Oklahoma Press, and Toronto: McClelland & Stewart, 1997.

———. *Fortune's a River: The Collision of Empires in Northwest America*. Madeira Park, BC: Harbour Publishing, 2007.

———. "James Cook and the Origins of the Maritime Fur Trade." *American Neptune* 38, 3 (1978): 217–24.

———. *The Northwest Coast: British Navigation, Trade and Discoveries to 1812*. Vancouver: UBC Press, 1992.

Gunther, Erna. *Indian Life on the Northwest Coast of North America: As Seen by the Early Explorers and Fur Traders during the Last Decades of the Eighteenth Century*. Chicago: University of Chicago Press, 1972.

———. "Vancouver and the Indians of Puget Sound." *Pacific Northwest Quarterly* 51, 1 (January 1960): 1–12.

Hacking, Norman. "Capt. Cook Missed Entrance to Strait." *Vancouver Province*, 27 December 1961.

Hewson, J.G. *A History of the Practice of Navigation*. Rev. ed. Glasgow: Brown, Son & Ferguson, 1963.

Hogarth, D.D., P.W. Boreham, and J.G. Mitchell. *Mines, Minerals and Metallurgy: Martin Frobisher's Northwest Venture, 1576–1581.* Ottawa: Canadian Museum of Civilization, 1994.

Householder, Michael. *Inventing Americans in the Age of Discovery.* Farnham, Surrey, UK: Ashgate, 2011.

Howay, F.W. "Early Navigation of the Straits of Fuca." *Oregon Historical Quarterly* 12 (1911): 1–32.

Inglis, Robin, ed. *Spain and the North Pacific Coast: Essays in Recognition of the Bicentennial of the Malaspina Expedition, 1791–1792.* Vancouver: Vancouver Maritime Museum, 1992.

Kendrick, John. *Alejandro Malaspina: Portrait of a Visionary.* Montreal and Kingston: McGill–Queen's University Press, 1999.

———. *The Men with Wooden Feet: The Spanish Exploration of the Pacific Northwest.* Toronto: NC Press, 1986.

Kessell, John L. *Spain in the Southwest: A Narrative History of Colonial New Mexico, Arizona, Texas, and California.* Norman: University of Oklahoma Press, 2002.

Lamb, W. Kaye, ed. "The Mystery of Mrs. Barkley's Diary" and "Documents Relating to the Mystery of Mrs. Barkley's Diary." *British Columbia Historical Quarterly* 6, 1 (January 1942), 31–59.

Loades, David. *England's Maritime Empire: Seapower, Commerce and Policy 1490–1690.* Harlow: Longman, 2000.

Manning, William A. *The Nootka Sound Controversy.* 1905. Reprint, New York: Argonaut, 1966.

Mathes, W. Michael. "The Province of Anian and Its Strait: Myth, Reality, and Exploration of the Pacific Northwest, 1542–1792." Typescript prepared for the Vancouver Conference on Exploration and Discovery, Simon Fraser University, 1992.

McDowell, Jim. *José Narváez, The Forgotten Explorer: Including His Narrative of a Voyage on the Northwest Coast in 1788.* Spokane: Arthur H. Clark, 1998.

McMillan, Alan D. *Since the Time of the Transformers: The Ancient Heritage of the Nuu-chah-nulth, Ditidaht, and Makah.* Vancouver: UBC Press, 1999.

Morgan, Murray. *The Last Wilderness.* Seattle: University of Washington Press, 1976.

Morison, Samuel Eliot. *Admiral of the Ocean Sea: A Life of Christopher Columbus.* Boston: Little, Brown, 1942.

Navarette, Martín Fernández de. *Noticia histórica de las expediciones hechas por los Españoles . . . con el objeto de reconocer el Estrecho de Fuca.* Madrid: Imrenta Real, 1802. This, published separately, is the historical introduction some have attributed to José Espinosa y Tello, *Relación* (see "Voyage Accounts" section, above).

Nokes, J. Richard. *Almost a Hero: The Voyages of John Meares, R.N., to China, Hawaii and the Northwest Coast.* Pullman: Washington State University Press, 1998.

Obee, Bruce. "Welcome to the Salish Sea." *British Columbia Magazine* 53, 4 (Winter 2011): 44–53.

Oleson, Triggvi. *Early Voyages and Northern Approaches, 1000–1632.* 1963. Reprint, Toronto: McClelland and Stewart, 1968.

Perry, M. Eugenie. "When Frances Barkley Came." *Western Home Monthly,* (July 1929): 15, 45.

Poolman, Kenneth. *The* Speedwell *Voyage: A Tale of Piracy and Mutiny in the Eighteenth Century.* Annapolis: Naval Institute Press, 1999.

Quinn, David Beers. *England and the Discovery of America.* London: George Allen Unwin, 1974.

Ramírez, Tristán. "Historiografía: Amarga derrota: el Trafalgar de 1905." *La Aventura de la Historia* 85 (November 2005): 107–9.

Roberts, John E. *A Discovery Journal of George Vancouver's First Survey Season on the Coasts of Washington and British Columbia 1792 Including the work with the Spanish Explorers Galiano and Valdés.* Victoria: Trafford, 2005.

Robinson, Leigh Burpee. *Esquimalt "Place of Shoaling Waters."* Victoria: Quality, 1948.

Ruskin, John. *The Stones of Venice.* Edited by Jan Morris. London: Folio Society, 2001.

Schurz, William. *The Manila Galleon.* New York: Dutton, 1959.

Scott, James W. *Pacific Northwest Themes: Historical Essays in Honor of Keith A. Murray.* Bellingham: Center for Pacific Northwest Studies, Western Washington University, 1978.

Skelton, R.A. *Captain James Cook after Two Hundred Years.* London: British Museum, 1969.

Souhami, Diana. *Selkirk's Island.* London: Phoenix, 2002.

Spate, Oskar H.K. *The Pacific since Magellan. Vol. I, The Spanish Lake.* Canberra: Australian National University Press, 1979.

Swan, James G. *The Indians of Cape Flattery, at the Entrance to the Strait of Fuca, Washington Territory.* Washington, DC: Smithsonian Contributions to Knowledge, 1870.

Taylor, E.G.R. *Tudor Geography, 1485–1583.* London: Methuen, 1930.

Taylor, Herbert C., Jr. "Incident at 'La Punta de los Mártires.'" In James W. Scott, ed., *Pacific Northwest Themes: Historical Essays in Honor of Keith A. Murray*. Bellingham, WA: Center for Pacific Northwest Studies, Western Washington University, 1978, 35–42.

Thurman, Michael. *The Naval Department of San Blas: New Spain's Bastion for Alta California and Nootka, 1767–1798*. Glendale, CA: Arthur H. Clark, 1967.

Tovell, Freeman M. *At the Far Reaches of Empire: The Life of Juan Francisco de la Bodega y Quadra*. Vancouver: UBC Press, 2008.

Villiers, Alan. *Captain Cook, The Seamen's Seaman*. 1967. Reprint, London: Penguin Books, 2002.

Wagner, Henry Raup. "Apocryphal Voyages to the Northwest Coast of America." *Proceedings of the American Antiquarian Society* new series 41 (1931): 179–234. Juan de Fuca's account is reprinted, with commentary, 179–90.

Waters, David W. *The Art of Navigation in England in Elizabethan and Early Stuart Times*. London: Hollis and Carter, 1958.

Whitebrook, Robert Ballard. *Coastal Exploration of Washington*. Palo Alto, CA: Pacific Books: 1959.

Williams, Glyndwr. *The British Search for the Northwest Passage in the Eighteenth Century*. London: Longman, 1962.

———. *The Prize of All the Oceans: The Triumph and Tragedy of Anson's Voyage Round the World*. London: HarperCollins, 1999.

Williamson, James A. "Michael Lok." *Blackwood's Magazine* 196 (1914): 58–72.

NOTES

Introduction

1. Sources for the Introduction include the following: *British Columbia Pilot*, 2nd ed. (1898); *United States Coast Pilot: Pacific Coast, California, Oregon and Washington*, 3rd ed. (1917); Anon., "Recollections of Six Months in Puget Sound," *Nautical Magazine* 21 (May–June 1852); James Wood, "Vancouver Island—British Columbia," *Nautical Magazine* 28 (December 1858); James A. Gibbs, *Shipwrecks Off Juan de Fuca* (Portland: Binfords and Mort, 1968); and John T. Walbran, *British Columbia Coast Names, 1592–1906* (1909; repr., Vancouver: J.J. Douglas, 1971).

2. Peter L. Griffes, *Pacific Boating Almanac 2004, vol. 1: Pacific Northwest* (Culver City: Pacific Boating Almanac, 2004), 226; also "Columbia River to Strait of Juan De Fuca, Washington," chap. 11 of *United States Coast Pilot 7*, ed. 43 (2011), online at www.nauticalcharts. noaa.gov/nsd/xml2html.php?xml=coastpilot/files/cp7/11.xml; retrieved 30 July 2011.

Chapter 1: A Conversation in Venice

3. Quoted in John Ruskin, *The Stones of Venice*, edited by Jan Morris (London: Folio Society, 2001), 15–16.

4. Throughout I have been guided by the interpretations of Warren L. Cook, who included the Lok account and attendant correspondence (Michael Lok to Juan de Fuca) in his *Flood Tide of Empire* (New Haven, CT: Yale University Press, 1973), 539–43, and discussion of same,

22–29. Lok's account first appeared in print in Samuel Purchas, *Hakluytus Posthumus; or, Purchas His Pilgrimes* (London, 1625), Book III, Part iv.

5. Cook, *Flood Tide of Empire*, 539–40.

6. Ibid.

7. In 1792 Captain Vancouver gave this inland sea the name Gulf of Georgia, in honour of King George III. "Gulf" was changed to "Strait" by surveyor Captain George Henry Richards in 1865, after he had been appointed hydrographer. Notwithstanding the alteration, for many years after it was locally spoken of as "the Gulf" (John T. Walbran, *British Columbia Coast Names* [1909; repr., Vancouver: J.J. Douglas, 1971], 204–5). According to Andrew Scott, "In the early 2000s, a First Nations-backed initiative to change the name of the feature to the Salish Sea . . . gained momentum. BC premier Gordon Campbell signalled acceptance of the idea in Mar 2008, saying that it was 'really a matter of political respect and recognizing that the history of BC goes well beyond the history of Europeans coming to these shores' . . . The Salish people, who live around the shores of the Salish Sea (and inland as far as Idaho), are those who speak one of the Salishan family of First Nation languages." From Scott, *Raincoast Place Names* (Madeira Park, BC: Harbour Publishing, 2009), 218, 519. Note, however, that the name "Salish Sea" was coined by Dr. Bert Webber, a professor of marine ecology at Western Washington University. By the mid-1990s, "Salish Sea" was in common use (Bruce Obee, "Welcome to the Salish Sea," *British Columbia Magazine* 53, 4 [Winter 2011]: 44–53). It is to be regretted that the term suffers from geographical overstretch: watershed (110,000 square kilometres) vs. sea surface (16,925 square kilometres). Although it is generally regarded that the Salish Sea meant the salt water area of these inland seas defined by coastlines, adherents to the idea are now calling it an enlarged watershed, or an ecosystem. According to this thinking, Salish Sea embraces all watersheds that flow to Juan de Fuca Strait, Puget Sound, Strait of Georgia and inland seawaters as far north as Point Chatham, Vancouver Island, where Discovery Passage meets Johnstone Strait.

8. Cook, *Flood Tide of Empire*, 539-40.

9. Ibid.

10. Further details may be found in James McDermott's biography of Lok in *Oxford Dictionary of National Biography*. See also D.D. Hogarth, P.W. Boreham and J.G. Mitchell, *Mines, Minerals and Metallurgy* (Ottawa: Canadian Museum of Civilization, 1994), 150; and K.G. Davies, *The North Atlantic World in the Seventeenth Century* (Minneapolis: University of Minnesota Press, 1974), 20.

11. On this matter, see the entry by Michael Brennan on Peter Martyr (1447–1526), the famous Italian historian of New World discoveries, in

Jennifer Speake, ed., *Literature of Travel and Exploration* (New York and London: Fitzroy Dearborn, 2003), 2:933–35, notably the bibliography. Specifically, Lok translated into English five or six texts, all part of an edition of Martyr's *The History of the West Indies*, published 1628.

12. Elizabeth Story Donno, ed., *An Elizabethan in 1582* (London: Hakluyt Society, 1976), 224.

13. The discoverers were, according to Robert Thorn the Younger, his father Robert Thorn and a Bristol merchant named Hugh Eliot. See Tryggvi J. Oleson, *Early Voyages and Northern Approaches, 1000–1632* (1963; repr., Toronto: McClelland and Stewart, 1968), 125.

14. Thomas Rundall, ed., *Narratives of Voyages towards the North-West* (London: Hakluyt Society, 1849), 9.

15. Quoted in Mary Alice Downie and Mary Hamilton, illustrated by Ernest J. Revell, *"And Some Brought Flowers"* (Markham, ON: Fitzhenry & Whiteside, 2002), xi. The authors note (ibid.): "The token that fired Frobisher's imagination was a glittering stone, which conjured up visions of great mineral wealth. Yet in many ways the flowers brought back were the true symbol of the country's wealth. Plants and trees were to provide settlers with food, shelter, medicine, transportation, and such necessary incidentals as dyes, barrel staves, baskets, and roofing materials."

16. See the prescient review by David Quinn of the first printing of Oleson's *Early Voyages and Northern Approaches*, included in the foreword to the second printing, pp. xii-xiii. The review appeared first in the *Canadian Historical Review*, March 1965. Two other reviews reprinted in the same foreword confirm the view that Inuit were not a culture derived from Icelandic influences but were of Asiatic origin adapted to local, northern conditions.

17. Michael Householder, *Inventing Americans in the Age of Discovery* (Farnham, Surrey: Ashgate, 2011), 17–18.

18. James McDermott, ed., *The Third Voyage of Martin Frobisher to Baffin Island 1578* (London: Hakluyt Society, 2001), 71–102.

19. Ibid., 102n.

20. Donno, *An Englishman in 1582*, 23.

21. On the Frobisher–Lok connection, see Alan Cooke, "Martin Frobisher," in *Dictionary of Canadian Biography* (Toronto: University of Toronto Press, 1966), 1:317–18, which includes Stefansson's comments.

22. *Calendar of State Papers, Colonial, East Indies, China and Japan* (1864), 2:63–67 (on British History Online website, www.british-history. ac.uk/).

23. Material on Jenkinson in this and following paragraphs is from John Appleby, "Anthony Jenkinson," in *Oxford Dictionary of National*

Biography (2004), 29:971–73. See also Foster Rhea Dulles, *Eastward Ho!* (1931; repr., Freeport, NY: Books for Libraries Press, 1969).

24. These and related details are from David Loades, *England's Maritime Empire* (Harlow: Longman, 2000), 116–18.

25. There is a fascinating conjunction of ship and name here, for Dowglas's charge, the *Ragosana*, is, in fact, a variant of *Argosy*, itself representative of the prevalence of trade with the Republic of Ragusa, then a powerful rival of Venice, whose name derived from that of the Illyrian port. It was one of the five great trading states of the Mediterranean, today's Dubrovnik. At the beginning of *The Merchant of Venice*, we find Shakespeare making reference to *Argosy* as a merchant-vessel:

> *There, where your argosies with portly sail,—*
> *Like signiors and rich burghers on the flood,*
> *Or, as it were, the pageants of the sea,—*
> *Do overpeer the petty traffickers.*

26. Corfu, Cephalonia, Zante, Cerigo, Cerigotto, etc., were held by Venice until the overthrow of that republic by Napoleon in 1797. In 1799 they were occupied by a joint Russian and Turkish force. In 1807 they passed into French hands, and then a British force was sent against them. The islands, formally known as the United States of the Ionian Islands, were then formed under British protection and remained an appendage to the British Crown until 1863, when they were ceded to Greece. Cephalonia and Ithaca together now form one administrative prefecture.

27. An article by Anthony Maroussis asserts that calling Juan de Fuca by the name Apóstolos Valerianos is a misconstruing and that his real name was Ioannis Phokas, of the village of Valeriano, Elaion valley, southwestern tip of Cephalonia; that while sailing for Spain, his name was adapted into Spanish as Juan de Fuca to disguise Christian Orthodox origins; and that Phokas family ancestors fled in 1453 from Constantinople to the Peleponnese and settled successfully after 1470 on Cephalonia. Anthony G. Maroussis, "Juan de Fuca—A Greek Pioneer," in Articles for Hellenes, website of the American Hellenic Educational Progressive Association, Firwood District 22 (Oregon/Washington), http://www.ahepad22.org/articles/JUAN_DE_FUCA.pdf; retrieved 21 July 2011.

28. The two islands are contiguous. "Ithaca and Cephalonia lie side by side—though the latter is much longer, indeed the largest island of the Ionian group . . . The channel between Ithaca and Cephalonia is about two kilometres broad," Lawrence Durell wrote in *The Greek Islands* (New York: Viking Press, 1978), 42. The shape and close alignment of the two islands suggest they once were one, and paleolithic findings show Cephalonia was

originally united with Ithaca, to its immediate east, and to the mainland. UK geological engineers, under Prof. John Underhill, are investigating sea levels and the landslide-filled isthmus of the Paliki peninsula to test the theory of a Homeric sea channel, and another Ithaca, on the western side of Cephalonia. "Coring for Ithaca: Geoscientist article describes drilling progress" (4 December 2010), at the Odysseus Unbound website, http://www.odysseus-unbound.org/news.html; retrieved 2 July 2011.

29. These definitions are taken from *The Observations of Sir Richard Hawkins* (1622); see J.B. Hewson, *A History of the Practice of Navigation*, rev. ed. (Glasgow: Brown, Son & Ferguson, 1963), 13.

30. Samuel Eliot Morison, *Admiral of the Ocean Sea* (Boston: Little Brown, 1942), 145.

31. Ibid., 186–87.

32. David Beers Quinn, *England and the Discovery of America* (London: George Allen & Unwin, 1974), 247–49.

Chapter 2: Pirates on Their Beat

33. In Zelia Nuttall, ed., *New Light on Drake* (London: Hakluyt Society, 1914), 318.

34. Quoted in Bruce Hutchison, *The Fraser* (Toronto: Clarke Irwin, 1950), 13–14.

35. Information on Cavendish is from David Quinn, ed., *Last Voyage of Thomas Cavendish, 1591–1592* (Chicago: University of Chicago Press, 1975). Cavendish's account of the capture of the *Santa Ana* is in Richard Hakluyt, *Voyages and Discoveries*, ed. Jack Beeching (Harmondsworth, Middlesex: Penguin Books, 1972), 286–87. Frustrated and despondent because of delays, Thomas Cavendish became paranoid and violent during his second voyage, in 1592, and died, possibly by his own hand.

36. At about the time Juan de Fuca had been in Chinese waters, an anonymous writer, of 1590, wrote this about the kingdom:

> The kingdom of China is situate most easterly [if approaching from India]; albeit certain islands, as Japan, stand more easter-ly than China itself . . . Almost no lord or potentate in China hath authority to levy unto himself any peculiar revenues, or to collect any rents with the precincts of his seignories, all such pow-er belonging only to the King, whereas in Europe the contrary is most commonly seen . . . This kingdom is most large and full of navigable rivers, so that commodities may easily be conveyed out of one province into another. This region affordeth especially sundry kinds of metals, of which the chief is gold, of which so many pesos are brought from China to India that I have heard say

that in one and the same ship, this present year, 2000 such pieces consisting of massy gold, as the Portuguese commonly call golden loaves, were brought unto us for merchandise, and one of these loaves is worth almost 100 ducats. Neither are these golden loaves only bought by the Portuguese, but also great plenty of gold-wire and leaves of gold, for the Chinese can very cunningly beat and extenuate gold into plates and leaves. There is also great store of silver. What should I speak of their iron, copper, lead, tin, and other metals, and also of their quick-silver. Of all which in the realm of China there is great abundance. But now let us proceed unto the silk, whereof there is great plenty in China . . . The king-dom of China aboundeth with most costly spices and odours, and especially with cinnamon, with camphire also, and musk . . . Let us now entreat of that earthen or pliable matter commonly called porcelain, which is pure white, and is to be esteemed the best stuff of that kind in the whole world for three qualities: namely, the cleanness, the beauty, and the strength thereof.

From "An excellent treatise of the kingdom of China, printed in Latin at Macao a city of the Portuguese in China, An. Dom. 1590," in Hakluyt, *Voyages and Discoveries*, 330–32.

37. Musk is an odoriferous reddish brown substance secreted in a gland by male musk-deer, which is used for perfumes and as a stimulant. Similarly, civet is a strong musky perfume from the anal glands of the civet-cat, a carnivorous quadruped somewhere between the fox and the weasel in size and appearance.

38. In 1718, George Shelvocke in the *Speedwell* used Puerto Seguro, at Cabo San Lucas, for a similar mission, perhaps reusing Cavendish's port of watchfulness. Kenneth Poolman, *The* Speedwell *Voyage* (Annapolis: Naval Institute Press, 1999), 147–49.

39. William Schurz, *The Manila Galleon*, paperback ed. (New York: Dutton, 1959), 308.

40. Ibid.

41. A true accounting of all the gold, pearls, silks and other goods, plus a valuable shipment of musk and civet destined for manufacturing of perfume in Europe, based on data from Román, the outraged and dis-tressed royal treasurer at Manila, is available from ibid.

42. For a general description, see John L. Kessell, *Spain in the Southwest* (Norman: University of Oklahoma Press, 2002), 89–93.

43. Schurz, *The Manila Galleon*, 307–9.

44. Ibid.

45. Statement of Bishop Salazar, in ibid., 312.

46. Quoted in ibid., 312.

47. Quoted in ibid., 313.

48. Although Elizabeth received him, she did not knight him, says historian David Judkins. See Judkins's entry at "Cavendish, Thomas (1560–1592)" in Jennifer Speake, ed., *Literature of Travel and Exploration* (New York and London: Fitzroy Dearborn, 2003), vol. 1.

49. Quoted in Glyndwr Williams, *The Prize of All the Oceans* (London: HarperCollins, 1999), 123.

50. "Lok's Account of Fuca's Voyage, 1592" in Warren L. Cook, *Flood Tide of Empire* (New Haven, CT: Yale University Press, 1973), 539.

51. Ibid.

52. "Homer called Odysseus' followers Cephalonians, not Ithacans, and Cephalonia claims Odysseus as a native son. Cephalonia furnished Venice with stately firs for her war galleys and firs still crown the principal mountain of the island." Philip Deane, *The Land and Isles of Greece* (New York: Doubleday, 1966), 165.

53. Lok's account, in Cook, *Flood Tide of Empire*, 543.

54. Ibid.

55. Ibid.

56. Ibid.

Chapter 3: Pursuing the Legends, Exploding the Myth

57. This is discussed in Michael Franks, *The Court, the Atlantic and the City* (Mapledurwell, Hampshire: South and West Books, 2009).

58. Catherine Drinker Bowen, *The Lion and the Throne* (Boston: Little, Brown, 1956), 97, 416.

59. Purchas worked collaboratively with Hakluyt during the latter's last years and was a self-appointed successor, though he suffered a comparative disadvantage: he was second in that line of work after the great master. On these points and others, see the commentary by C.R. Steele, in David Quinn, ed., *The Hakluyt Handbook* (London: Hakluyt Society, 1974), 1:74–96. On Lok, specifically, see p. 92.

60. Samuel Purchas, *Hakluytus Posthumus; or, Purchas His Pilgrimes* (London, 1625), Book III, Part iv, p. 808.

61. Samuel Bawlf, *The Secret Voyage of Sir Francis Drake, 1577–1580* (New York: Walker & Co., 2003), 329.

62. Thomas James, *The Dangerous Voyage of Capt. Thomas James*, 2nd ed. (London, 1740), 121–22. This work was first published in 1633.

63. William Dampier, *A New Voyage Round the World* (1686).

64. On piratical activities at this time, see Diana Souhami, *Selkirk's Island* (London: Phoenix, 2002), 146–53.

65. The term is Pierre Berton's.

Chapter 4: British Merchant Mariners on Discovery

66. John C. Beaglehole, ed., *The Journals of Captain James Cook* (3 vols.; Cambridge: Hakluyt Society, 1967), Vol. 3, Part 2, 1187–88 (hereafter cited as *Cook's Journals*).

67. These observations on Cook and sailing treacherous shores on discovery are drawn from R.A. Skelton, *Captain James Cook after Two Hundred Years* (London: British Museum, 1969).

68. James Burney, *A Chronological History of North-Eastern Voyages of Discovery* (London: John Murray, 1819), 203.

69. For further details see Barry Gough, *The Northwest Coast* (Vancouver: UBC Press, 1992), 40–43.

70. Beaglehole, *Cook's Journals*, Part 1, 293.

71. The Makah website is at http://www.makah.com. Eugene Arima and Alan Hoover's *The Whaling People of the West Coast of Vancouver Island and Cape Flattery* (Victoria: Royal BC Museum, 2011) is also an introduction to the Makah.

72. The Makah indigenous tribal lands are regarded to stretch as far east as Lyre River and as far south as the lands shared with the Quileute.

73. Alan D. McMillan, *Since the Time of the Transformers* (Vancouver: UBC Press, 1999), 37–38. Also, information from Grant Keddie.

74. From time to time they enact this right, although the Tribal Council does not always authorize a hunt. Indeed, differences have arisen between those engaging in the practice and those on the Tribal Council, who have not authorized it in recent times.

75. See Anna M. Renker and Erna Gunther, "Makah," and Gary Wessen, "Prehistory of the Ocean Coast of Washington," in *Handbook of North American Indians*, vol. 7, *Northwest Coast*, ed. Wayne Suttles (Washington: Smithsonian Institution, 1990).

76. Information from geologist Ray Weldon, in University of Oregon press release, 28 December 2004.

77. I owe this observation to Murray Morgan in *The Last Wilderness* (Seattle: University of Washington Press, 1976), 11–12.

78. Ivan Doig, *Winter Brothers* (New York: Harcourt Brace Jovanovich, 1980), 75.

79. James G. Swan, *The Indians of Cape Flattery, at the Entrance to the Strait of Fuca, Washington Territory* (Washington, DC: Smithsonian Contributions to Knowledge, 1870), 61.

80. Beaglehole, *Cook's Journals*, Vol. 3, Part 1, 294.

81. See, for example, Barry Gough, "James Cook and the Origins of the Maritime Fur Trade," *American Neptune* 38, 3 (1978): 217–24.

82. Dalrymple attracted controversy and still has an unsettled position

in the historiographical record. Alan Villiers, otherwise a reliable authority on sailing matters, took many swipes at Dalrymple in an attempt to venerate Cook at Dalrymple's expense. On this point, see Alan Villiers, *Captain Cook* (London: Penguin, 2002), 68–71, and elsewhere. Wiser counsel shows that Dalrymple's careful assembly of geographical and historical detail guided Cook's discoveries of Terra Australis and those waters. See Simon Baker, *The Ship* (London: BBC, 2002), 228–33.

83. Richard Glover, "Hudson Bay to the Orient," *The Beaver* 281 (December 1950): 47–51.

84. Robert Galois, ed., *A Voyage to the North West Side of America* (Vancouver: UBC Press, 2004), 109.

85. M. Eugenie Perry, "When Frances Barkley Came," *Western Home Monthly*, (July 1929): 15, 45.

86. This famous paragraph has been reprinted many times. I have relied on W. Kaye Lamb's copy, which he obtained from a transcript Captain John T. Walbran sent to F.W. Howay, 5 May 1910. W. Kaye Lamb, ed., "The Mystery of Mrs. Barkley's Diary" and "Documents Relating to the Mystery of Mrs. Barkley's Diary," *British Columbia Historical Quarterly* 6, 1 (January 1942): 49–50.

87. The standard account, based on Bodega y Quadra's and the pilot Mourelle's reports of 1775, is Warren L. Cook, *Flood Tide of Empire* (New Haven, CT: Yale University Press, 1973), 72–77. Important discussions of Quinault war practices and the location of this event are in Herbert C. Taylor, Jr., "Incident at 'La Punta de los Mártires,'" in *Pacific Northwest Themes*, ed. James W. Scott (Bellingham: Center for Pacific Northwest Studies, Western Washington University, 1978), 35–42, esp. 39–40.

88. Lamb, "Mystery of Mrs. Barkley's Diary," 50–51. For discussion, see Richard J. Nokes, *Almost a Hero* (Pullman: Washington State University Press, 1998), 184–85.

89. Here I follow Walbran's explanation. See John T. Walbran, *British Columbia Coast Names, 1592–1906* (1909; repr., Vancouver: J.J. Douglas, 1971), 34. Walbran, as diligent a historian as he was a hydrographic surveyor, saw the diaries of Frances Barkley before they were lost in a fire. He also saw the original log of the *Imperial Eagle*. Howay, Lamb and others have attempted, with success, to reconstitute the story but all rely necessarily, as I have done, on Walbran.

90. Alexander Dalrymple, *Plan for Promoting the Fur-Trade* (London, 1789), 21. Also, F.W. Howay, ed., *The Dixon-Meares Controversy* (Toronto: Ryerson, 1929), 49–50.

91. Bern Anderson, ed., "The Vancouver Expedition," *Pacific Northwest Quarterly* 30 (1939): 190; also Erna Gunther, "Vancouver and

the Indians of Puget Sound," *Pacific Northwest Quarterly* 51, 1 (January 1960): 2–3.

92. Meares's instruction to Duffin, 13 July 1788, and Duffin's journal are printed in John Meares, *Voyages made in the Years 1788 and 1789 from China to the North West Coast of America* (London, 1790), unpaginated but appendices no. 3 and no. 4, respectively.

93. Charles Duncan to George Dixon, n.d., recounting proceedings and complaining of Meares's misappropriations of discoveries, quoted in Galois, *A Voyage to the North West Side of America*, 265. Also, Richard E. Wells, *Calamity Harbour* (Sooke, BC: the author, 2002), 182–89.

94. Walbran, *British Columbia Coast Names*, 270.

95. Cook, *Flood Tide of Empire*, 29.

96. "Re: Important discoveries made by Captain Duncan on the N.W. Coast of America 1787/8," HO 42/13 (57), UK National Archives, Kew.

97. Dalrymple, *Plan for Promoting the Fur-Trade*, 21–22.

98. No sooner was Duncan back in London, where he was in discussion with Dalrymple about these geographical prospects, than a new expedition was worked up to probe the Hudson Bay coast with a view to finding where Juan de Fuca might have entered salt water on the Atlantic side of the continent. Duncan was instructed to find a water communication from Hudson Bay to Yathked Lake. If that proved impossible, he was to search out Chesterfield Inlet and probe overland, if necessary, so as to reach Arathapescow Lake (Great Slave Lake, first seen by Samuel Hearne in 1771–72) and Nor'wester Peter Pond's reported find of March 1790, Slave Lake, both on the Mackenzie River. Duncan sailed that summer of 1790 to join the sloop in Hudson Bay in which he would make his intended examination. He found the vessel in no state of fitness, however, so returned to England in the autumn. The next year, 1791, in the Hudson's Bay Company's brig *Beaver*, he did all that his instructions demanded of him. No prospects of a waterway existed where he sailed or trod. It is said that he was so disappointed and overwrought by his experiences that he tried to commit suicide on the return voyage. But he did not abandon the possibilities of there being such a passage, so firmly rooted was he in the beliefs of Juan de Fuca and of de Fonte's account. The best discussion of this is Howard T. Fry, *Alexander Dalrymple (1737–1808) and the Expansion of British Trade* (Toronto: University of Toronto Press, 1970), 219–21.

99. Dalrymple, *Plan for Promoting the Fur-Trade*, 22. See also Fry, *Alexander Dalrymple (1737–1808)*, 207.

Chapter 5: Boston Traders and the Strait: The Links to China
100. "The Northwest Fur Trade by the Hon. William Sturgis [1846],"

in Briton C. Busch and Barry M. Gough, eds., *Fur Traders from New England* (Spokane: Arthur H. Clark, 1997), 88.

101. John Dewhirst, "Nootka Sound, a 4,000 Year Perspective," in *nu-tka: The History and Survival of Nootkan Culture*, ed. Barbara S. Efrat and W.J. Langois, *Sound Heritage* 7, 2 (1978): 1.

102. Philip Drucker, "Northern and Central Nootkan Tribes," *Bureau of American Ethnology, Bulletin 144*, House Documents, vol. 49 (Washington, DC: GPO, 1951), 240–43.

103. "John Hoskins' Memorandum on the Trade at Nootka Sound," in F.W. Howay, ed., *Voyages of the* Columbia *to the Northwest Coast 1787–1790 & 1790–1793* (Portland: Oregon Historical Society Press, 1990), 485–86.

104. "Haswell's First Log," in Howay, *Voyages of the* Columbia, 74.

105. Ibid., 75.

106. "Boit's Log," 4 June 1791, in Howay, *Voyages of the* Columbia, 369.

107. Ibid., 371.

108. Ibid.

109. Ibid., 380.

110. The following discussion of Ingraham and the voyage of the *Hope* is drawn from Mark Kaplanoff, ed., *Joseph Ingraham's Journal of the Brigantine "Hope"* (Barre, MA: Imprint Society, 1971).

111. C.F. Newcombe, ed., *The First Circumnavigation of Vancouver Island*, Memoir 1 (Victoria: Archives of British Columbia, 1914), plates 5 and 6 and captions.

112. Tim Flannery, ed., *The Life and Adventures of John Nicol, Mariner* (New York: Atlantic Monthly Press, 1997), 103–8. First published 1822.

113. Lord Amherst headed a similar mission in 1816. When he got to Peking he was turned away without even an audience. In 1833 the British tried again, and their intended chief superintendent of trade, Lord Napier, backed by two warships and quite ignorant of Chinese customs, found himself trapped in the river. Outmanoeuvred by Chinese officials, he was forced to make humiliating apologies. Then came the so-called Opium Wars and forceful diplomacy, and only in 1860 did the British and the French force their way to Peking and obtain the right of permanent embassies in the Chinese capital. Perhaps presciently, the Chinese, much alarmed by the sight of a British man-of-war, often told John Nicol (see note 112), "Englishman too much cruel, too much fight."

Chapter 6: The Spanish Press South from Nootka

114. Mark Kaplanoff, ed., *Joseph Ingraham's Journal of the Brigantine "Hope"* (Barre, MA: Imprint Society, 1971), 210.

115. Ibid. 213–14.

116. Ibid., 210.

117. For further details, see Barry Gough, *Fortune's a River* (Madeira Park, BC: Harbour, 2007), 116–22.

118. Barry Gough, *The Northwest Coast* (Vancouver: UBC Press, 1992), 87–145, esp. 126–45.

119. Useful to the inquisitive on this subject are the lists of Spanish ships used in the North Pacific, many built in Mexican ports (chiefly San Blas), to be found in Warren L. Cook, *Flood Tide of Empire* (New Haven, CT: Yale University Press, 1973), 550, which supplants the nonetheless still useful Robert Ballard Whitebrook, *Coastal Exploration of Washington* (Palo Alto, CA: Pacific Books: 1959), 123–26. Also, Michael Thurman, *Naval Department of San Blas* (Glendale, CA: Arthur H. Clark, 1967), 203n.

120. Information from Gordon Miller. At the conclusion of the 1791 Eliza survey of Juan de Fuca and Georgia Straits, *Santa Saturnina* sailed for San Blas and ended her days as a supply vessel.

121. Jim McDowell, *José Narváez, The Forgotten Explorer* (Spokane: Arthur H. Clark, 1998), 167–68, gives some of the details on this vessel, which are not entirely finite or clear.

122. Captain Mayo's painting is a fine representation of the age of sail that has nearly vanished, but which is still preserved in the parade of vessels we now call Tall Ships, seen most recently in Victoria in 2008, and in the important work of S.A.L.T.S. (Sail and Life Training Society) of Victoria, the La Conner Sea Scouts and, indeed, all who promote the good work of ASTA, the American Sail Training Association. We have not lost entirely this wooden world or the age in which they knew that the wind was free.

123. Thurman, *Naval Department of San Blas*, 341–43.

124. See my list of books on place names in the Sources.

125. Ten years later, Maquinna, with great sorrow, told John Jewitt, the armourer who was hostage there in 1803, that they had found themselves compelled at the behest of a stranger to quit the homes of their forefathers. But Jewitt, Nootka's first ethnographer and historian, wrote that "with equal joy did they repossess themselves of it when the Spanish garrison was expelled by the English." Derek G. Smith, ed., *The Adventures and Sufferings of John R. Jewitt*, from the Edinburgh 1824 ed. (Toronto: McClelland & Stewart, 1974), 49. It is a fine point, but one worth making, that the Nootka crisis and its consequences obliged the Spanish to leave with the British. It is a nicety of British diplomatic affairs that this event is called "the mutual abandonment of Nootka." Fair to say that the Spanish, in one of the great showdowns of history, submitted to British muscle.

126. Also 19° 28' W of San Blas. Cecil Jane, ed., *A Spanish Voyage to Vancouver and the North-West Coast of America* (London: Argonaut, 1930). This is the translation of the 1802 Spanish edition.

127. Quimper's letter to the viceroy with an account of his voyage, 13 November 1790, at San Blas, trans., in Henry Raup Wagner, ed., *Spanish Explorations in the Strait of Juan de Fuca.* (Santa Ana, CA: Fine Arts, 1933), 77–136.

128. John T. Walbran, *British Columbia Coast Names, 1592–1906* (1909; repr., Vancouver: J.J. Douglas, 1971), 465. Captain Henry Kellett in HMS *Herald* made a survey in 1846. He gave the names of his officers to the points, islands and spit; John George Whiffin was ship's clerk.

129. Quoted in Leigh Burpee Robinson, *Esquimalt "Place of Shoaling Waters"* (Victoria: Quality, 1948), 15.

130. Quoted in Whitebrook, *Coastal Exploration of Washington*, 56.

131. Jane, ed., *Spanish Voyage*, 38.

132. W. Colquhoun Grant, "Description of Vancouver Island, by its First Colonist," *Journal of the Royal Geographical Society* 27 (1857): 281.

133. Walbran, *British Columbia Coast Names*, 411–12.

134. Information from Heather Harbord.

135. He has rightly been called the forgotten explorer. See McDowell, *José Narváez.*

136. Wagner, *Spanish Explorations in the Strait of Juan de Fuca*, 32.

137. For commercial transactions at this time, see McDowell, *José Narváez*, 56–68.

138. Because Spanish charts of this coast were little known and never used after 1792, their place names almost disappeared, gradually giving way to English ones. Point Grey replaced Punta Langara. Burrard Inlet triumphed over Canal de Sasamat. Many of the Spanish names were supplanted by British hydrographers who worked this coast on their extensive surveys in the nineteenth century. Captain George Henry Richards, Royal Navy, commemorated the location of the meeting between Captain Vancouver and Alcalá Galiano and Valdés in Spanish Banks and English Bay. False Creek was named by the Spaniards, and the name was anglicized by Richards. (And remember that for every Spanish name lost there are a thousand First Nations place names that never appeared on a European chart.)

139. McDowell, *José Narváez*, 60.

140. Quoted in Jane, ed., *Spanish Voyage*, 4.

Chapter 7: Alcalá Galiano and Valdés: The Final Quest for the Elusive Passage

141. A. Malaspina, "Plan for a Scientific and Political Voyage around

the World, 1 September 1788," in *The Malaspina Expedition 1789–1794*, ed. Andrew David et al. (London: Hakluyt Society in association with Museo Naval Madrid, 2001–2005), 1:312.

142. For further details, see David et al., *Malaspina Expedition*, 2: appendix ("Ferrer Maldonado Fantasy"); also Barry Gough, *Fortune's A River* (Madeira Park, BC: Harbour Publishing, 2007).

143. In G.F. Barwick, trans., *Viaje de las Goletas Sutil y Mexicana* (1802; typescript in library of Maritime Museum of BC), 27.

144. On the genesis of these instructions, see Warren L. Cook, *Flood Tide of Empire* (New Haven, CT: Yale University Press, 1973), 330–31. And see next note.

145. Revillagigedo to Galiano and Valdés, 31 January 1792, and instructions from Malaspina, 6 December 1791, in John Kendrick, ed., *The Voyage of Sutil and Mexicana 1792* (Spokane: Arthur H. Clark, 1991), 39–54, quotation at 40–41.

146. Donald Cutter, introduction, in Andrew David et al., *Malaspina Expedition*, 1:lxviii.

147. Cecil Jane, ed. *A Spanish Voyage to Vancouver and the North-West Coast of America* (London: Argonaut, 1930), 16.

148. Diary extract [report of proceedings by Alcalá Galiano and Valdés] in Henry Raup Wagner, ed., *Spanish Explorations in the Strait of Juan de Fuca* (Santa Ana, CA: Fine Arts, 1933), 210.

149. Ibid.

150. *Vancouver Province*, 6 July 1925.

Chapter 8: Captain Vancouver and the Salish Sea

151. I have explained these complicated shifts in British plans as they responded to the crisis with Spain in my *The Northwest Coast* (Vancouver: UBC Press, 1992), chs. 7 and 8, to which the reader is directed for much fuller particulars than can be stated here.

152. Thomas Manby, *Journal of the Voyages of the H.M.S. Discovery and Chatham* (Fairfield, WA: Ye Galleon Press, [1988]), 60–62.

153. W. Kaye Lamb, ed., *George Vancouver: A Voyage of Discovery to the North Pacific Ocean and Round the World, 1791–1795* (London: Hakluyt Society, 1984), 2:497–98 (hereafter cited as *Voyage of George Vancouver*).

154. Ibid., 2:500–501.

155. [Alexander Dalrymple], Memorandum for Mr. Nepean, n.d., HO 42/17 (89), UK National Archives, Kew.

156. Lamb, *Voyage of George Vancouver*, 2:501.

157. Ibid., 2:502.

158. Ibid., 4:1618. Here I have italicized the ship names.

159. Ibid., 2:502.

160. Ibid., 2:505.

161. Ibid., 2:504n4.

162. Ibid., 2:504–5.

163. Draft plans of this area at the time of Cook's visit are in Andrew David, ed., *The Charts and Coastal Views of Captain Cook's Voyages*, vol. 3, Hakluyt Society Extra Series (London: Hakluyt Society, 1997).

164. Lamb, *Voyage of George Vancouver*, 2:503.

165. Robin Fisher, *Vancouver's Voyage* (Vancouver: Douglas & McIntyre, 1992), 4.

166. Lamb, *Voyage of George Vancouver*, 2:508–9.

167. Manby, letters, 30 April 1792, in Lamb, *Voyage of George Vancouver*, 2:508n3.

168. Lamb, *Voyage of George Vancouver*, 2:509.

169. It is claimed, with eminent good sense, that John Meares named Mount Olympus, at elevation 7,980 ft (2,432 m) the tallest of Washington State's Olympic Range, as a further tribute to the mariner from Cephalonia.

170. James Johnstone's journal, 29 and 30 April 1792, Adm. 53/335, 169–70.

171. Lamb, *Voyage of George Vancouver*, 2:513.

172. Influenza, measles, tuberculosis and smallpox reduced populations in the Pacific Northwest tribes from 180,000 to 35,000, according to anthropologist Robert T. Boyd's research on epidemiology and social impacts. Boyd, *The Coming of the Spirit of Pestilence* (Vancouver: UBC Press, 1999).

173. Lamb, *Voyage of George Vancouver*, 2:540.

174. Ibid., 2:541–43.

175. Johnstone's journal, Adm. 53/335.

176. C.F. Newcombe, ed., *Menzies' Journal of Vancouver's Voyage April to October 1792*, Memoir 5 (Victoria: Archives of British Columbia, 1923), 50.

177. Ibid., 51.

178. Ibid., 53.

179. W. Kaye Lamb, ed. *Vancouver Discovers Vancouver* (Burnaby: Vancouver Conference on Exploration and Discovery at Department of History, Simon Fraser University, [1989]), 5–6.

180. Joseph Whidbey to [Henry Dundas], 2 January 1793, in Hardin Craig, Jr., ed., "A Letter from the Vancouver Expedition," *Pacific Northwest Quarterly* 41, 4 (October 1950): 353.

181. Lamb, *Voyage of George Vancouver*, 2:569.

182. John T. Walbran, *British Columbia Coast Names* (Vancouver: J.J. Douglas, 1971), 205.

183. Lamb, *Vancouver Discovers Vancouver*, 10.

184. Lamb, *Voyage of George Vancouver*, 2:581.

185. Charles Hill-Tout, *The Salish People*, vol. 2, *The Squamish and Lillooet* (Vancouver: Talonbooks, 1978): 29.

186. Here I rely completely on ibid.

187. Lamb, *Vancouver Discovers Vancouver*, 13.

188. Ibid., 14.

189. George Vancouver, *Voyage of Discovery to the North Pacific Ocean and Round the World* (London: C.J. and J. Robinson; J. Edwards, 1798), 2:189–94. Charles Hill-Tout, *The Far West* (London: Archibald Constable, 1907), 19.

190. Vancouver, *Voyage*, 1:312. For a slightly different version, see Edmond S. Meany, ed., *Vancouver's Discovery of Puget Sound* (New York: Macmillan, 1907), 206–7.

191. Newcombe, *Menzies' Journal*, 62–63.

192. Lamb, *Voyage of George Vancouver*, 2:592.

193. Ibid., 2:595n1.

194. Ibid., 2:597–98.

195. Lamb, *Vancouver Discovers Vancouver*, 14.

196. Whidbey to [Dundas], 2 January 1793, in Craig, "A Letter from the Vancouver Expedition," 354.

197. Lamb, *Voyage of George Vancouver*, 2:604.

198. Ibid., 2:614.

199. Ibid., 2:615n4.

200. Newcombe, *Menzies' Journal*, 78.

201. Lamb, *Voyage of George Vancouver*, 2:615.

202. Ibid., 2:616.

203. Ibid., 2:617.

204. Ibid., 2:621.

205. Ibid., 2:627.

206. Ibid., 2:633.

207. Ibid., 2:647.

208. A. Menzies journal, British Library Add. Ms. 32,641, 177.

209. Menzies to Sir Joseph Banks, 1 and 14 January 1793, printed in Lamb, *Voyage of George Vancouver*, 4:1619.

210. Ibid., 4:1619–20.

211. Ibid., 4:1620.

Chapter 9: Nootka Sound 1792

212. C.F. Newcombe, ed., *Menzies' Journal of Vancouver's Voyage April to October 1792*, Memoir 5 (Victoria: Archives of British Columbia, 1923), 118.

213. Five years' training as an officer cadet would have covered

navigation, seamanship, ship handling, manoeuvres, geometry, trigonom-etry, calculus, astronomy, cosmography, geography, cartography, artillery, naval construction and fortifications. See Freeman M. Tovell, *At the Far Reaches of Empire* (Vancouver: UBC Press, 2008), 8.

214. For more on this expedition, see Herbert Beals, ed., *For Honor and Country* (Portland: Western Imprints/Oregon Historical Society, 1985).

215. The following discussion of the Nootka Convention is based on William R. Manning, *The Nootka Sound Controversy* (New York: Argonaut, 1966), which for all its pro-Spanish biases and other faults remains the best account. (It must be remembered that the United States inherited Spanish claims to discovery and possession, by treaty with Spain, in 1819.) See also Barry Gough, *The Northwest Coast* (Vancouver: UBC Press, 1992), 165–66, and, particularly for the Spanish motives and documentation, Christon I. Archer, "Retreat from the North," *BC Studies* 18, 3 (1973), 19–36.

216. Mark Kaplanoff, ed., *Joseph Ingraham's Journal of the Brigantine "Hope"* (Barre, MA: Imprint Society, 1971), 219–20. For discussion of motives, see Gough, *Northwest Coast*, 101–2.

217. Boit calculated that at a meal for fifty-four guests, 270 sterling silver plates had been used. Warren Cook comments that among Lima's aristocracy, "sterling table service was not unusual, given the abundance of silver in Peru, but it understandably awed the Americans and Englishmen encountering such opulence at remote Nootka." Cook, *Flood Tide of Empire* (New Haven, CT: Yale University Press, 1973), 360–61.

218. Janet R. Fireman, "The Seduction of George Vancouver," *Pacific Historical Review* 56, 3 (August 1987): 427–43.

219. Quoted in ibid., 439.

220. Tovell, *At the Far Reaches of Empire*, 330.

221. For further discussion, see Barry Gough, *Fortune's a River* (Madeira Park, BC: Harbour Publishing, 2007), 126–27.

222. Bodega y Quadra to Vancouver, 29 August 1792, printed in W. Kaye Lamb, ed., *George Vancouver: A Voyage of Discovery to the North Pacific Ocean and Round the World, 1791–1795* (London: Hakluyt Society, 1984), 4:1569–70 (hereafter cited as *Voyage of George Vancouver*).

223. Ibid., 4:1570. Orders from Mexico City about the Strait, "Revillagigedo's Instructions to Bodega for the Expedition of the Limits," are Appendix B of Tovell, *At the Far Reaches of Empire*, 339–42.

224. Vancouver to Bodega y Quadra, 1 September 1792, printed in Lamb, *Voyage of George Vancouver*, 4:1570–71.

225. Bodega y Quadra to Vancouver, 2 September 1792, and, in

reply, Vancouver to Bodega y Quadra, 10 September 1792, printed in ibid., 4:1572.

226. Bodega y Quadra almost immediately sent to Viceroy Revillagigedo his report of the negotiations with a folio of charts and drawings. See Appendix C, "History and Description of Bodega's *Viaje*: The Official Report of the Expedition of the Limits," in Tovell, *At the Far Reaches of Empire*, 343–47. The text of the journal is published in Freeman M. Tovell, Robin Inglis, and Iris H. Wilson Engstrand, eds., *Voyage to the Northwest Coast of America, 1792* (Norman: University of Oklahoma Press, 2012).

227. The Convention is printed in Hubert H. Bancroft, *History of the Northwest Coast* (San Francisco: History Press, 1886), 1:300–301. The key papers are published in John Forsyth, ed., "Documents Connected with the Final Settlement of the Nootka Dispute," *British Columbia Historical Federation Second Annual Report*, 1924, 33–35. For further particulars, see Archer, "Retreat from the North," 19–36.

228. James A. Gibbs, *Shipwrecks off Juan de Fuca* (Portland, OR: Binfords and Mort, 1968), x.

229. See the disputants' claims and counterclaims in F.W. Howay, *The Dixon-Meares Controversy* (Toronto: Ryerson, 1929), which includes material from Duncan, including a regrettably cropped version of Duncan's plan of the entrance.

230. Colnett's knowledge of the rediscovery of the Strait of Juan de Fuca lies outside the bounds of this work. However, the following explains his comprehensive understanding of developments in regard to the strait. Colnett drew a chart based on his own information and what he could collect from officers and men of the *Princess Royal* and other ships' boats in 1787, 1788 and 1790. His chart is in the UK Hydrographic Office, Ministry of Defence (Navy), Taunton, Somerset, Reference P24 Press 87. He explains that he had copied "These Straights" from Quimper in 1790 "after the Spaniard had captured the *P[rincess] Royal* & Stole our Inform[ation]." He had fallen in with Quimper in the Hawaiian Islands. He adds: "Before I got this copy the Chief of Clioquot informed me he had been as far to the Sº in these Straights as to get Sugar Cane and to the N . . ." Other comments on this chart, equally interesting and doubtless by Dalrymple, say "*Prince of Wales's* & Sloops Boat over haul[e]d [worked over, or cleared out in trade] those Inletts in 1787 & *P[rinces]s Royal* in 1788." (The *Prince of Wales* was Colnett's command.) Dalrymple was speaking not of the Strait of Juan de Fuca but of the inlets on the north coast, in the latitudes of Haida Gwaii. "The Openings & Chanels appear'd to have no End—Sound[ing]s . . . no Bottom." Dalrymple noted that Duncan and others thought these inlets communicated with Hudson Bay.

Dalrymple contended that the "Straights of Juan De Fuca joins with all these Inlets to the Northward." He also had every reason to believe that the Northwest Coast as far north as Prince William Sound was only a body, or cluster, of islands, and that the mainland lay much farther to the eastward than was generally believed; also that on account of this world of islands a great probability existed of a large sea between those islands and the mainland. He noted the perpendicular rise of tide from 14 to 20 feet, the flood tide coming from the westward.

231. Lamb, *Voyage of George Vancouver*, 4:1553.

232. Ibid., 4:1554.

233. W. Kaye Lamb, ed., *The Journals and Letters of Sir Alexander Mackenzie* (Cambridge: Hakluyt Society, 1970), 380.

234. Personal communication 1992. Also, W. Michael Mathes, "The Province of Anian and Its Strait" (typescript prepared for the Vancouver Conference on Exploration and Discovery, Simon Fraser University, 1992).

235. John Crosse, "Honour Juan de Fuca Too," *Vancouver Sun*, 13 June 1972.

236. M. Wylie Blanchet, *The Curve of Time* (1961; repr. North Vancouver: Whitecap Books, 1987), 161–62. Blanchet differs only slightly from the original as given in Purchas, *Hakluytus Posthumus; or, Purchase His Pilgrimes*, Book III, Part iv.

237. Norman Hacking, "Capt. Cook Missed Entrance to Strait," *Vancouver Province*, 27 December 1961.

Epilogue: To the Totem Shore and Beyond: A Historian's Odyssey

238. For a survey of these, see Warren L. Cook, *Flood Tide of Empire* (New Haven, CT: Yale University Press, 1973), 179–81, 375–79.

239. José Mariano Moziño, *Noticias de Nutka*, trans. and ed. Iris H. Wilson Engstrand (Seattle: University of Washington Press, 1991), 77–80.

240. When Malaspina arrived safely at Cadiz on 21 September 1794, having completed his voyage of scientific inquiry, the Spanish court was in flux. Carlos III, the great enlightenment enthusiast, had died in 1788. Spain would not see his like again, and the country passed through several changes of prime minister. On the fall of Floridablanca, first Aranda and then the notorious Manuel Godoy, the so-called Prince of Peace and paramour of the corrupt queen, Maria Luisa of Parma, came to the fore to dominate the affairs of the Spanish empire. Malaspina was soon sailing rougher seas in the dangerous waters of the Spanish court than he ever saw on the lee shore of the iron-bound Northwest Coast. He found himself tangled up in a web of conspiracy to replace Godoy as head of state. Malaspina, according to evidence presented at the time, was to assume that office and obtain the personal affections of the queen. Other persons

of high rank and influence were involved in the plot. In his apparent inti-
mate relationship with the queen, Malaspina was induced to write a letter
exposing Godoy's incompetence. Unhappily, the letter fell into Godoy's
hands. Malaspina's bright future came to a crashing end. He was tried,
condemned and imprisoned at Coruña, Galicia, Spain, for eight years,
then released on condition that he not set foot in Spain again. He returned
to Lunegiana, in northern Italy, where he continued to write on enlightenment themes until he died in 1810. He was denied honour for his accomplishments. As historian Donald Cutter wrote, "He who as a glorious
mariner had brought so much prestige to the Spanish Royal Navy died in
obscurity. It is easy to agree with the Baron von Humboldt that 'this able
navigator is more famous for his misfortunes than for his discoveries.'"
Cutter, "Malaspina's Grand Expedition," *El Palacio: Quarterly Journal of
the Museum of New Mexico* 82, 4 (Winter 1976): 41.

241. Edward Fraser, *The Enemy at Trafalgar* (London: Chatham,
2004), 49.

242. Translated by author from Benito Pérez Galdós, *Trafalgar*
(Madrid: Arlanza, 2005). This work was first published in 1905 and is
emblematic of the melancholia, patriotism and romantic nostalgia of that
age. Part of the despair of the times, and the glorification of the heroes of
Spain who fought at Trafalgar, may be accounted for on grounds of the loss
of Cuba and the Spanish defeat at the hands of the United States (principally its navy) in the Spanish-American War of 1898. On this subject, see
Tristán Ramírez, "Historiografía: Amarga derrota: el Trafalgar de 1905,"
La Aventura de la Historia 85 (November 2005): 107–9.

243. Donald Cutter, "The Malaspina Expedition and Its Place in the
History of the Pacific Northwest," in Robin Inglis, ed., *Spain and the North
Pacific Coast* (Vancouver: Vancouver Maritime Museum, 1992), 6–7.

244. He outlived the king's reign and eventually returned to Spain to
live out his days in honour in a top position at Cadiz and as head of the
Spanish navy.

245. Barry M. Gough, "The Chains of History: Canada, 1992
and Christopher Columbus," *IDEAS '92: A Journal to Honor 500 Years
of Relations among Spain, Latin America and the United States* 8 (Spring
1991): 45–55.

246. Newspaper clippings re: Vancouver exposition at Vancouver
Maritime Museum, VMM Library and Archives.

INDEX

Illustrations indicated in **bold**